Reforming
the Labor Market in a
Liberalized Economy

Gustavo Márquez
Editor
IESA, Venezuela

Published by the Inter-American Development Bank
Distributed by The Johns Hopkins University Press

Washington, D.C.
1995

D1279759

The views and opinions expressed in this publication are those of the authors and do not necessarily reflect the official position of the Inter-American Development Bank.

AUTHORS

Allen, Steve
Professor of Economics and Human Resources, Director of the Graduate Management Program, North Carolina State University. Researcher, Grupo de Estudios en Economía, Organización y Políticas Sociales (GEOPS), Montevideo, Uruguay.

Amadeo, Edward J.
Professor, Economics Department, Pontificia Universidad Católica, Rio de Janeiro, Brazil.

Betancourt, Keila
Researcher, Instituto de Estudios Superiores de Administración (IESA), Caracas, Venezuela.

Camargo, José Márcio
Professor, Economics Department, Pontificia Universidad Católica, Rio de Janeiro, Brazil

Cassoni, Adriana
Adjunct Professor, Economics Department, Universidad de la República, Uruguay. Researcher, Grupo de Estudios en Economía, Organización y Políticas Sociales (GEOPS), Montevideo, Uruguay.

Echevarría, Cristián
Adviser, Ministry of Labor, Santiago, Chile.

Freije Rodríguez, Samuel
Researcher, Instituto de Estudios Superiores de Administración (IESA), Caracas, Venezuela.

González, Pablo
Researcher, Corporación de Investigaciones Económicas para Latinoamérica (CIEPLAN), Santiago, Chile. Division Chief, Planning and Budget Unit, Ministry of Education, Chile.

Labadie, Gastón J.
Director and Researcher, Grupo de Estudios en Economía, Organización y Políticas Sociales (GEOPS), Montevideo, Uruguay. Dean, School of Management and International Affairs, ORT Institute, Uruguay.

Márquez, Gustavo
Coordinator, Instituto de Estudios Superiores de Administración (IESA), Caracas, Venezuela.

Mendonça, Rosane
Researcher, Instituto de Pesquisa Econômica Aplicada (IPEA) and Instituto de Pesquisas Econômica e Social (INPES), Rio de Janeiro, Brazil.

Paes e Barros, Ricardo
Professor, Yale University. Researcher, Instituto de Pesquisa Econômica Aplicada (IPEA) and Instituto de Pesquisas Econômica e Social (INPES), Rio de Janeiro, Brazil.

Romaguera, Pilar
Professor, Department of Industrial Engineering, Universidad de Chile. Researcher, Corporación de Investigaciones Económicas para Latinoamérica (CIEPLAN), Santiago, Chile.

FOREWORD

Institutional and regulatory reforms of the labor market are an essential component of economic liberalization processes. The labor market is important because sustained growth can only result from a continued increase in labor productivity. Labor market policies must encourage, and regulation must permit, the mobility required to make the most of the increased efficiency that results from the complementarity between capital and labor.

At present there is a general inconsistency in the nature and functioning of labor market regulations. These regulations impose rigid inefficiencies on individual labor contracts, restrict the capacity of negotiating collective contracts, and lead to a high degree of conflict. In general, the institutions responsible for labor administration are very inefficient and lack the necessary human and financial resources, notwithstanding the large number of functions and responsibilities conferred on them by these regulations.

From this discouraging outlook emerges a strong need for regulatory and institutional reforms to permit the labor market to function more efficiently. The main objective of such a reform is to provide a regulatory framework that will stimulate an increase in labor productivity while preserving the civil and political rights inherent in a democratic society.

This reform has often been presented as oriented towards making the labor market more flexible, without defining whether the desired flexibility should be interpreted on the macroeconomic level, or should refer to the restrictions on hiring and firing, or to the formulation of job descriptions. With respect to the macroeconomic aspect, this book has found that real wages show downward flexibility, allowing the market to adjust to severe adverse shocks without excessive growth in unemployment. As far as restrictions on hiring and firing are concerned, the labor market is considered overly flexible, since the penalties for dismissals create incentives for management and labor to maintain short-term labor relations without providing training. With respect to job descriptions or functional flexibility, the book considers that the regulations and mechanisms for participating in hiring and collective disputes hinder the flexibility required for adopting more up-to-date and productive technologies.

The reforms proposed in this report are therefore oriented towards the following:

- Defining the scope of legal regulations and the area that should be left to negotiation between management and labor.

- Producing a transparent atmosphere that will stimulate rational conduct and discourage political lobbying in the negotiation of collective contracts and the resolution of collective disputes.
- Reforming and strengthening institutions responsible for labor policies.

With respect to the first aspect, general legal regulations should be restricted to creating the minimum conditions required for guaranteeing due process in labor relations. Where heterogeneity in labor is important (in terms of the observance of the productive effort and the capital specificity required), contractual regulations are more efficient, since they permit the parties to design optimal contracts as a function of the special characteristics of the labor relation. Penalties for dismissal should be eliminated and replaced by social security systems that function on the basis of competition, minimizing anti-labor incentives. At the same time, retraining and placement services should be opened to competition with the objective of improving the flow of information into the labor market.

With respect to the second aspect (hiring and collective disputes), the aim of the proposed reform is to reduce conflict and widen the scope for negotiation. It should therefore eliminate regulations such as the "improvement" of the contract in force, which does not guarantee greater well-being for workers. At the same time, there should be a precise limit on the capacity of the labor authorities to intervene by means of clear and transparent laws that encourage the parties to develop cooperative behavior and avoid incentives to political lobbying. This reform will permit the development of functional flexibility while preserving the interests of the workers.

With respect to the reform of the institutions responsible for labor policies, their functions should be precisely defined in order to give them a realistic mandate, and to expand the human and financial resources available to these institutions. Institutional reform is a crucial task, since these institutions exercise the legal authority to implement labor policies and, therefore, to define the operative contents of the regulations.

None of these reforms will be possible without a social pact based on sustainable and credible macroeconomic policies, and on a stable, equitable political system. Without guarantees that today's sacrifices will be translated into a reasonable share of future benefits, there can be no hope that workers and unions will accept and participate in the reform process. Curiously, these very conditions have often been acclaimed as those necessary for reactivating private investment.

Nohra Rey de Marulanda, Manager
Department of Integration and Regional Programs

CONTENTS

CHAPTER ONE

REFORMING THE LABOR MARKET
IN A LIBERALIZED ECONOMY

Gustavo Márquez

The importance of the labor market lies in the fact that sustained growth can only come about with continuous increases in labor productivity. Liberalization of trade, financial reform and, in general, expansion of the role of market competition in resource allocation constitute measures that are essential to creating a macroeconomic climate conducive to growth. As the most recent period of Latin American history shows, however, without significant reforms in the rules and operation of the labor market, those measures can lead to worsening income distribution and more widespread poverty.

In the final analysis, growth depends on the availability of better-qualified and more productive human resources with skills adequate to the increasingly sophisticated investment in material capital needed to participate successfully in the international marketplace. The labor market must keep the players informed about a diversified work force that can be tapped for a wide range of tasks. Labor market policies must encourage, and labor standards permit, the mobility necessary to take advantage of the greater efficiency resulting from complementarities between capital and labor. In addition, the institutional framework through which labor rules and policies operate must be capable of functioning as intended.

Regulation of the labor market and its effects on efficiency and welfare are subjects of extensive and widespread concern in Latin America. Protective laws designed in the 1930s and 1940s are questioned in light of the challenges posed by globalization and the development of more competitive market economies. This concern has given rise to reform processes in countries as diverse as Colombia and Uruguay, not to mention Chile, which has pioneered reform in Latin America. In other countries of the hemisphere efforts to reform the labor market have failed for the moment, as in Venezuela, or produced very partial reforms, as in Brazil.

This debate transcends the borders of Latin America. In the past year the subject of labor market regulation surfaced repeatedly on the front pages of the world's leading newspapers. The debate is taking place at two different levels, both equally important for our purposes.

The first issue under scrutiny is the impact of labor standards on the efficiency of the labor market and on job creation. The countries of Western Europe, recovering from an apparently endless recession, find that unemployment is not diminishing and that long-term unemployment has increased substantially. The European Union's "Delors Report" points out that this situation is rooted in excessive protection of job security and a generous system of unemployment benefits. In the United States, by contrast, active debate is underway about the effect that the absence of legal protection of job security has had on slowing the rise in productivity, at least compared to countries such as Japan. In Eastern Europe, whose labor market reflects the heritage of its statist past, reforms have to contend with a system in which employment is the basis of an individual's existence as a citizen, conditioning his or her access to social services and even the exercise of civil and political rights.

Secondly, the signing of the Free Trade Agreement (FTA) and the end of GATT's Uruguay Round placed the issue of labor standards at the center of the discussion about international free trade agreements. The developed countries, perceiving that their domestic producers may be faced with competition from products from poorer countries, maintain that the competitive advantage of cheap labor is based on failure to meet labor standards set by their own laws.[1] As to the FTA, it led to the signing of an additional protocol establishing a set of control and arbitration mechanisms to resolve relevant disputes. Similarly, labor standards figure prominently in the agenda of the embryonic World Trade Organization.

Not surprisingly, given the profound political and social implications of all these discussions, the debate has not always been based on the best information and the clearest analysis. The political and economic interests of the various groups, historic prejudices, and the usual rivalries have frequently obscured the picture and turned the debate into exchanges of rhetoric.

The studies contained in this volume seek to clarify the issues. They do so first by providing a complete description of the legal framework and the customs and procedures that regulate labor relations in these four countries. Furthermore, the authors study the effects of those factors on the operation and efficiency of the labor market. The authors attempt to answer two questions: What effects do existing labor market regulations have in their countries? And

---

[1] The concept of cheap labor has been used in a questionable manner in this discussion, ignoring the vast differences in productivity existing between the two groups. What actually ought to be compared are not the labor costs per worker but the unit labor costs (by unit of output). The inference that the lower labor costs per worker in the poorer countries translate into lower labor costs per unit than in the developed countries is debatable, to say the least, given the higher productivity of the latter.

what reforms are necessary to allocate resources more efficiently in the labor market?

The answers to these questions are as varied as the national contexts and histories surrounding them. The common denominator, however, is the conviction that, as the exposure to international trade confronts economies with dynamic changes, there is a need for regulations that allow for more rapid and efficient reallocation of resources among different activities. Those changes are aimed not so much at eliminating standards as at changing them and giving a broader role to bargaining between employers and workers in the definition of working conditions within a regulatory framework that guarantees the human, civil, and labor rights intrinsic to democratic societies.

One of the more interesting (and paradoxical) conclusions of this volume is that the legal guarantees of job security imposed by labor laws are responsible for an extreme "flexibility" in the labor market, in the form of jobs of short duration without any provision for in-service training. This is associated with the slow rise in productivity and wages, which ultimately undermines the well-being of workers.

This chapter offers an overview of the shared and divergent findings yielded by the subsequent country studies on Brazil, Chile, Uruguay and Venezuela. Accordingly, the next section will be devoted to a comparative presentation of labor standards in force in the four countries analyzed. The one following analyzes the impact of those regulations in terms of the flexibility and efficiency of the labor market. The analysis includes a look at the meanings assigned to the word "flexibility" and the implications of the current normative system for each of those meanings. The third section briefly sets forth the policy recommendations resulting from this process. The final section summarizes the conclusions drawn from the chapter.

Regulation of the Labor Market

One of the assumptions on which our research is premised is that regulations are essential for the efficient operation of the labor market. The transactions conducted in that market do not fit the paradigm of perfectly competitive "spot" markets,[2] which economists are apt to point to as efficient markets. Furthermore, even in markets such as stock exchanges—models of perfectly competitive spot markets—transactions are strictly regulated and sophisticated conflict-resolution mechanisms are used. Those institutions and standards are efficient in the sense

---

[2] Spot markets, as the term is used here, are characterized by instantaneous single transactions between buyer and seller, without any need for subsequent contact.

that they offer the market and the conduct of transactions greater scope than would be possible in their absence (Coase, 1990).

Labor contracts have special characteristics that make the role of institutions and regulations more important. Two features, present in varying degrees in different types of labor contracts, are particularly important in this regard: uncertainty with respect to the precise nature of the object of the transaction, and investment in specific capital.

With respect to the first feature, businesses can achieve control over a certain portion of the worker's time, but they cannot always measure without cost the level of effort applied by the worker during that time. The more costly it is to measure the worker's effort, the greater the possible conflicts. As noted by Williamson (1985), the presence of this type of uncertainty calls for conflict-resolution rules that would preclude opportunistic behavior by the party possessing greater information. These conflict-resolution mechanisms are very specialized, given the highly specific nature of the information necessary to resolve the conflicts. Hence the existence of legal mechanisms (formal and informal) specifically designed for labor-related matters.

With respect to the second feature, problems connected with the definition of property rights in situations involving substantial investments in specific capital could hinder the implementation of certain agreements. For businesses, the process of seeking, selecting and training workers represents a specific capital investment in the sense that the process must be repeated for the next worker to be hired. For the worker, the accumulation of training without market value outside the firm is also a form of specific capital investment. As the business cannot obtain property rights over the worker and the worker cannot obtain them over the job, there will be no contract unless safeguards are provided against its opportunistic termination (Williamson, 1985).

Although the uncertainty and specificity of capital necessitate a set of regulations, the fundamental question with respect to those standards is to what extent they have to be legal (instruments of public policy regulating all transactions without exception) or contractual (private policy instruments covering transactions conducted between the signatory parties). Returning to the example of stock exchanges, the prevailing regulatory structure there is a mix of legal provisions and contractual and customary arrangements, with the latter predominating. The diversity of transactions and the speed with which they have to be concluded would make a purely legal regulatory system impossible (or too cumbersome). In this connection, the effects on the efficiency and scope of the labor market of a predominantly legal regulatory system are not trivial.

In the four countries under examination, labor market standards are highly formalized in labor codes or laws that regulate a broad range of contractual forms and establish special legal and administrative jurisdictions for the settlement of disputes. The exception to this rule is Uruguay, where labor legislation has never coalesced into a single body of law. Nevertheless, while remaining a disconnected assortment of legal and jurisprudential instruments, the legislation regulates individual labor contracts in detail. In all cases, those regulatory bodies have a "protective" philosophy based on the presumption of the workers' "juridical inferiority." This philosophy is expressed in very specific legal principles[3] that seek to reestablish a balance of power between parties that are presumed to be contractually unequal (Caldera, 1960).

Tables 1.1 to 1.5 summarize labor laws in the four countries under examination with reference to individual contracting, termination of labor contracts, contracting and collective conflicts, and the special regulations governing public employees.

Individual labor contracts are strongly regulated in all cases, even where there is variety as regards permissible forms. The laws show a marked preference for contracts of indefinite duration, restricting fixed term contracts. That restriction affects both probationary periods (during which the contract can be dissolved without any cause) and financial penalties incurred by the firm at the end of the contract.

The law generally assumes the existence of a labor contract on the simple basis of work done on the employer's premises. In Brazil and Chile the absence of a formal, registered contract can lead to legal penalties. In all cases, labor law constitutes the minimum labor agreement, in the sense that all its clauses are defined in the law, and contracts are not permitted that are more favorable to the employer and less favorable to the worker than provided for by law.

The levels and forms of public intervention in setting wages are closely associated with each country's inflation history. In general, the state acts to set a minimum wage, with different levels for rural, urban, and domestic workers. Chile also differentiates by age. In Brazil, wages (including the minimum) are generally indexed. Uruguay has centralized bodies in which the government, employers, and labor unions meet to discuss wage standards. In Chile and Venezuela, wages are open to discussion through collective bargaining.[4]

None of the countries has *estabilidad propia* or "actual security," defined as the prohibition on terminating any labor contract, although in practice it has occasionally been used during certain periods in Venezuela. There are restrictions on the termination of contracts with pregnant women, and they extend for different periods following childbirth. Termination of contracts with workers

---

[3] An interesting principle is that of *in dubia pro operario*, which shows a striking parallel with the penal principle *in dubia pro reo* but in this case breaks with the principle of the contacting parties' equality before the law.

[4] In Venezuela from 1975 to 1989, decrees increasing wages also set raises for the rest of the wage structure. This practice was abandoned in 1992.

Table 1.1. Individual Contracts

	Brazil	Chile	Uruguay	Venezuela
Probationary period	Three months	Two weeks, only private house workers	Up to three months	No
Duration of fixed-time contracts	Maximum two years, subject to a one-time renewal for the same term	One year, except managers and professionals and apprenticeship contracts (two years)	Open, with successive extensions. Contracts create the same rights as contracts of indefinite duration	Up to one (unskilled workers) or three years (skilled and white-collar workers). May be extended twice. Entail same compensation as contracts of indefinite duration
Hiring without offering benefits	No	No	Personnel undergoing retraining, redundant public sector employees and foreigners in free zones	No
Minimum Wage	Yes	Yes, with different levels determined by age (under 18, 18-65 years old and over 65), private house workers, and apprentices	Yes, with different levels for national, urban, rural, and domestic workers (every four months)	Yes, with different levels for urban and rural workers
Wage-setting mechanisms	Wages in the formal sector are indexed by the Wage Law	Individual and collective bargaining. Minimum income according to the Executive Branch law	Individual and collective bargaining. Executive Branch for minimum wages and in wage councils (government, workers and governments and businesses)	Minimum wage committees appointed by the Executive Branch, executive orders, collective agreements and personnel policy of the firm
Employment guarantee	Maternity: 120 days. Union members, in office and one year afterwards	Maternity: during pregnancy and one year following maternity leave (18 weeks). Labor union tribunal: members in a representative capacity and workers in collective bargaining and on strike (varying durations)	Maternity: job held for three months. Double compensation for dismissal after that period	Maternity: during pregnancy and one year following leave (18 weeks). Labor union tribunal: members in a representative capacity and workers engaged in collective bargaining or on strike (varying duration)

Source: Prepared by the author.

Table 1.2. Termination of the Labor Relationship

	Brazil	Chile	Uruguay	Venezuela
Prior notice	One month to five years of seniority	One month if dismissal attributable to the employer	No, only some collective agreements	From one week to three months depending on seniority
Severance pay				
Voluntary retirement	Accrued in the Time in Service Guarantee Fund (8% of wages deposited monthly by the employer)	One month of wages per year of service up to a limit of 11 years if the reason for dismissal is attributable to the employer	No	Ten days up to one month's wages per year of seniority or six-month portion
Dismissal for cause	No	No. If the dismissal results from reduction in force, voluntary retirement provisions apply	Does not exist	Same provisions as voluntary retirement
Dismissal without cause	Forty percent of the amount accrued in the Time in Service Guarantee Fund	On appeal by the employee, the court may order payment of IAS (one month of wages for time in service) increased by 20% to 50%	For layoffs in industry and commerce: one month's wages for each year or fraction thereof of work, up to six years. Doubled or tripled in case of illness or accident. Six months for pregnancy, variable for union activity	Twice the severance pay for voluntary retirement plus twice for prior notice
A firm's economic difficulties are considered just cause	No	Yes	No, but layoffs are allowed in all cases	No
Reemployment upon proof of dismissal without just cause	No	Only workers subject to labor union tribunal, if the tribunal does not authorize the term of the contract. With right to readjusted compensation and benefits	No	Yes, with right to back pay (except firms with less than 10 employees)
Indemnity for unemployment insurance	Yes, 1-3 weeks 80%, 3-6 weeks indemnity 3.5 weeks plus the difference, six or more weeks indemnity 4.5 weeks	No, but unemployment subsidy is available: $13,922 for 3 months; $9,282 for the 4th to 9th month, and $6,961 from 10th to 12th month	Yes, 50% of the average wage for the last six months and 70% for workers with family responsibilities	Yes, 60% of the benchmark social security wage (three times the minimum wage)

Source: Prepared by the author.

Table 1.3. Collective Labor Conflicts

	Brazil	Chile	Uruguay	Venezuela
Who makes the decision to go on strike?	Union leadership in consultation with the union members (no majority required)	The absolute majority of the workers involved	It is voted on at a union assembly meeting	The union representing the majority of the workers
Who takes part in the bargaining?	The labor courts when one of the parties ceases to negotiate and seeks a decision from the court	Labor organizations or workers comparably organized, businesses and the Directorate of Labor	Union officials, employer's representatives and National Directorate of Labor (Ministry of Labor and Social Services - MTSS)	Unions, employers and Inspector of the Ministry of Labor
Resolution mechanisms	Labor arbitration agencies	Legal time limit for negotiation (45 days), mediation, arbitration, extension of the previous contract	There are no provisions governing resolution. Agreements between the parties mediated by MTSS (conciliation, voluntary arbitration, and consultation by secret vote)	Conciliation, voluntary arbitration and compulsory arbitration declared by the Executive Branch in connection with essential services
Duration of strikes	Unlimited	Indefinite	Unlimited	Indefinite
Suspension of the work contract	No, payment of wages continues	Yes. There is no obligation to render services or pay wages. Temporary work outside the firm is allowed	Yes, but only temporarily	Yes, but without obligation to perform services or pay wages (although they are usually paid owing to union pressure)
Conditions governing replacement of workers	As decided by the firm	May be replaced as of the first or the 15th day, depending on the employer's offer	No regulations	Not permitted
Job protection during strikes	Yes, provided the strike is not abusive	Yes, from 10 days prior to presentation of the draft collective agreement until signing	Yes, but subject to court decision	Yes, when the established administrative procedures have been carried out

Source: Prepared by the author.

Table 1.4. Collective Agreement or Hiring

	Brazil	Chile	Uruguay	Venezuela
Who negotiates?	Labor unions and employer associations	Unions or comparably organized workers and employers	Unions by branch or firm, elected workers' delegates, employers or business organizations	Union by branch or firm (absolute majority of workers), employers or employers' association
Maximum duration	One year	None. The minimum is two years	None, but one or two years in practice	Two to three years
Whom does it bind?	Firms represented in employers' associations that took part in the bargaining	Firm where the bargaining starts. If more than one firm is involved, the matter must be previously agreed upon	Hiring unit (employers and workers)	Signatories, except in the case of agreements covering a branch
Scope of negotiation	Remuneration and a broad range of working conditions	Remunerations and benefits, and in general the "common" working conditions	Unrestricted	Working conditions intended to improve those established by law
Who benefits from it?	All workers, unionized or not	All workers, unionized or not, except apprentices, managers, supervisors, agents, attorneys in fact, and persons authorized to hire and fire or invested with higher management and inspection responsibilities	Hiring unit	Workers, except for representatives or employers and employees in positions of trust
Limitations	Not to weaken working conditions established by law	Matters that would restrict the employer's power to organize, direct, and administer the firm, and those matters alien to the firm	No	Not to weaken working conditions under the law. Frequent exclusion clauses and limits of functional versatility

Source: Prepared by the author.

Table 1.5. Some Public Sector Regulations

	Brazil	Chile	Uruguay	Venezuela
Wage increase mechanism	Legal indexing, individual and collective bargaining	Administrative, as provided for under Chilean law, and specific laws to cover special circumstances	Administrative (by rendering of accounts) and collective bargaining	Only administrative career. Executive and collective bargaining
Severance pay	No	Only permanent staff	No	Only administrative career. Time in service: half of last annual salary or fraction (eight months). Dismissal: five to 15 days wages through time (three months–one year or fraction of eight months)
Voluntary retirement	No	No	The principle of tenured employment prevails	
Dismissal without cause	Forty percent of the *Fundo de Garantia por Tempo de Serviço* and one month's prior notice	Appeal of sanctions to higher authorities (immediate supervisor, agency head or the office of the Comptroller General of the Republic		
Agency action in the resolution of collective conflicts	Labor law organs	As there is no legal provision for collective action in the public sector, the law contains no conflict resolution mechanisms	Unions, Executive Branch and/or the National Directorate of Labor (MTSS), and the Planning and Budget Office of the Ministry of Economic Affairs	Only administrative career. Unions, national executive branch, public agencies, National Inspectorate of the Ministry of Labor, CORDIPLAN, Ministry of Finance, Office of the Attorney General of the Republic, and OCP
Most frequent clauses in collective contracts		Collective contracts do not exist. The economic authorities and the unions engage in bargaining to adjust remuneration	Minimum wages and working conditions (public enterprises)	Only administrative career. Wage tabulator (absolute) and subsidies to unions

Source: Prepared by the author.

whose collective contracts are under discussion and union members protected by the labor tribunal is similarly restricted.[5]

Even in the absence of actual security, termination of individual labor contracts carries heavy penalties. Jurists describe existing job protection systems in Latin America as *estabilidad impropia* or false security, as contracts can be terminated by the unilateral decision of the employer. There are three types of termination initiated by employers: dismissal with cause, dismissal without cause, and indirect dismissal. Some of the laws studied provide for resignation with cause (termination initiated by a worker with cause), which subjects the employer to the same penalties as dismissal without cause.

Causes for dismissal are specifically defined in legislation, and generally involve bad conduct. In this respect, Chilean legislation is the only one that recognizes the needs of the firm as cause for dismissal. Indirect dismissal, on the other hand, comes about when changes in working conditions or pay adversely affect the worker. In this case the worker can petition the appropriate judicial authority for a declaration of dismissal, which confers the same indemnities and penalties as those that apply to dismissal without cause. In all cases of termination, indemnities and penalties are governed by the worker's seniority.

Termination of the contract through resignation of the worker gives rise to a number of payments to the worker in Brazil, Chile and Venezuela. These payments are based on savings credited to the worker in a centralized fund in Brazil (FGTS) and in a fund charged to the firm in Venezuela. In Brazil and Venezuela, dismissal with cause carries the same rights to severance pay as resignation, while in Chile payment follows only if the cause is "needs of the firm." The rationale in the Brazilian and Venezuelan cases is, of course, that the payments are deferred wages.

Dismissal without cause triggers severance pay described in the third section of Table 1.6, including actual indemnities, penalties charged to the savings funds (in Brazil and Venezuela), and periods of prior notice (generally paid and not worked). In all the cases studied these penalties are in addition to unemployment insurance, which varies greatly in coverage and amount.

The regulations on collective contracts fundamentally affect the degree of centralization of wage-setting (Calmfors and Driffil, 1988). In the four cases studied, collective hiring is highly decentralized, even when the possibility of establishing general regulations on the part of the government or in agreement with workers and businesses varies considerably from one country to another. In Brazil, collective hiring is by definition the action engaged in by the hiring group (which can include firms that did not bargain directly), while in Venezuela the

---

[5] The labor tribunal establishes special protections for labor leaders and organizers in order to facilitate union organizing efforts.

Table 1.6. Severance Pay for Different Types of Dismissal of a Private Sector Worker After One Year of Service
(As percentage of the basic annual wage)

	Brazil	Chile	Uruguay	Venezuela
Voluntary retirement				
Disbursement of accumulated funds				
(FGTS, benefits) IAS	8.00			9.93
Dismissal for cause	8.00	8.33[a]		9.93
Dismissal without case or retirement for cause				
Actual severance pay (layoff)	8.33	8.33		9.93
Double payment for seniority	3.20	1.67	9.03	8.33
Prior notice penalty with respect to FGTS, IAS		4.17		

Source: Prepared by the author.
[a] Only if the cause is the needs of the firm.

term "collective contract by branch of industry" covers all the firms of the branch. The administrative authority may classify a collective contract as a contract by branch if the signatories represent most of the branch's workers and firms. At the other end of the spectrum, collective hiring in Chile affects only the firm and the signatory workers. The contract can cover only firms that have not participated in the discussion by prior agreement. In Uruguay, meanwhile, collective hiring and collective labor rights in general are subject to very little regulation. Nevertheless, a relatively centralized bargaining tradition rooted in the tripartite *Consejos Salariales* or wage councils permits bargaining by branch when sufficient pressure is mounted by the labor unions.

With respect to the duration of collective contracts, Brazil sets a maximum of one year and Chile a minimum of two years. In both cases, obviously, the length of the contracts is used as a price policy tool.

In the cases of Brazil and Venezuela, the law limits the topics to be discussed through the "no worse" clauses of working conditions under the existing contract, without establishing criteria and standards of comparison. The result is that collective contracts turn into long lists of cumulative clauses, which make it considerably more difficult to adapt collective hiring to new conditions in the firm or the economy. In these two cases numerous clauses limit the definition of workers' positions, functional versatility, and recruitment practices (establishing union privileges in the selection of new workers).

In all the cases studied, the right to strike exists if collective bargaining does not lead to an agreement between the parties or if any part of an agreement is not complied with. In Brazil and Venezuela, the union leadership may call a strike without directly consulting the rank and file. In Chile and Uruguay, an absolute majority of the workers concerned must support any strike. However, this right to strike is strictly regulated. Failure to follow the steps and procedures laid down by law can lead to the strike being declared illegal and the suspension of all the regulations.

Except in Brazil, all provisions of the labor contract are suspended during the strike, including payment of wages. The replacement of workers during the strike is permitted in Chile for a period that depends on the employer's offer. In Venezuela it is expressly prohibited, and in Brazil it is at the firm's discretion. In Uruguay it is not regulated. In all cases, however, the jobs of striking workers are protected and they cannot be legally dismissed.

In all cases the legal duration of strikes is unlimited. In order to limit them and achieve a settlement of the dispute, the laws grant the administrative labor authority a wide field of action, except in Chile, where precise rules govern the return to work of individual workers. The entire bargaining process is strictly regulated as to term and form, which grants both sides the broadest scope for negotiation.

This situation contrasts with that of the other countries, where precise rules governing the terms and forms of dispute settlement are absent, but very detailed regulation of procedures give the administrative and judicial labor authority broad scope for intervention. This authority to intervene stems from the need to protect the interests of the workers, assumed to be the party with the weaker bargaining position. To better protect those interests, the authority to intervene is very far-reaching, lending itself to arbitrary action that is more reflective of the immediate interests of the responsible authority (or of the government), which neither invariably nor necessarily coincide with those of the workers.

In all the countries under study there are special regulatory bodies that govern labor relations in the public sector. By and large, these regulatory bodies tend to restrict management's control over personnel to a considerable degree. In part this relates to the development of civil service systems (which tend to protect employees against arbitrary dismissal), although part of this greater regulatory rigidity relates to the union's greater power within the public sector and the weaker budgetary restrictions faced by the public agencies.

Law enforcement agencies and the administrative labor authority were in general considered inefficient or ineffective in the country studies, with the partial exception of Chile. By and large, the administrative labor authority is considered unsophisticated and very politicized, with budgets and staff spread very thin in relation to the highly ambitious objectives laid down in the legislation. This is a particularly serious problem considering the role assigned by law to the administrative and judicial authority in the individual and collective resolution of conflicts associated with labor relations.

Two different intervention procedures are in effect in Brazil and Venezuela. In Brazil, labor tribunals are responsible for most interventions in individual and collective conflict resolution, while in Venezuela the judicial authority intervenes mainly in individual disputes, with the administrative authority handling collective disputes.

Agencies connected with employment policies (including those handling placement, unemployment insurance, and retraining) also scored poorly in the country studies. Retraining is generally carried out as a monopoly of the state, which in some cases permits the waiving of taxes tied to the training by contracting for courses or programs in private institutions. Unemployment insurance systems were found to provide insufficient coverage and, in the case of Brazil, to be plagued with moral hazard problems (through simulated dismissals that allow evasion of payroll taxes and collection of insurance). Uruguayan jurisprudence avoids the moral hazard problem with the concept of fictitious dismissal. In Venezuela, unemployment insurance provides insufficient coverage and the benefits are very low, as they cannot exceed the ceiling on social security payments. The placement agencies were found to be inefficient, possibly in part because of the low efficiency of the retraining agencies.

Payroll taxes are high in all the cases studied, at least in relation to direct tax rates. The practice is to set aside the major part of payroll taxes as paid by the employer. Clearly, however, the payroll tax burden depends essentially on the elasticities of labor supply and demand, regardless of how the law reads (Márquez, 1994). These levies are generally regressive, since in many cases they are based on a constant marginal rate up to a maximum contribution,[6] with marginal rates equal to zero for wages exceeding that cap. The result is that the average rate of contribution shrinks significantly for total wages exceeding the social security cap, which creates a strongly regressive effect.

Table 1.7 summarizes the payroll taxes levied in each of the countries studied. A breakdown of the total labor cost appears at the end of this chapter, including allowances, contributions, and provisions for penalties for dismissal without cause.

Table 1.7 shows that one of the most important taxes is the levy for financing pensions and health insurance. Here again Chile is the exception as regards the method of collection: the contribution is paid directly by the worker, there is no cap on contributions, and the firm pays only for work accident insurance. In all the other cases the firm pays for part of the tax.

An important effect of payroll taxes is the difference they make between total labor costs, total wages, and workers' disposable income. Figure 1.1 shows

---

[6] This is the usual situation in the case of social security contributions. Many other contributions are similarly capped.

Table 1.7. Payroll Tax Contributions, 1992
(For a private sector worker with one year of service, in percentages of the basic annual wage)

	Brazil	Chile	Uruguay	Venezuela
Employee contributions:	**20.00**[a]	**19.84**[a] **to 20.7**	**18.41**[b]	**6.64**[c]
Pension fund		12.84 to 13.7		
Compulsory social security	20.00		14.8	4.77
Health insurance				
(SESI, SES)		7.00	3.25	
Involuntary unemployment insurance				0.60
Housing policy law				1.19
Training INCE, SENAI, SENAC				0.08
Payroll tax			1.08	
Employer contributions:	**27.60**	**0.85 to 6.80**	**23.95**	**21.09**
Work accident insurance	2.00	0.85 to 6.40		
Compulsory social security	20.00		17.87	14.30
Health insurance	1.50		5.00	
(SESI, SESC)				
Involuntary unemployment insurance				2.03
Housing policy law				2.38
Assistance to small and medium-sized				
business (SEBRAE)				
Education training	0.6			
INCE, SENAI, SENAL	3.50			2.38
Payroll tax			1.08	

Source: Prepared by the author.
[a] Based on the basic wage (100).
[b] Based on the basic wage plus bonus.
[c] Based on the basic wage plus vacations plus utilities.

how the total labor cost breaks down into employer contributions, employee contributions, deferred payments (paid out at the time of separation), and take-home pay. These calculations apply to a private sector worker with one year of service. In the Uruguayan and Brazilian cases take-home pay represents around 65 percent of the total labor cost, which implies an average tax rate similar to the highest marginal income tax rate in those countries. Take-home pay in Venezuela and Chile makes up around 80 percent of the total labor cost.

These taxes are intended to finance a package of services (social security, training, unemployment insurance, etc.) and, in principle, form part of the worker's consumption. However, an appraisal of the quality of those services in Brazil, Uruguay and Venezuela reveals that they are inefficient public monopolies of poor quality, which means that workers are compelled by law to transfer resources to inefficient producers of services who stand to profit from their position as

Figure 1.1. Payroll Tax Contributions
(As a percentage of total labor cost)

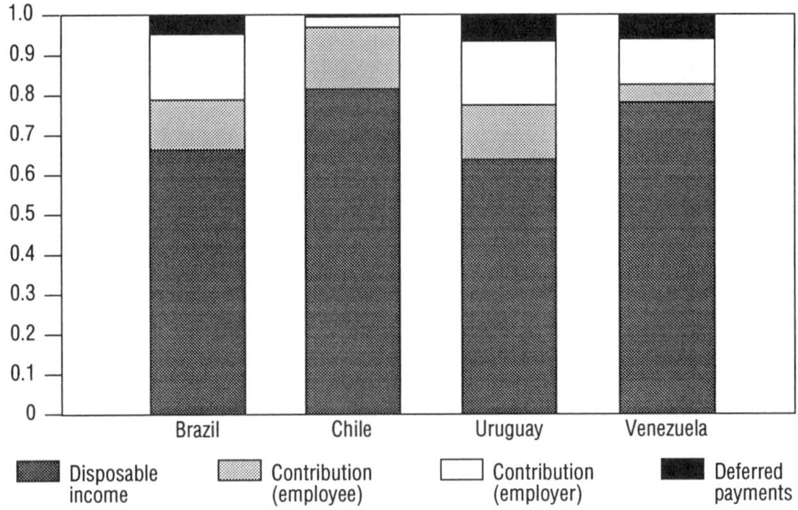

| Disposable income | Contribution (employee) | Contribution (employer) | Deferred payments |

Source: Prepared by the author.

monopolists. Again the Chilean case is different, inasmuch as the major share of the contributions goes to the pension and health insurance systems, which are rated as satisfactory, largely because there is competition among the producers of those services.

Flexibility and Efficiency in the Labor Market

In a sense, current discussion about regulation of the labor market revolves more around instruments than objectives. The market's "flexibility," however that is defined, is basically no more than an instrument. The end goal of labor market reform is a regulatory structure that will permit continuing and sustained increases in productivity. As described in the previous section, the present regulatory structure is rigid, in the specific sense that it seeks to impose a common, single framework on the very varied labor relations dealt with in the market, and complicates negotiating processes by an ambiguously defined and arbitrarily executed intervention of the state in the settlement of disputes.

The development of policies designed to adjust the labor market to the exigencies of the economic liberalization process requires a more precise definition of "flexibility" than is used for this term in the current debate. This section is intended to contribute to this clarification by discussing three issues that are generally associated with flexibility in the labor market, and to consider the extent to which existing labor market regulations are furthering or impeding the necessary flexibility.

At least three meanings of the notion of flexibility turn up in the literature. The first, macroeconomic flexibility, refers to the real wage variability necessary for the prevention of sharp and lasting rises in the unemployment rate following shocks that affect labor demand. The second is flexibility in hiring and firing, in the sense of freedom from provisions that might penalize termination of the labor contract, usually by the employer. The third is functional flexibility, in the sense of freedom from restrictions on the actors' ability to determine job contents and functions.

Macroeconomic Flexibility

Evaluating the efficiency of the labor market in macroeconomic terms is an elusive task. The theoretical argument posits that a perfectly competitive labor market leads to a Paretian optimum, provided that all other markets (goods and capital) are also perfectly competitive. However, Paretian optimality does not guarantee that the resulting income distribution (based on the initial distribution of resources) will be congruent with a society's distributive preferences. In addition, one of the dominant characteristics of developing countries is that neither the goods nor the capital market functions in a competitive fashion. Furthermore, as shown in the first section, labor markets do not lend themselves to a simplistic application of the competitive mechanism, for the transactions conducted in them are marked by uncertainty and high specificity of capital, conditions under which the conclusions of the competitive model are not borne out.

From the policy standpoint, the long history of interventionist episodes should make it very clear that these societies do not assign a very high value to Paretian optimality. To arrive at convincing policy conclusions it may therefore be necessary to use more ambivalent arguments and focus on the ways in which the labor market deals with the tensions imposed by macroeconomic stabilization processes. As Horton, *et al.* (1991) suggest, "it is better to approach the analysis with a precise notion of what to expect from the labor market, given the structure of the other markets and the policy problems under consideration."

In the process of economic stabilization, the principal problem is how to line up national income and expenditure. In the presence of a negative external shock that reduces national income (such as a drop in the price of an export product, a rise in interest rates, or a curtailment of international credit), the stabilization policy is simply a set of macroeconomic measures designed to trim national expenditure. The main task of the labor market is to ensure that the cut in spending causes as small a reduction as possible of the national product in real terms.

To accomplish this task efficiently, real wages have to decline enough to reduce labor costs to a level at which output does not falter and unemployment does not rise. In all the cases studied, the economies underwent a shock in the form of falling demand due to rising international interest rates and tightening international credit which, in the case of Venezuela, were aggravated by falling oil prices. As shown by Figure 1.2, real wages responded by moving in the expected direction. Given the last decade's trend in real wages, as reflected here, it seems implausible to speak of rigid real wages. Actually, real wages have shown extreme downward flexibility in all the countries except Brazil. In Uruguay and Venezuela, real wages are well below the levels reached early in the decade, whereas in Chile they reached those levels only in 1990. In this respect Brazil is the exception, with real wages rising sharply in the middle of the decade but falling back to their original levels by 1990.

How successful was this drop in real wages in averting a rise in unemployment? In theory, if real wages are flexible enough, visible unemployment will not increase in relation to its baseline rates in the presence of adverse demand shocks. The data presented in Figure 1.3 shows us that the unemployment rate was relatively stable in the four countries studied, returning swiftly (i.e., in two or three years) to the baseline levels prior to the common shock experienced in the early 1980s.

It is tempting to conclude that the labor markets of these four countries functioned "efficiently" in the various stabilization processes, reacting as expected to shrinking national income and avoiding sharp and sustained increases in unemployment. From our point of view, such an assertion raises two basic questions.

The first question relates to the progress of real wages: 10 years of stagnation in real wages are not a certain indication of a properly functioning labor market, but rather of a very effective adjustment mechanism by which the economy can be stabilized on the basis of continuous reductions in real wages. But these reductions make it more difficult to return to a sustained growth path, as they destroy a good part of the incentives in favor of increased productivity—incentives usually associated with rising, not falling, real wages. In other words, reducing real wages may be efficient for purposes of stabilizing the economy, but it is highly inefficient for purposes of generating the structure of incentives necessary for a sustained rise in productivity, the ultimate source of any sustained growth.

The second question concerning labor market efficiency, as reflected by a relatively stable unemployment rate, relates to the fact that the labor markets in these countries are not homogeneous. They are made up of two segments which differ in terms of their capitalization, their productivity, and the formal organization of their production units: the modern sector and the informal sector. In the two cases where we have complete data for the decade with respect to the size of the informal sector, it is clear that this sector has played an essential role in the labor market's adjustment to the various shocks which those economies have

Figure 1.2. Trends in Average Real Wages
(National currency indexes, 1980 = 100)

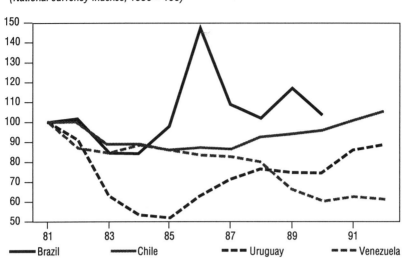

Source: Prepared by the author.

experienced. In both cases an adjustment pattern is discernible in which, as adverse demand shocks occur, the informal sector expands by absorbing part of the labor force squeezed out of the modern sector, thus averting a rise in the open unemployment rate.

Figures 1.4 and 1.5 show the unemployment rate (horizontal axis) and the informal sector's share of total employment (vertical axis) for each of the years in our sample. The solid arrows between two years indicate a contraction and pointed ones an expansion. An expansion (contraction) of informal employment accompanied by an increase (reduction) in the unemployment rate is represented by movement in a NE (SW) direction. This is the type of movement that would dominate the adjustment process in the labor market if the informal sector acted as a cushion, absorbing part of the work force displaced from the modern sector in a contraction and releasing workers toward the modern sector in an expansion. The NE and SW movements would indicate that the informal sector and unemployment complement each other, in the sense that when the demand for labor increases (declines) the informal sector and unemployment shrink (grow) simultaneously.

The information on Brazil in Figure 1.4 shows mainly NE and SW movements, which indicates that both the informal sector and unemployment grew in response to contractions and shrank during expansions. The exception to this rule is the year 1987, in which an expansion produced a decline in the informal sector,

Figure 1.3. Open Employment Rates
(As a percentage of the economically active population)

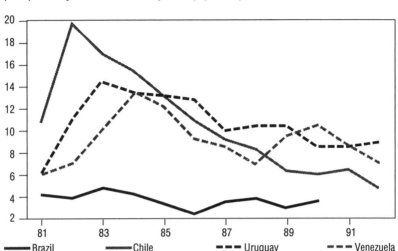

Source: Prepared by the author.

accompanied by rising unemployment. The creation in 1986 of the current unemployment insurance system in Brazil could suggest that unemployment rose in that year, thus producing this anomalous movement. However, the information available for that date does not permit firm conclusions in that regard.

As regards those examples in the Venezuelan case, they leave no doubt as to the predominance of the pattern of movement suggested by the informal sector's cushioning role. An expanding informal sector in Venezuela, and to a lesser extent rising unemployment, tended to absorb slowdowns in growth, while upswings in growth were reflected in considerable measure by informal job losses.

The implication of these trends is that the relatively stable unemployment rate seen in Figure 1.1 was the result of a complex pattern of adjustments in which the diversity of the labor market played a fundamental role. If the added analysis of real wages and unemployment suggests the efficient behavior of a perfectly flexible labor market, the introduction of the informal sector into the analysis suggests rather an adjustment pattern in which adverse demand shocks drive down employment and wages in the modern sector. The expansion of the informal sector in these conditions tends to cushion the impact that the contraction of the modern sector has on the unemployment rate.

It is difficult to determine to what extent these labor market characteristics derive from the current regulatory system. The size and the very presence of the

Figure 1.4. Unemployment and the Informal Sector in Brazil
(Percentages)

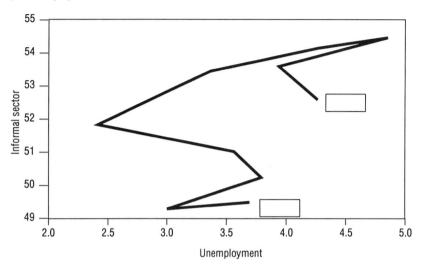

Source: Prepared by the author.

informal sector are no doubt associated with lack of access to credit and imperfect monitoring and enforcement of the rules. In this connection, our conclusions seek not to identify causal relations (along the lines of "the regulations cause the informal sector"), but to show how the regulation of the labor market will be influenced primarily by the diversity of the labor market. As we shall see in the next subsection, the fact that the informal sector exists makes the impact of certain regulations on distribution and efficiency very different from what it would be if that sector were not present.

Flexibility in Hiring and Firing

In all the cases analyzed there are regulations on separation and dismissal that significantly penalize employers when they dismiss workers without just cause (separation on other than legally established grounds). In general, just cause for dismissal is precisely defined (linked to "bad conduct") and, except in Chile, does not include a slump in business. In all cases, penalties for dismissal increase with seniority and wage level.

The specific enumeration of causes of dismissal and the principle that the employer bears the burden of proof give rise to a strong tendency to litigate, to which employers respond by habitually resorting to dismissal without cause. The

Figure 1.5. Unemployment and the Informal Sector in Venezuela
(Percentages)

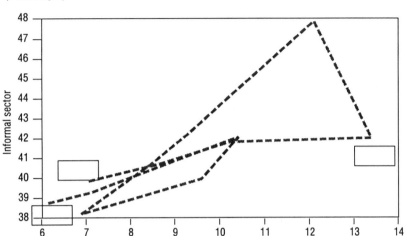

Source: Prepared by the author.
Note: The year 1985 was excluded because it is out of the rank of representation.

argument for this conduct is delineated in the following Nash diagram, in which the rows and columns represent the strategies open to the worker and the employer, respectively.

	Dismiss with cause	Dismiss without cause
Do not litigate	$I, -I$	$(I+P), -(I+P)$
Litigate	$I+(P+SC)*\pi - L,$	$(I+P)-L, -(I+P)$
	$-(I+(P+SC)*\pi+C)$	

I = severance pay for dismissal with cause ($I \geq 0$)
P = penalty for dismissal without cause ($P > 0$)
SC = back pay covering period of litigation ($SC \geq 0$)
L = worker's litigation cost, including unpaid time ($L > 0$)
C = cost of legal counsel ($C>$ only for the employer, as the worker is entitled to legal assistance free of charge)
π = probability that the worker will win the case ($0<\pi<1$)

If the employer adopts the "dismissal with cause" strategy, the worker's optimal response is "litigate," since this strategy's pay-off is greater than that of "do not litigate" for any admissible value of P, SC and π (all of which are positive by definition) if L is sufficiently small, as it generally is. The worker generally has access to a public defender free of charge; if he loses the case he does not have to pay court costs, and if he wins it he obtains more severance pay and, in Venezuela, reinstatement plus back pay for the period of litigation. If the employer adopts the "dismissal without cause" strategy, the worker's optimal response is "do not litigate." By dint of eliminating rows and columns one arrives easily at the conclusion that "dismiss without cause" and "do not litigate" are the dominant strategies. This implies that businesses are prepared to pay the penalties for dismissal even when just cause exists, given the value of litigating anticipated by each party.

In this sense, the cost of analyzing the impact of the rules that limit the flexibility of hiring and firing is that of dismissal without cause shown in Figure 1.6.

The data reflect the amount of the penalties (in months of the last wage) paid by the employer at the time of the dismissal without cause, based on the worker's years of service. Those penalties include severance pay for the dismissal itself, plus payment for the period of prior notice to the employee in cases where this is required of the employer. These are the minimum amounts received by the employee at the time of dismissal; more is paid out in the form of other funds accumulated during the period of the labor contract (in Brazil the *Fundo de Garantia por Tempo de Serviço* makes an annual payment to the firm, but the worker receives it only at the time of dismissal).

These payments hold very specific incentives for both businesses and workers and ultimately lead to short work relationships and an almost total absence of on-the-job training. The effect of severance pay on labor costs depends on the amount of the penalty (P) and the probability (γ) of incurring it. The amount of the penalty is a function of the worker's last wage (w) and the worker's time in service (T). More formally,

$$P = P(w,T); \ \frac{\delta P}{\delta W} > 0; \frac{\delta P}{\delta W} \geq 0$$

and, therefore, the total labor cost (CLT) is a random variable with a mathematical expectancy of

$$E[CLT] = W + E [\ \gamma * P (W,T)]; \ \frac{\delta CLT}{\delta \gamma} > 0; \frac{\delta CLT}{\delta T} \geq 0; \frac{\delta CLT}{\delta W}$$

The firm has an incentive to try to make T as small as possible. Even when the worker's productivity rises with years in service, the higher value of the marginal

Figure 1.6. Severance Pay for Dismissal for Cause
(Months of the last wage per year of service)

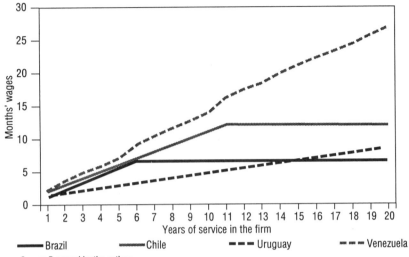

Source: Prepared by the author.
Note: In Chile, the needs of the firm are deemed just cause for dismissal.

product cannot be reflected completely in the wage, as part of it must cover the expected increases in the total labor cost. The firm therefore has an incentive to reduce the duration of employment and not to train workers (which increases their time in service and wages) in the absence of penalties for dismissal without cause. It is easy to imagine the regressive distributive impact of incentives that work against on-the-job training in societies where a substantial part of the population's skills is acquired outside the formal educational system.

Workers, meanwhile, have an incentive for types of behavior (minor breaches of discipline, absenteeism, uncooperativeness) that prompt businesses to terminate their contracts for reasons not listed as just cause for dismissal. To be dismissed increases their current income, because of both the access it gives them to the forced saving funds (FGTS in Brazil, social benefits in Venezuela) and actual severance pay.

Furthermore, the environmental conditions of the economy fundamentally affect the probability (γ) of incurring penalties for dismissal, which rises with the frequency of adverse demand shocks encountered by the firm or of the technological changes that are being introduced. This effect is particularly important in open economies or in ones in the process of opening up, where businesses face a much more uncertain microeconomic climate. Businesses most vulnerable to penalties for dismissal are those that are trying to penetrate new markets or introduce technological changes into their processes and products. In either case the firm usually has to modify the composition of its work force by changing job descriptions and the knowledge and skills required of its employees.

An additional effect derives from the differences in the enforcement of dismissal penalties based on how "visible" any given business is to the authorities concerned. If all businesses were equally "visible" before the law, the effect of the penalties would simply be to reduce employment first, followed by cuts in the real wages of the workers affected, which would again align the value of those workers' marginal product with the total labor cost (equal to wages plus the expected value of dismissal penalties).

However, deficiencies in official oversight as well as differences in the size, capital intensiveness, and formal structure of firms prevent their all being equally "visible" to the enforcement agencies. Larger and more formally organized concerns are visited more frequently by the oversight agencies and therefore tend to develop more formal labor relations and to abide by legally established rules regarding job security. Smaller and more informal firms are visited less often (if ever) and tend to develop labor relations outside the legally established framework.

The more the labor cost of the more formal firms is driven up by dismissal penalties, the more those firms' labor demand shrinks. Workers who cannot find employment there will "invent" jobs with informal businesses that are smaller and less highly capitalized. Since the productivity of those jobs is lower, the wages are lower too, and income distribution will worsen. Therefore, given the diverse range of businesses, the distributive effects of job security regulations are neither neutral nor negligible.

Functional Flexibility

Functional flexibility refers to the capacity to redesign and redefine jobs, including the ability to change the type of work done by each worker in the production process. In this sense functional flexibility is essentially a microeconomic problem that defines the scope of management authority for the definition of tasks within the production unit.

The topic of functional flexibility arises as a management demand in the midst of processes of economic liberalization and industrial reconversion, translated into demand by the development of "flexible," generalist, or multifunctional workers. All these terms describe workers capable of developing themselves with reference to comprehensive job descriptions, with pay scales based on knowledge and skills and employees broadly familiar with the entire production process rotating from one to another of several positions (Beer, *et al.*, 1985). In a pioneering study on competitiveness, Perrin (1992) defines the ability to "attract and retain flexible employees" as one of the most important contributions of human resource management to successful competitiveness.

A recent study conducted in Venezuela (Granell, *et al.*, 1994), in which the opinions of more than 700 managers in medium-sized and large businesses are analyzed, shows a clear trend in the most modern enterprises to set up training systems and incentives designed to develop workers with multiple skills capable of handling different tasks and possessing a general familiarity with the firm's production process.

The process of privatizing the major public enterprises has brought to light a number of clauses common to contracts issued by them, which limit the composition of work teams and the definition of those teams' tasks[7] in ways that greatly complicate the modernization of the enterprises. Although these are the examples that have received the most public attention, some studies (such as Granell, *et al.*, 1994) discuss these regulations' effects on the introduction of functional flexibility.

The introduction of functional flexibility is directly impeded by regulations in two areas. First, most of the laws examined contain the concept of "indirect dismissal," which is defined as a change in working conditions or job description. Second, the regulations governing collective contracts stipulate that the new collective contract may not "be worse" than the preceding one, without specifying how its "worse" quality is to be measured. Both provisions hobble technological change, which inevitably entails the redefinition of jobs and incentives established in the collective contract. Additionally, the customary use of "union preference" clauses, which provide that a certain portion of the enterprise's contracts must be awarded to candidates put forward by the union, similarly limits an enterprise's ability to adapt to changing conditions by altering the composition of its work force.

Naturally, all these limitations are likely to be questioned in the process of technological change and modernization (which are bound to occur eventually, if only to ensure the survival of the enterprise and its jobs), creating innumerable opportunities for disputes. That these disputes must be brought before the administrative or judicial labor authority for settlement underscores the inadequacy and inefficiency of these systems, which all the country studies point out in greater or lesser degree. The penalties for dismissal and the system of incentives, which foster litigation, also place obstacles in the way of this kind of flexibility by giving workers incentives to engage in dysfunctional conduct, which prompts the enterprises to terminate the work relationship through dismissal without cause.

---

[7] In interviews with managers of the recently privatized Venezuelan telephone company, we find that under the collective contract the repair crew should consist of nine workers (with narrowly defined tasks assigned to each, such as driving a particular type of vehicle and not another one) and the crew may not effect more than eight repairs daily.

It is certain that functional flexibility tends to give management more latitude in the work relationship. The resulting shift in the balance of forces is reflected in current collective contracts and in the explicit or implicit job descriptions. Given the "protective" spirit of labor law in general, this shift is perceived as counter to the interests of the workers, even if it leads to increases in productivity that ultimately benefit them. In this sense the elimination of incentives to litigation and the curtailment of the administrative or judicial labor authority's power to intervene arbitrarily has to be accompanied by greater autonomy in bargaining between businesses and their workers, which should allow jobs to be redefined and at the same time protect the interests of workers who might be affected by that redefinition.

As Mertens (1990) and Calero (1991) have stressed, this entails fundamental change in the organization and interests of the unions, which must convert themselves from organizations devoted primarily to political lobbying to instruments for organizing workers in accordance with their productive activity.

It is precisely the lack of that bargaining autonomy and the constant recourse to the administrative or judicial authority that complicates the necessary negotiation over job descriptions and working conditions in general. From the point of view of public policy, the best course of action is undoubtedly to make the labor authority less arbitrary and union organizing easier. That may allow significant advances in this field, which is essential to the viability of changes necessary for a sustained increase in productivity and wages.

Recommendations for Regulatory Labor Market Reform

Analysis of labor market regulations has been and continues to be plagued with conceptual imprecision, subtly disguised defense of vested interests, and pure and simple prejudices (both anti- and pro-union) of long standing. We have seen not only that the regulations have evolved away (sometimes in revolutionary directions) from the common labor movement inherited from the last century, but we have also seen the form in which the various national contexts mold the influences that the regulations have on the operation of the market.

As we complete this analysis of the operation of the labor market, we are left with the impression of a market in which efficiency—in terms of the stability of the unemployment rate—has huge costs reflected in low wages and a slow rise in productivity. Behind this discouraging result we find a number of regulations that govern bargaining between businesses and workers beyond what can be reasonably demanded in the name of fairness and social justice, and also beyond any prudent acknowledgment of the importance of costs and incentives. By no means do we intend to suggest that the principles of fairness and justice which inspired labor legislation in the 19th century are less important now than they were then. But it is only common sense to recognize that now, a century later, greatly changed market conditions require a new approach to fair and efficient regulations.

A burgeoning informal sector, low wages, and low productivity all give rise to dissatisfaction with the way the labor market is operating. That same dissatisfaction is spurring the search for new forms of regulation that will enable us to avoid the trap of restrictive rules that spawn unproductive behavior, correction of which is then sought through even more restrictive regulations. Recognition of the premise that bargaining between businesses and workers must be the center and the matrix for new forms of labor relations is crucial. For that mechanism to function it is more imperative to devise incentives than to legislate results.

Recommendations for reform growing out of this argument can, for purely expository purposes, be broken down into three basic categories: individual contracts, collective contracts and disputes, and legal and regulatory enforcement mechanisms. The following presentation attempts not to summarize the recommendations made in the country studies but rather to outline a general approach to regulatory reform.

Regulations Concerning Individual Contracts

Labor laws are often defined as the minimum collective contract, in the sense that they regulate and limit the possible designs of individual labor contracts. If this interpretation is correct, labor laws should be more modest in scope and leave the individual details of labor contracts to bargaining between businesses and workers. The basic criterion for how far the law should reach is twofold. First, the spheres generally covered should be those pertaining to the civil and political rights underlying due process in labor relations aimed at limiting management's authority in areas not directly concerned with production (but preserving and broadening it in areas directly involving production). Second, those spheres in which varied work is an important element (in terms of poor or costly observability of effort and of substantial investment in specific capital) should remain subject to collective bargaining, for the imposition of uniform rules would hold up the conclusion of contracts and lead to reduced productivity.

In this connection the law should address issues such as the minimum wage, leave, and working hours, but without laying down a single pattern for all activities and situations; the parties should be left to work out the details through bargaining, within the legally established limits. The law ought to focus on protecting labor's right to organize and on facilitating the organization of workers within the productive unit. All provisions designed to set up a union monopoly preventing groups of workers from negotiating directly with their employers should be eliminated. Also important is the protection of particularly vulnerable groups (pregnant women, mothers with newborn infants, minors) in order to prevent businesses from "externalizing" the costs of their actions. In addition, the law should permit the design of contracts for special groups (youth, apprentices) whose personal characteristics make it difficult for them to enter the labor market because of the high wage costs associated with minimum wages and payroll taxes.

An example of the type of change needed in terms of risk coverage is the protection against risks that are associated with working conditions and work accidents. Coverage can be achieved more efficiently through insurance, an area where the law must be limited to establishing standard minimum coverage for all activities, leaving the insurance market free to set premiums based on the risks associated with each activity. Obviously, that entails changes in the manner of providing this insurance, which at present is for the most part handled monopolistically by public agencies.

In order to get rid of the current system's perverse incentives to create short-term employment without training, the private dismissal penalties must be abolished, and it would be advisable to make the needs of the firm a just cause for dismissal. The private penalties should be replaced by unemployment insurance with broad coverage, possibly integrated with retirement systems. The unemployment and retirement systems must operate through a system of insurance policies offered competitively by public and private producers. The law must set minimum benefits and payment schedules and specify an agency to monitor the financial condition of the providers in this market. Businesses and workers can negotiate for services over the minimum, using them as part of their incentives system.

Nevertheless, income replacement is only one necessary function of an employment policy. The best protection an unemployed worker can obtain is a new job, and often that requires training and retraining. This makes it necessary to modify the retraining and placement systems, allowing alternative producers to participate and eliminating the monopoly that some public agencies wield over the service. The placement agencies should work more closely with businesses and workers, while businesses—the final users of these workers' services—should be encouraged to provide training, thus improving the flows of information in the market.

Provisions Linked to Collective Contracts and Conflicts

The issue of contracts and collective conflicts is crucial in terms of functional flexibility, because normally the definition of contracts is what determines working conditions and the structure of compensation considered as a whole, and collective conflicts are where the disputes associated with these conditions are settled. A good part of the problems evident in this context are associated with union activity focused on political lobbying and with a management attitude in which workers are viewed as competitors in the appropriation of revenue.

The existing regulations in most cases are highly interventionist and tend to increase the climate of conflict and inject uncertainty into the bargaining process. The clauses calling for "improvement" of the previous contract and the unregulated possibility of intervention by the administrative or judicial labor authority create an atmosphere of uncertainly and introduce incentives to resolve disputes through political lobbying and not through negotiation between the two sides. The rationale for this type of intervention is the omnipresent "economic inferiority" of the workers, but it must be acknowledged that this type of intervention serves primarily to defend the government's circumstantial interests, which do not always necessarily coincide with those of the workers.

In this connection the reforms must aim primarily at creating a climate of transparent and predictable bargaining for the parties, based on clear and universal procedures and terms, and limiting the labor authority's power of intervention to situations affecting public order and essential services. These two exceptional situations must be strictly spelled out in the law, so as to prevent their indiscriminate use by the labor authority.

A good example of the type of regulation desired is that of Chile, where the employer's wage offer determines the terms and procedures in discussions and disputes, should these arise. This type of regulation allows the parties to act in a rational manner by evaluating costs and benefits of alternative actions and thus avoiding the temptation of resorting to political lobbying as a pressure tactic.

Two additional rules are required for the regulatory system to work properly. First, it must be understood that those bound by the collective contract are the signers, so that the parties or the labor authority are not free to extend the obligations and benefits of the contract to nonsignatory businesses and workers as can currently be done under collective contracts "by branch of industry." That would permit appropriate decentralization of the wage negotiation process and useful discussion of productivity-related issues that can be more easily focused on at the company level.

In the second place, all decisions concerning contracts or collective conflicts should be taken by the workers by secret ballot under procedures prescribed by law. Incredible as it may seem, in several of the countries we studied, these decisions can be taken by the union officers or by a show of hands, both procedures open to all sorts of distortions widely recognized in the political system.

It is necessary also to limit the role of the labor authority in authorizing the formation of unions, by clearly spelling out the reasons for which it may withhold legal recognition from a labor organization. The long history of political manipulation in this type of recognition primarily reflects the unions' lobbying role, and has done nothing to improve their negotiating ability.

Legal and Regulatory Enforcement Mechanisms

The scope of the labor authority's powers are not generally consistent with the budget allocations or staffing of the responsible agencies. One often finds the labor authority operating on a very low budget (in many cases with most of its resources earmarked for social security) and inadequately staffed for the very broad authority vested in it by law.

Given the litigious tendencies arising from the severance rules, the labor authority tends to get overburdened by litigation and neglect its important responsibilities in the areas of industrial safety and labor standards. Meager funding and staffing also inhibit inspection efforts, which renders evasion and violation of legally established labor standards less "costly."

Given the impact of these inefficiencies and incapacities on the entire labor relations system, it is clear that institutional reform should be a matter of prime concern. Such reform should be aimed at improved regulatory effectiveness. In view of the limited resources available, the functions of these institutions should be realistically defined and they should not be loaded down with formal functions they cannot implement. To protect the institutions from political lobbying, it is necessary to abandon the practice of turning over their functions to union or business representatives designated because of the ideological stance of the government in power.

Three functions are crucial to labor policy: the resolution of individual and collective disputes; industrial safety inspection and enforcement; and employment policy as such (training and placement). The first two functions are actually public, in the sense that the private sector has no incentives to provide them, and it is here that the labor authority should focus its effort and develop an adequate intervention capability. The last, by contrast, can be supervised and regulated by the labor authority but produced and distributed by public or private agencies that act in a decentralized and competitive fashion.

An institutional reform of this magnitude obviously requires heavy investment in material needs (infrastructure and operational equipment) as well as in human resources. The crucial consideration is that without these investments there is little we can do in terms of creating an efficient regulatory system through which labor policy decisions can be executed in a predictable and efficient manner.

Conclusions

The research presented in this book sheds additional light on the discussions referred to in the introduction to this chapter. The necessary labor market reforms are much more complex than what the words "flexibility" and "deregulation" so appealingly suggest. The range of contexts and historical situations in which the debate on labor market reform is taking place, and the very nature of labor relations, call for skepticism regarding simplistic panaceas. The four country cases analyzed within Latin America present sufficient variety to show the wide range of approaches and standards necessary.

This does not imply that guides and pointers are absent and that any reform must be essentially *ad hoc* in nature. On the contrary, greater acknowledgment of the diverse range of transactions in the labor market and the consequently greater negotiating autonomy for individuals and groups is the underlying theme of the recommendations set forth in the preceding section. This in turn implies that the state must develop more effective regulatory action that encroaches less on the freedom of action of the parties involved and at the same time that relies more on clear rules than undefined authority to engage in arbitrary intervention. It also entails a shift in union activity from political lobbying to organizing workers.

None of that can come about without a sustainable economic strategy and an equitable political system. As Nelson (1991) notes, the conditions for union participation can be summarized under three headings: economic viability, political viability, and guarantees that today's sacrifices will lead to a fair share in tomorrow's rewards. Curiously, those requirements are identical to the ones put forward by business to revive private investment.

What does our discussion of the problem of labor standards and their relationship with free trade agreements tell us? In the first place, it indicates that labor standards clearly are not universally complied with in the countries examined; this is reflected in the size of the informal sector, where the rules are evaded. In three of the four cases (Brazil, Chile and Venezuela), the available data suggest that this sector generates a third or more of total employment. However, these sectors are oriented to trade and services and therefore fill at most an indirect role in exports, an area where formal businesses that do comply with those standards are the major players. In the second place, our analysis shows that labor market regulations in these four countries are considerably more restrictive than in the United States, particularly as regards penalties for dismissal that are contractual in the U.S. but legal in Latin America (Addison, 1986). The extent to which those penalties complicate the attempts of firms to adapt to the ever-changing conditions of the international marketplace is so great that it is unclear where the greatest competitive disadvantages lie: in the United States, with its (arguably) higher labor costs, or in Latin America, with its much more restrictive labor regulations.

Bibliography

Addison, J. T. 1986. Job Security Provisions in the United States: Law, Collective Bargaining, Policy, and Practice. *British Journal of Industrial Relations* 24 (3): 381-418.

Beer, M., B. Spector, *et al.* 1985. *Human Resources Management: A General Manager's Perspective.* New York: The Free Press.

Caldera, R. 1960. *Derecho del trabajo.* Buenos Aires: Librería El Ateneo.

Calero, F. (coordinator). 1991. *Nuevos retos del sindicalismo.* Caracas: Editorial Nueva Sociedad.

Calmfors, L., and J. Driffil. 1988. Centralization of Wage Bargaining. *Economic Policy* (April).

Coase, R.H. 1990. *The Firm, the Market, and the Law.* Chicago: The University of Chicago Press.

Granell, E., *et al.* 1994. *Recursos humanos y competitividad en organizaciones venezolanas.* Caracas: CDRH (IESA) and Hay Group, Ediciones IESA.

Márquez, G. (ed.) 1994. *Regulación del mercado de trabajo en América Latina.* Santiago: CINDE.

Mertens, L. 1990. *Crisis económica y revolución tecnológica.* Caracas: Editorial Nueva Sociedad.

Nelson, J. 1991. Organized Labor, Politics, and Labor Market Flexibility in Developing Countries. *The World Bank Research Observer* 6 (1): 37-56.

Perrin, T. 1992. *Priorities for Competitive Advantage, an IBM Study.* New York: IBM.

Williamson, O. 1985. *The Economic Institutions of Capitalism.* New York: The Free Press.

Appendix Table 1.A.1. Composition of Total Labor Cost, 1992
(For a private sector worker with one year's seniority)
(Percentages)

	Brazil	Chile	Uruguay	Venezuela
Annual basic wage	100.00	100.00	100.00	100.00
Leave	16.00 [a]	4.1	5.6	7.22 [a]
Annual bonus	8.33	25.0 to 39.6		
Christmas bonus			8.3	
Profits				16.67
Transportation allowance				10.00
Day-care center				16.2
Other	10.00 [b]			0.80 [c]
(minus) employee contributions:	**20.00** [d]	**19.84** [d] **to 20.7**	**18.41** [e]	**6.64** [f]
Retirement fund		12.84 to 13.7		
Compulsory social security	20.0		14.08	
Health insurance (SESI, SESC)		7.00	3.25	4.77
Involuntary insurance				0.60
Housing policy law				1.19
Training INCE, SENAI, SENAC			1.08	0.08
Payroll tax				
WORKER'S TAKE-HOME PAY	**114.33**	**108.4 to 123.84**	**95.49**	**144.25**
Employer's contribution:	**27.60**	**0.85 to 6.80**	**23.95**	**21.09**
Work accident insurance	2.00	0.85 to 6.80		
Compulsory social security	20.00		17.87	14.30
Health insurance (SESI, SESC)	1.50		5.00	
Involuntary unemployment insurance				2.03
Housing policy law				2.38
Assistance to small and medium-sized business (SEBRAE)	0.60			
Training and education: INCE, SENAI, SENAC	3.50			2.38
Payroll tax			1.08	
Accumulated fund (FGTS, IDP, seniority)	8.00		9.03	9.93
LABOR COST	**169.9**	**129.95 to 150.08**	**146.88**	**181.91**
Contingent penalties: (dismissal without just cause) IAS				
double pay for seniority		8.33		
prior notice				9.93
FGTS, IAS penalties	8.33	8.33		8.33
	3.20	1.67 to 4.17		
MAXIMUM TOTAL COST	**181.43**	**148.28 to 170.91**	**146.88**	**200.17**

Source: Prepared by the author.
[a] Including payment in kind (days off) and in cash (extra pay).
[b] Estimation of average additional costs that depend on specific characteristics of workers such as family allowances, perinatal leave, transportation allowances, etc.
[c] Perinatal leave, (18 weeks) by the probability of employment in the private sector (26.7 percent) by the weighted fertility rate of female employment (8.6 percent).
[d] Calculated on the basic wage (100).
[e] Calculated on the basic wage plus Christmas bonus.
[f] Calculated on the basic wage plus leave plus profits.

CHAPTER TWO

BRAZIL

Edward J. Amadeo
Ricardo Paes e Barros
José Márcio Camargo
Rosane Mendonça

The theoretical literature on labor holds that when the standards and laws guiding the behavior of firms and workers are stringent, then a country's labor markets are usually rigid—meaning that real wages and labor turnover are low and also that the duration of unemployment is high or that the labor market is segmented, or both. But despite Brazil's rigid labor regulations, the Brazilian labor market is flexible, with high levels of labor turnover and mobility between the formal and informal segments of that market. And the extent to which the segmentation of Brazil's labor market results from institutional rigidities or from other factors is difficult to assess.

Brazilian Labor Legislation: Private Sector Firms and State Enterprises

The main body of Brazilian labor law regulating capital-to-labor relations in the private sector and the treatment of labor in state enterprises was introduced in the 1940s and was consolidated into a Labor Code (the *Consolidação das Leis do Trabalho*, CLT) in 1943 by the Getúlio Vargas administration.

Three important changes in this legislation have occurred since then that have greatly affected capital-to-labor relations in the country. In 1965, a wage adjustment law was introduced to determine the minimum rate of wage adjustments of all workers in the economy. In 1966, a dismissal fund *(Fundo de Garantia por Tempo de Serviço*, FGTS) was created to replace a clause forbidding dismissal (firing) of workers with more than 10 years of tenure. And in 1986, the unemployment insurance program was created.

Two important aspects of the Labor Code must be kept in mind to understand how it functions. The first is the coexistence of individual and collective contracts. Each worker is supposed to have an individual contract with his or her employer that clearly states wages, working conditions, hours, and the like. It is illegal for a firm or person to hire a worker without a signed contract (although the actual enforcement of this legislation is somewhat weak, as described later in the section on the informal sector). At the same time, firms are also supposed to sign a collective contract with their workers' unions. Collective contracts, which are negotiated yearly, stipulate baseline or minimum work-related standards in the interest of union members. Individual contracts can determine only better (not worse) conditions (wages, working conditions, shorter work hours, and so forth) than those stipulated in the collective contracts and those mandated by the Labor Code. On the other hand, workers without individual contracts are not covered by the collective contracts.

The second important aspect of Brazil's labor legislation is the pivotal role played by the labor courts in individual and collective contracts, clauses, enforcement, and collective bargaining settlements, making the Brazilian labor relations system one that is very much based on legal procedures (even though collective bargaining has gained an increasingly important role since the end of the 1970s). Understanding how labor courts function is an important step towards understanding how the actors in the Brazilian labor market behave collectively and individually.

Individual Labor Contracts and Minimum Labor Standards

Brazil's Labor Code is a very comprehensive set of rules covering individual and collective rights and duties of workers, unions and firms. Individual contracts and the rights of individual workers and firms are covered in Titles II through IV of the code. The law states that each worker must have a booklet in which his or her individual labor contract and its changes over time are registered by the employer. An employer who does not sign this booklet can be prosecuted by the worker or by the worker's union at any time until five years after the end of the work relationship. (Before the 1988 Constitution, this period covered only two years after the end of the work relationship.)

In addition to the employer's obligation to sign the booklet, the law establishes a set of basic conditions which any employment arrangement must observe, including the following: a ceiling on the number of a worker's hours per week and on overtime; a minimum wage and minimum payment for overtime work; paid annual vacations; special protection for women and children; prohibition of the dismissal of pregnant women; the mother's right to paid leave before and after childbirth; special work conditions for night shifts; a one-month notification before firing; protection against unjustified dismissal; on-the-job safety, including special rules for certain occupations; an annual bonus (introduced in 1962); a family allowance (introduced in 1963); unemployment benefits (introduced in 1986); and a father's right to a five-day leave upon the birth of his child (introduced in 1988).

Until 1988, the law had established a maximum work week of 48 hours and a two-hour-per-day ceiling on overtime work, with the minimum payment for overtime set at 20 percent higher than normal wages. Maternity leave was for three months, one before and two after childbirth. Each worker had the right to a 25-working-day prepaid vacation per year of work in the same firm. In 1962, a one-month bonus (13th wage) was created for all private sector workers, to be paid half in November and half in December; the value of this bonus was equal to one-twelfth of the value of the worker's wage in December of each year, multiplied by the number of months of employment in the enterprise in that year. The family allowance was calculated on the basis of family size and as a percentage of the minimum wage and was financed through employer contributions.

In 1988, many important changes were introduced by the new Constitution. The maximum number of hours of work per week was reduced from 48 to 44, and the minimum payment for overtime increased from 20 percent to 50 percent of workers' normal hourly wages. For continuous work shifts, the maximum workday was reduced from eight to six hours. A vacation bonus of one-third of a worker's wages was created. Unemployment benefits were liberalized. Maternity leave was increased to 120 days and a five-day paternity leave was introduced.[1]

The protection against unfair dismissal is of special interest and will be analyzed separately. Until 1965, if a worker was fired without proper justification, the employer had to pay him or her one month of wages for each year worked in the firm, calculated on the basis of the highest wage received during the work contract. It was the responsibility of the employer to prove that the dismissal was justified, and the conditions for justified dismissals were clearly defined in the law. After 10 years in the same enterprise, dismissals were forbidden by law, unless properly justified. If a worker was accused by the employer, the worker's contract could be interrupted and an inquiry opened to determine if the accusation was correct. If the inquiry determined that the accusation was not well-founded, the dismissal was overruled and the worker had to be reinstated by the firm. In the event that an enterprise was closed, the monetary compensation of the tenured worker was two months of wages per year of work, calculated on the basis of the highest wage received during the work contract. Thus, it was very difficult to fire workers with more than 10 years of service in the same company.

In 1966, this entire system of protection against unjustified dismissals was changed with the creation of the FGTS, the capitalization fund. When contract-

---

[1] Two other clauses were introduced in the Constitution, to be implemented when specific laws were approved by Congress. Those covered profit-sharing and a change in the previous notification of firing from one month to a period proportional to seniority in the enterprise. These two clauses were not yet in effect as of May 1994.

ing a worker, the firm had to open a bank account in the worker's name and deposit 8 percent of the value of the monthly wage in the account every month. These resources constituted a fund adjusted for inflation and earning 3 percent interest a year. When fired (unless the firing was a result of some serious breach as defined in the law), the worker could withdraw this money and also receive a lump sum additional compensation corresponding to a fine of 10 percent of the total amount of the fund, paid by the employer. In 1988, this percentage was increased to 40 percent. Besides this use, the fund could also be drawn on by the worker to buy a house and upon retirement. The system is in place up to the present (May 1994). After this legislation, firing became much easier and more inexpensive for companies, and in turn, hiring new workers also became much easier.

The foregoing are the minimum individual rights of Brazil's private sector and state enterprise workers. These basic working conditions can be improved by introducing new clauses in the individual or collective contracts, whether through negotiations between the individual worker and the firm or through collective bargaining.

Union Organization, Collective Bargaining, and Collective Contracts

The negotiation of collective contracts in Brazil is carried out between workers' unions and firms or between workers' unions and employers' unions. Clauses in individual contracts cannot by law be worse for workers than clauses in collective contracts. In this sense, Brazilian labor legislation sees individual contracts as a complement to collective contracts. Collective contracts establish a floor for individual contracts.

To understand how collective contracts and collective bargaining are undertaken in Brazil, it is important first to know how unions are organized. Title V of the Labor Code defines the structure of union organization in the country. By this statute, unions for workers and for employers are organized along parallel lines. Unions are defined on the basis of occupation (for the workers) and economic category (for the employers), as determined by the Ministry of Labor, using criteria of similarity of work characteristics and business activities. Until 1988, it was forbidden by law to group different occupations and different economic categories into one single union. Furthermore, all unions had to be registered with and approved by the Ministry of Labor.

Once recognized by the Ministry of Labor, a union was to have a monopoly of representation for its particular occupation or economic category at the geographical base defined, and all collective bargaining had to be carried out with the participation of the workers' union. The smallest geographical base is the city, and the confirmation of statewide (provincial) and interstate unions was also allowed, but up to 1988 only on an exceptional basis was a union allowed to have a national jurisdiction. Disputes regarding representation were resolved by the Ministry of Labor.

A federation could be created by five or more unions, and more than one federation could be created for the same occupation or economic category. The federations did not, however, have the right to stand in for a member union in collective bargaining, unless there were no unions to represent the worker in question. The geographical base for a federation is the state (or province). A grouping of three or more federations can form a confederation at the national level. A central union, grouping many different occupations at the national level, was not allowed by the Labor Code.

Union affiliation is not compulsory for either firms or workers, but a compulsory fee applies to all firms and all workers in order to finance the unions. The financial resources collected through this fee were to be divided among the union (60 percent), the federation (15 percent), the confederation (5 percent), and the Ministry of Labor (20 percent). The use of these resources was clearly defined by law. They could be used for social welfare objectives (libraries, funeral relief, education, scholarships, consumer cooperatives, and the like) but never for political objectives (such as constituting a strike fund or helping in collective bargaining).

Besides this compulsory fee, unions were authorized to collect a voluntary contribution from their associates. The value of this contribution was to be determined by each union's general assembly. The resources originating from this source could be utilized by the unions at their discretion.

Union boards were to be elected through secret ballot, and the quorum for the election was two-thirds of the associates for the first ballot, half for the second, and two-fifths for the third. If these quorums were not constituted, then the Ministry of Labor itself could name a new board and a new election would be called. Once registered as candidates for the board of directors, workers could not be fired. If elected, the worker could not be fired during the year following the end of his mandate. Unemployed workers were not eligible to serve on the board of directors.

The Ministry of Labor had the right to intervene in a union and depose the board of directors for many reasons, the most important of which were the board's use of the compulsory contribution resources for objectives not allowed by law and the board's calling of an unauthorized strike or lockout. A union had the obligation "to act in cooperation with the government and other social institutions in the interest of improving social solidarity and to subordinate its own economic and occupational interests to the national interest" (CLT, Art. 518.c). The union could be closed by the president of the country in case it created "any obstacle to the implementation of the governmental economic policy" (CLT, Art. 555.c).

Collective bargaining was defined as mandatory and as a monopoly of the workers' unions, which were also to represent workers at collective disputes in the labor courts and to sign collective agreements and conventions. Collective bargaining is mandatory once a year at the "data base" between the occupational union and the employers' union or company. In the first case, the signed contract is called a convention; in the second, it is called an agreement. Bargaining is at the level of the workers' union (if the employer is represented by a union) or at the level of the firm (if the employer is an enterprise).

Although a specific union membership representation was limited by geographic area and by members' occupation or economic category, collective agreements and conventions were not limited in the same way. In principle, collective agreements and conventions could cover any geographic area and any occupational or economic category, if many unions negotiated and signed the same convention or agreement. It is common to have workers from different occupations in the same firm signing the same collective contract. The law did declare "not valid any clause of a collective agreement or convention that directly or indirectly goes against any disciplinary rule or prohibition of the government's economic policy or the wage policy in force" (CLT, Art. 623).

Although the Labor Code had no explicit rules on calling a strike or a lockout, severe penalties were prescribed for individuals or unions that implemented or incited such strikes or lockouts before an explicit authorization was issued by the labor courts. These penalties could range from a fine to the Ministry of Labor's direct intervention in the union and the removal of the board of directors, or even imprisonment of the leaders of the movement.

Because the representation of workers in collective bargaining was the monopoly of unions and because unions were constituted on an occupational and citywide basis, most collective bargaining was carried out at this dual occupation/city level or at the firm level (of course, some unions were constituted on a multicity, state [provincial], or multistate basis). Thus, collective bargaining was as a rule very decentralized and went down usually to the occupation/city level or even to the company level. Before the 1980s, very little bargaining was carried out at a higher level of aggregation (we shall later discuss in some detail the evolution of this structure).

Finally, one very important aspect of collective contracts in Brazil is that the Labor Code made them mandatory for all workers and firms in the geographical area and occupation and economic category represented, regardless of whether or not the worker or firm was formally affiliated with the union that negotiated and signed the contract.

Important changes in this original overall structure defined by the Labor Code were implemented in the mid-1960s by Brazil's military government and in 1988 by the new Constitution. Two of the mid-1960s changes were of particular significance: a strike law and a wage adjustment law.

One of the first decisions of the military government that followed the military coup of March 1964 was the creation of a strike law. The main objectives of this law were to regulate the right to strike (something not covered in the Labor Code) and to create rules that had to be followed in order for a strike to be considered legal. To be considered legal, the strike had to be approved by the union's general assembly, which had to be convoked through the press. The period between the calling of the general assembly and it being held had to be at least 10 days. To be valid, the general assembly had to reach a quorum of two-thirds of the union's members in the first calling and one-third in the second. For those unions representing more than 5,000 workers, the quorum in the second calling was to comprise one-eighth of the members. Between the first and the second callings, the minimum period required was two days. Secret balloting was mandatory.

If the strike was approved, the union had to notify the employer, who had a five-day period to accept the demands of the workers before the strike could be started. Certain economic activities were considered essential (defined by law), and in these particular activities the grace period was increased to 10 days.[2] If the unions followed all these steps, the strike could be declared legal by the labor courts, and the workers could not be dismissed or replaced during the strike period. Wages were due during legal strikes.

This law was changed in 1989, in order to make it compatible with the new Constitution of 1988, which declared strikes a social right of all workers. With this change, the concept of a legal strike became obsolete. Instead of determining the legality of a given strike, the new law introduced the concept of "abuse of the right to strike" and significantly reduced the restrictions on this right to strike. The notification to the employer was reduced to 48 hours in all sectors except "essential sectors," where the period is 72 hours. The general assembly quorum necessary for voting on a strike was left to the unions discretion to define. Peaceful picketing was allowed. During a nonabusive strike, firing continued to be forbidden and wages were due. The union was responsible for the maintenance and protection of the firm's equipment. In the essential sectors, as defined in the law, the workers' and employers' unions were both responsible for the provision of the minimum services needed to guarantee the levels considered indispensable to the community. (This is the law still in effect as of May 1994.)

A second important mid-1960s change in the Labor Code was the introduction of a wage adjustment law in 1965. Before this date, wage adjustments had

---

[2] Essential activities included water supply, energy and gas services, communications, transportation, funeral services, hospitals, food shops, and industries considered essential for national defense, at the government's discretion. This list was increased in 1978 to include all public services. In these sectors, the authorities are required to take all the necessary measures to keep strikers working during the strike.

been decided through collective bargaining between the workers' and the employers' unions (at the data base) and through individual negotiations between one worker and his or her employer. Only the minimum wage itself was directly determined by the president of the country.

The wage adjustment law gave the government the right to determine the minimum rate of adjustment of all wages in the formal sector of the economy. The first wage law stipulated that nominal wages should be adjusted once a year, at the data base of each occupation, following a formula that took the past and expected future rates of inflation and the growth rate in per capita GDP as the base for the adjustments. The specific formula and the adjustment period were changed many times through the years, as the rate of inflation increased. Crucial changes occurred in 1979, when the period of wage adjustment was reduced from one year to six months and a productivity index, negotiated by each occupation, replaced per capita GDP as part of the calculation process.

Other changes were made in 1986, when an automatic wage adjustment clause began to go into effect whenever the rate of inflation reached 20 percent. After 1987, when the rate of inflation accelerated sharply, this clause was discontinued, and the wage adjustment period was further reduced to one month. Since then, indexation to past inflation has not been perfect for higher wages; the limit varies, depending on the period, from three to six minimum wages. Adjustments in individual contracts above those stipulated in the wage law are negotiated by the firm with its workers. Although the wage adjustment period was progressively reduced from one year to one month between 1979 and 1987, collective bargaining continued to be held annually, as before. In 1990, the wage adjustment law was discontinued but was reintroduced the following year, when the rate of inflation increased once more.

The Constitution of 1988 changed many of the old Labor Code restrictions on union organization and collective bargaining. The first important change was the prohibition of government intervention or interference in union activities; unions are now completely free of government control. Second, the right to strike was (as noted earlier) turned into a constitutional right of all workers in the country, and changes in the strike law had to be made. Third, the Constitution allowed the formation of national unions, or central unions, which also gained the right to argue the constitutionality of a law or act of government in the Supreme Court of Justice. Fourth, in enterprises with more than 200 employees, the workers gained the right to organize an elected workers' council that could negotiate with the employer (this last point is still to be regulated by law).

These were clearly important changes in the formal legislation, and many of them had in fact already been common practice in the country. Meanwhile, the compulsory fee, the monopoly of representation, and the extension of collective contracts to all workers regardless of their affiliation or nonaffiliation with a union—some of the pillars of Brazilian union organization—were not changed.

Thus, many of the most important characteristics of union structure and collective bargaining were maintained even after the changes.

Labor Courts

Labor courts have three important functions in the Brazilian labor relations system. First, every dispute concerning compliance with the law has to be resolved through the labor courts. Second, they are responsible for resolving all disputes concerning compliance with individual and collective labor contracts. Third, the labor courts are also responsible for conciliation, arbitration and judgment related to collective bargaining. These three very important roles make the labor courts a key element in the Brazilian labor relations system.

The Brazilian labor court system has three branches: boards of conciliation and judgment; area-wide labor courts; and the superior labor court. A board of conciliation and judgment is composed of one labor lawyer, one worker representative, and one employer representative; these last two members are named by the president of the area-wide labor court where the board is located.

The area-wide labor court is composed largely of labor lawyers and also of worker and employer representatives chosen by the president of the country. The area-wide labor courts evaluate and issue decisions on the demands of workers and employers. These decisions in turn may be appealed to the superior labor court by workers or the employer.

The members of Brazil's superior labor court are named by the president of the country and are approved by the Senate. This court is made up of three worker representatives, three employer representatives, and 11 labor lawyers, who have a lifetime mandate. The decisions of the superior labor court are final, unless the dispute concerns a Constitutional principle, in which case the decision can be appealed to the Supreme Court of Justice.

At the individual level, an agreement made between a worker and an employer that resolves a dispute about compliance with an individual contract or with the law is considered valid only if it is made through the pertinent board of conciliation and judgment. This means that any firing of a worker has to be done in the judge's presence if the employer wants to be sure the worker will not later claim any right supposedly not observed by the employer during the work relationship. Since 1988, the worker has had a five-year period in which to file such a claim. If that happens, it is the burden of the employer to prove that he or she did indeed honor the contract or the law. If the employer is unable to do so, the judge is free to decide if the claim is acceptable. If the judge decides that the claim is indeed acceptable, the employer will have to compensate the worker for not having observed the rights the worker is claiming. Only monetary claims are acceptable, since the worker cannot demand to be rehired by the employer.

At the collective bargaining level, disputes between the labor union and the firm over compliance with collective contracts are resolved through a labor court. Here again, it is the employer's burden to prove that the law was observed. Conciliation and arbitration during collective bargaining are also important functions of the labor courts. If the negotiations arrive at a stalemate, the courts have the final decision (at the area-wide or the national level).

The main function of the courts regarding collective bargaining is to promote conciliation and judgment vis-à-vis points of conflict between bargaining parties in their jurisdiction. If at any time a collective bargaining process arrives at a stalemate, any of the parties can unilaterally declare a *dissídio* (point of conflict). The dispute then goes to the board of conciliation and judgment located in the area where the bargaining is being carried out. If conciliation at this level is not possible, a decision is arrived at by the board. Workers and employers can appeal such decisions up the hierarchical ladder of courts.

Conciliation and arbitration follow no special rules or principles. When the dispute concerns noncompliance with the law, arbitration is based on the law; otherwise, previous decisions of the same board or court can be used as a guide. And in many instances, judgment is based on political grounds; in fact, the Brazilian labor justice system is the only branch of the entire Brazilian justice system that has normative power in the sense that it can actually make a law, instead of just having to apply an existing one.

Labor Legislation and the Behavior of the Brazilian Labor Market

The foregoing section presented a description of Brazilian labor legislation. Let us now examine how this legislation influences the behavior of workers, employers and unions and how the Brazilian labor relations system has developed over time.

Individual Contracts, Costs of Dismissals, Flexibility and Informality

Given the importance of individual labor contracts, any analysis of the Brazilian labor relations system must consider how labor legislation affects individual contract negotiations and other related determinations. The major elements governing individual labor contracts in the country are the following: (i) the individual rights of workers (defined in the Labor Code and the 1988 Constitution) and the nonwage costs of labor; (ii) the role of labor courts in individual contract disputes; (iii) the costs (monetary or other) of firing workers; and (iv) the unemployment insurance scheme and its effects on the behavior of the labor market. Let us examine each of these four elements in turn.

Individual Rights and Nonwage Costs of Labor

The Labor Code and the 1988 Constitution establish a very comprehensive set of minimum standards any individual labor contract must meet in order to be legal. The rules are quite rigid in the sense that they do not provide room for negotiation between the employer and the worker. The idea implicit in this rigidity is that the employer-worker relationship is asymmetrical, with the employer having more power than the worker. If conditions were left to be negotiated between the employer and the worker, the final result would probably not be fair. In order to protect the worker, a rigid set of minimum rules has been adopted that reduces the flexibility of the labor market and its capacity to adapt to changes in the economic environment.

Besides the increase in labor market rigidity, these rules imply nonwage costs for the employer. The cost of labor in Brazil can be disaggregated as follows: (i) the basic wage, which includes the contractual wage, plus the annual one-month bonus (13th wage), plus the employer's contribution to the workers' capitalization fund (FGTS), plus the contribution paid by firms to finance a workers' assistance service (SESI); (ii) hours paid but not effectively worked, because of vacations and leave (an important share of labor costs); (iii) the employer's contribution to Brazil's official labor-training system (SENAI and SENAC) and to an institution that assists small enterprises (SEBRAE) (such financial resources and institutions are administered by the employers' union federations and confederations); and (iv) the employer's contribution to social security, educational services *(salário educação)*, and an on-the-job accident insurance fee that is mandatory for all firms and proportional to the payroll.

The first aggregate of total labor costs to the employer is received by workers directly as wages, through a capitalization fund, or indirectly through the use of facilities of SESI. SESI differs from the other two modes in that it is a social service that not all workers use, while the basic wage and the capitalization fund are directly appropriated by every individual worker. Similarly, the second aggregate—paid vacations and leave—also directly benefits the individual worker.

The third aggregate of total labor costs to the employer—the contribution to the official labor training systems, SENAI and SENAC—is difficult for workers to receive directly, but these training systems do benefit them indirectly because they help increase workers' skill and salary levels. These systems also increase labor productivity, and thus the employer also benefits from this contribution. The fact that the financial resources coming from this contribution and from the training institutions are administered by the employers' union federations and confederations might suggest that employers are more directly favored by this contribution than are workers, and in reality, a share of the contribution is used to finance these federations and confederations. But this arrangement might well also be simply the result of historical contingencies, since it was the employers who lobbied for the labor-training systems in the first place.

The fourth aggregate of total labor costs to the employer consists of the contributions that go to the federal government to finance social security, education, and work accident insurance. In principle, the workers are the final beneficiaries of these contributions, but the quality of these government services in Brazil is so low that workers perceive little benefit. Still, the social security contribution does help to finance future retirement benefits for contributing workers and a pension system for old workers who are not able to provide for their own retirement.

Table 2.1 shows the composition of hourly labor costs in the Brazilian industrial sector in 1992. The table is divided between those contributions that entail a direct benefit to workers and those that do not.

The total labor cost to the employer in the Brazilian industrial sector is 186.9 percent of the basic wage. From this cost, 48.2 percentage points over the basic wage go directly to the worker in the form of direct or indirect wages and paid vacations or leave. The difference between the total cost of labor (186.9 percent of the basic wage) and the amount directly appropriated by the worker (148.2 percent of the basic wage) is partly appropriated by the worker, partly appropriated by the employer, and partly appropriated by society through the government.

Labor Courts and Individual Contract Disputes

As discussed earlier, it is always the burden of the employer to prove that all the laws and conditions of the individual labor contract were followed during the work relationship. Workers, or a workers' union, can always sue the employer in the labor courts if they believe the contract or the law was not respected. All agreements between individual workers and employers relating to disputes on individual contract compliance or on compliance with the law are valid only if made through a board of conciliation and judgment. This means that any firing of a worker has to be made in the judge's presence if the employer wants to be sure the worker will not later claim any right not observed by the employer. Since 1988, the worker has had a five-year period in which to file a claim in the labor courts.

Any individual dispute starts when a worker or his or her union files a complaint with the board of conciliation and judgment. The employer is notified and asked to provide the documents to prove that he is not guilty. The complaint and the documents are analyzed by the judge, who then calls the worker and the employer to a conciliation meeting. The process at this level is quite bureaucratic. The judge asks the employer if he or she wants to make a counterproposal to the worker. If the answer is yes, the judge asks the worker if the counterproposal is acceptable. If so, the dispute is over. If the employer does not make a counterproposal or if the one made is not accepted by the worker, then the judge

Table 2.1. Brazil: Worker's Pay and Labor Cost
(Monthly with normal number of hours = 44 weekly)

	Percentage	Total
Basic wage		100.0
Annual bonus	0.083	
FGTS	0.080	
SESI	0.015	
Others[1]	0.100	
Total pay to workers (monthly)		127.8
Paid leisure	0.160	
Paid to worker plus leisure		148.2
SENAI/SEBRAE	0.016	
INSS + accident insurance + education	0.245	
Total labor cost[2]		186.9

Source: Prepared by the authors based on data taken from the Brazilian Constitution and Labor Code.
[1] These include benefits that cannot be calculated for all workers, since they depend on gender, kind of work done, economic sector, and the like. These include family allowances, pregnancy leave, transport subsidies, etc.
[2] Employees contribute with 20 percent of their gross wages to social security. For workers who earn 20 minimum wages or more, the contribution is 20 percent of 20 minimum wages.

ends the hearing. After several months or even years, a decision is pronounced and sent to the parties in dispute. Once the decision is received, the employer must pay within seven days if the worker's demands were accepted by the judge or if a negative finding was successfully appealed to the area-wide labor court. In the end, the final decision can take years to be handed down and executed.

Institutions That Regulate the Firing of Workers

Another important element that can affect employer-worker relations at the individual contract level is the cost of funding the institution that buffers workers after firing—the FGTS. The main limits on firing in the Brazilian labor relations system (besides the required one-month warning period) are monetary limits. If the firing was not caused by a serious breach by the worker, then the employer has to pay a fine corresponding to 40 percent of the total amount of money deposited by the employer in the worker's FGTS account while he or she was working in the firm. As noted, in addition to this fine, the employer also has to notify the worker one month before the firing; this is the *aviso prévio* or prior notice of termination.

Thus, for Brazilian firms, the cost of dismissing workers has two components—namely, the FGTS aspect and the aspect of prior notice. During the month after the worker has received prior notice, he or she is allowed, according to the law, to take two hours a day to look for a new job. This arrangement implies an automatic minimum cost of 25 percent of the worker's monthly wage. In fact, the actual cost is usually higher, since the firms often end up paying a "termination notice fee" to the worker and dismissing him or her immediately. When this is not done, the worker's productivity usually declines sharply anyway during this period, making the actual cost of notice of termination fall between 25 percent and 100 percent of the monthly wage.

Thus, the total cost of dismissal to the employer is the sum of two components: 25 percent to 100 percent of the dismissed worker's monthly wage and 40 percent of the FGTS. The actual cost depends on the number of months the employee has worked for the firm, since the 40 percent fine is levied on the monthly deposits by the firm into the FGTS. Table 2.2 shows the costs for the firm to fire a worker, in numbers of monthly wages and according to the number of years of the worker's contract, under the assumption that the full cost of the notice of termination is borne by the firm.

The Unemployment Insurance Program

The Brazilian unemployment insurance program was created in 1986, as part of the well-known Cruzado Plan. The program initially had very low coverage and no secure source of resources. It was substantially improved in 1990, with changes that both reduced the eligibility requirements (producing a sharp increase in the proportion of the labor force covered) and provided a secure mechanism to fund the program. This new mechanism was based on the creation of a specific fund—the *Fundo de Amparo do Trabalhador* (FAT)—financed with taxes on the revenues of the firms (PIS/PASEP). Besides financing the unemployment insurance program, 40 percent of FAT's revenue is capitalized through the Brazilian Development Bank (*Banco Nacional de Desenvolvimento Econômico e Social* [BNDES]) and utilized to finance investment projects; the resources transferred to BNDES must give a rate of return of 5 percent a year, after correction for inflation. The fund also pays an annual bonus of one minimum wage for all formal sector workers receiving less than two minimum wages a month.

FAT's average monthly revenues increased from \$535.7 million to \$1.004 billion between 1991 and 1993, as a result of increases in the interest paid by BNDES and in financial revenues from FAT resources maintained at the Central Bank (public debt titles). Even though FAT's tax revenues declined during the period as a result of the increasing recession, its expenses remained smaller than revenues. The surplus was used to buy public debt titles, which are deposited at the Central Bank. FAT's unemployment insurance expenditures declined in real terms in 1993 as a result of the reduction in the number of unemployed workers covered by the insurance and in the average value of the benefit itself.

The unemployment insurance program offers partial coverage for up to four

Table 2.2. Brazil: Total Cost of Firing a Worker
(In number of monthly wages)

Contract period	Years							
	1	2	3	4	5	10	15	20
FGTS fine	0.41	0.84	1.27	1.72	2.19	4.72	7.66	11.07
Previous notification	1.00	1.00	1.00	1.00	1.00	1.00	1.00	1.00
Total	1.41	1.84	2.27	2.27	3.19	5.72	8.66	12.07

Source: Prepared by the authors.

months of unemployment.[3] The value of the benefit cannot be lower than the value of the minimum wage; it is adjusted monthly for inflation; and it is related to the average wage received by the worker in the last three months on the previous job.

A sharp increase took place in the number of workers covered by unemployment insurance during the 1986-93 period, at least as compared with the number of applicants. After the rapid increase between 1986 and 1988, which can be explained primarily by the fact that the insurance was created in 1986 and workers only gradually became aware of the program, the total number of applicants again increased sharply in 1990, this time as a result of the reduction in the eligibility requirements and because of the recession that started in 1990 and persisted through 1992. In 1992, the unemployment insurance program covered 3.85 million workers.

Coverage can be estimated as a percentage of total number of dismissed formal-sector workers can be estimated. In Brazil, every legally registered enterprise with more than five employees is obliged by law to register monthly, in the Ministry of Labor, every new labor contract signed (admission) and every labor contract ended (dismissal). With these data, the Ministry of Labor keeps a file of the total number of admissions and dismissals by legally registered enterprises. These total dismissed numbers can be compared with the number of dismissed workers actually receiving unemployment insurance benefits during a given period. The percentage of dismissed workers actually receiving the benefit has increased steadily since 1989. In 1993, 77.1 percent of all workers fired in the

---

[3] To become eligible to receive the benefit, the worker must meet the following criteria: (a) dismissal without a just cause; (b) formal labor contract during the last six months or legal self-employment for at least 15 months; (c) status as unemployed for at least seven days; (d) no other pension; and (e) no other type of income sufficient to guarantee his or her own subsistence and that of his or her family.

formal labor market were receiving unemployment insurance benefits. Of course, these data should be interpreted with care, since they cover only firms with more than five employees, but they do show that the Brazilian unemployment insurance program is quite important for the country's unemployed formal sector workers.

Individual Contract Regulations and Labor Market Incentives

The foregoing description of how individual labor contracts are regulated suggests many important points regarding the way these regulations can create incentives for individual workers and employers in the labor market and how such incentives can affect labor market behavior.

From this point of view, the most important aspect to be considered is axiomatic. Clearly, the structure of the regulations is based on the assumption that there exists a pronounced power asymmetry in the employer-worker relationship. Workers are weaker than employers and thus should be protected if the objective is to arrive at a fair employer-worker relationship. This viewpoint explains why there is no room for negotiation on minimum working conditions, the way labor courts function, or other such factors. On the other hand, this non-negotiability does generate rigidities and incentives to agents in the labor market that tend to induce behavior not conducive to productivity growth. Take, for example, the way labor courts behave. The process is quite awkward, both for the employer and the worker. On the one hand, the worker has no costs if he or she sues the employer, except the cost of going to the hearings.[4] This means that anytime a worker is fired, he has a strong incentive to sue the employer. He cannot lose anything but can perhaps win the suit. Thus, from the worker's point of view, the process provides good protection against unlawful practices but creates incentives to ride roughshod over the employer. So workers tend not to complain while they are employed, for fear of being fired, but they are as a rule very active in the labor courts if they do get fired.

Employers, on the other hand, tend to appeal the decisions of the board of conciliation and judgment, since they believe that at this level the sentences in general favor the workers. And, in fact, it is common knowledge that the system is quite paternalistic, and so the employers are correct in their belief.

The end result is very congested labor courts, with millions of cases per year (Pastore and Zylberstajn, 1988), which ends up impairing the workers' rights, since the final judgment can take years to be pronounced. Furthermore, the current situation generates difficult employer-worker relationships, with employers

---

[4] In general, labor lawyers determine their remuneration as a proportion of the value of the lawsuit, if the decision is favorable to the worker.

always afraid of being sued in the labor courts, and with very little incentive for cooperation and mutual worker-employee trust at the firm level.

This situation is exacerbated by the lawmaking power of the labor courts. Any decision handed down by the superior labor court that is not already specified clearly in the law becomes new law. Thus, certain concepts, such as the viewing of fringe benefits as part of a worker's regular wage, become a normal procedure in the courts and take on the force of law. This has resulted thus far in the exacerbation of tendencies toward a quite rigid and distrustful work relationship between workers and employers, at least at this level.

Given that employer-worker relationships are asymmetrical, a more workable alternative might be to create regulations that would induce an increase in workers' power, so as to make the relationship more symmetrical. At the individual level, this would mean an increase in the degree of qualification of the labor force, combined with an increase in the importance of workers' unions and more room for the definition of minimum work standards through collective contract negotiation at all levels, including the firm level. Direct negotiations between employers and workers might also be an important way to solve conflicts as they arise. The labor courts should have a much less dominant role to play, and workers' councils at the firm level would be of fundamental importance for improving workers' bargaining power and inducing continued negotiations at the plant level. In such a structure, workers' councils could be the forum for negotiating working conditions at the firm, for verifying that the employer effectively observes minimum working conditions, and for carrying out other related functions. This would constitute a system with more communication and conflict resolution between workers and the employer at the firm level. Certainly, the individual labor contract could only be made much more flexible in many dimensions.

Although current laws would seem to imply rigidity in the dimensions of work standards and employment, regulations actually tend to generate incentives for a very flexible real wage and employment relationships. This is so for two reasons. First, because the costs of firing are only monetary, there exists no important real non-monetary disincentives against firing, apart from the termination notice fee. Second, and maybe even more importantly, the FGTS mechanism provides an incentive for very short-run individual labor contracts. If fired, a worker can enjoy the FGTS money deposited by the employer and also receive the 40 percent fine the employer has to pay upon dismissal. If the worker never changes employment, he or she will never receive the fine and will be able to use the FGTS money only when retiring (or buying a house). For unskilled workers in jobs without clear promotion opportunities, being fired means an immediate income flow that can be substantial, depending on how long they have held the job. This revenue ordinarily would become available only upon retirement. For these workers, the optimum strategy is to do an on-the-job search for another position and to seek to be fired from the present one—reducing the amount of effort dedicated to the current job and, consequently, reducing the present firm's productivity. Incentive to "job hop" this way is highest when the unemployment rate is low, since the probability is greater then that the worker will quickly find another job.

Because short-term work relationships constitute the optimal strategy for the worker, the best strategy for the employer is to get the most the worker can give in this short period of time and never to invest in the worker for the long run. The firm's probability of losing the investment made in worker training and qualification is very high. Thus, the optimal strategy for the firm is to provide the minimal amount of training to unskilled workers and to exploit them as much as possible.

Under these circumstances, worker-firm relationships are expected to be of short duration. The firm has no interest in providing training for workers, and workers do not identify with the firm's objectives. The employment relationship is very flexible, but there is very little room for growth in labor productivity through training and on-the-job learning. Table 2.3 shows the turnover rate of Brazilian formal sector workers during the 1985-93 period. The turnover rate is calculated as the minimum between admissions and dismissals, divided by the total labor force. Thus, it shows the percentage of jobs that have been filled by different workers during a given period. The table shows the average monthly turnover rate and the annual turnover rate for the periods for which data are available.

The data should be read as follows. In 1985, on the average, 2.8 percent of the positions in all legally registered firms in Brazil (i.e., those with more than five employees) were vacated and refilled with a different worker in the period of one month. In 1989, 39.66 percent of the positions in all legally registered firms in Brazil (again, with more than five employees) were vacated and refilled with a different worker in this year. In the 1989-93 period, 28 percent or more of the legally registered firms' jobs experienced worker turnover in the period of one year.

The period of time covered by Table 2.3 is too short for more elaborate statistical inferences, but the turnover rates shown by the table are very interesting—and strikingly high. On the one hand, the data show high employment flexibility in the Brazilian formal labor market. On the other, they suggest that—given such high worker turnover rates—training and on-the-job learning must not be very common in that same labor market. Of course, this situation cannot be wholly attributed to the FGTS mechanism, but that mechanism is most likely one of the single most important causes.

One of Brazil's key labor regulations discussed earlier was the unemployment insurance program (FAT). As noted, this program functions more like a monetary transfer program to formal workers than do the traditional European or

Table 2.3. Turnover Rates in Brazilian Formal Labor Market, 1985-93

Year	Labor turnover (Monthly average)	Labor turnover (Annual average)
1985	2.80	n.a.
1986	3.67	n.a.
1987	3.72	n.a.
1988	3.80	n.a.
1989	3.49	39.66
1990	3.26	38.20
1991	2.69	35.75
1992	2.26	28.05
1993[a]	2.73	32.81

Source: Ministry of Labor, Law 4.923.
[a] January-October, 1993.
n.a. Not available.

U.S. unemployment programs, which link the right to receive the benefit to some specific duties, like accepting any job offered by the government employment service or being available for retraining. But the fact that Brazil's program functions like a monetary transfer program for unemployed formal sector workers does create an incentive for workers and firms to convert signed labor contract jobs into temporary (during the four months the benefit is received by the worker), unsigned labor contract jobs. (We shall later discuss more fully the importance of unsigned labor contracts in the Brazilian labor market.)

This practice is possible because, during the four months in which the worker receives the FAT benefit, the unemployment board has no control over the activities of that "unemployed" worker. Thus, if the worker finds an informal (or unsigned contract) job during these four months, there is no way the benefit can be discontinued. If the new job is a signed-contract job, the unemployment board could, in principle, discover that the person is employed, and thus cut the benefit, although in reality that is never done, maybe because the processing costs would be greater than the amount of the benefit paid. For the employer, on the other hand, it is always less expensive to have an unsigned contract worker than a signed contract worker, because of the considerable nonwage costs discussed earlier.

Thus, a coalition can be formed between workers and employers to informalize the labor force. If the contract is discontinued during the four months that the FAT benefit is received but the worker maintains the job, he or she will keep the wage and also receive the unemployment benefit. Actually, the agreement could also include the payment of the FGTS (firing fund) to the worker and the negotiated informal repayment of the bonus 40 percent fine of the FGTS to the employer. Thus, both employer and worker could realize a financial gain at the expense of the government.

These developments could help to explain, at least in part, the surprising fact that the introduction of an unemployment insurance program in Brazil did not result in a tendency to increase the rate of unemployment or in a reduction in the percentage of workers with an unsigned contract job. Labor market models had predicted that unemployment insurance benefits would increase the rate of unemployment and decrease the percentage of workers with unsigned contract jobs for at least two reasons: because the benefit would at least temporarily reduce the utility of work versus leisure (for a good critical survey of these models see Atkinson and Micklewright, 1991) or because, as the workers receive the benefit, they can refuse worse employment opportunities in the unsigned contract labor market to provide their subsistence while unemployed (i.e., the buffer function of the unemployment insurance program).

Figure 2.1 shows the evolution of the rate of unemployment (y axis) versus the evolution of the percentage of workers without a signed contract (x axis) between May 1982 and October 1993. These are data from monthly household surveys (*Pesquisa Mensal de Emprego*, IBGE) for the six greater metropolitan areas of the country (São Paulo, Rio de Janeiro, Belo Horizonte, Recife, Salvador, and Porto Alegre). Each point in the curve represents the combination of the 12-month moving averages of the rate of unemployment and the percentage of workers without a signed contract, for a given period. For instance, point 1 represents the moving average between May 1982 and April 1983 of these two variables, point 2 for the period May 1983 through April 1984, and so forth. The slope of this curve shows the relative behavior of these two variables. The steeper the slope, the more the unemployment rate constitutes the labor market adjustment variable than does the percentage of workers without signed contracts. Points 1 and 2 correspond to the strong recession of the beginning of the 1980s (1982-84). Points 3 through 8 represent the years 1985-90, which is a period of both rapid economic growth (1985-86) and of relatively slow growth, without a recession (1987-89). Finally, points 9 through 11 represent the recession period of the beginning of the 1990s. As can be seen from the figure, there is a clear change in the reaction of the Brazilian labor market in the two recession periods (points 1, 2, and 3 as compared with points 9, 10, and 11). In the first recession, the rate of unemployment was the main labor market adjustment variable, but in the second, the percentage of workers without signed contracts took its place as the main labor market adjustment variable. The unemployment rate saw its labor market adjustment function sharply reduced in this later period. Very little of the adjustment in this second period was made through the increase in the rate of unemployment. Although this behavior cannot be entirely attributed to the unemployment insurance system, the fact remains that the unemployment rate became a less important labor market adjustment variable after the creation of the

Figure 2.1. Brazil: Open Unemployment and Informality, May 1982-October 1993
(As a percentage of the economically active population)

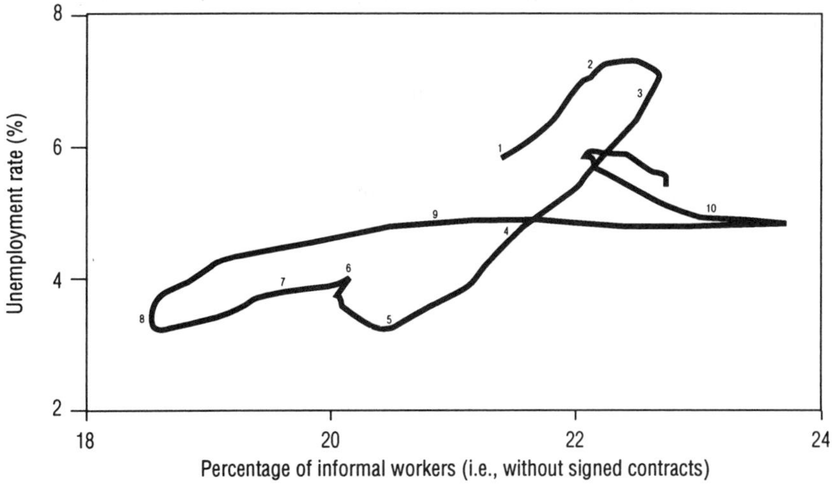

Source: Pesquisa Mensal de Emprego, IBGE.

unemployment insurance program—a quite unexpected result and contrary to most economic models of labor market behavior. Thus, the supposition that the Brazilian unemployment insurance system actually creates incentives for an increase in the share of unsigned labor contract workers is highly supported by the data shown in Figure 2.1.

Summing up, the individual labor contract is an important instrument of the Brazilian labor relations system. The paternalistic character of the laws governing the individual contract, together with the great importance of the labor courts, tend in principle to generate rigidities in work standards practices by employers. But the lack of effective nonmonetary restrictions on firing and the relatively small cost of dismissing workers—combined with institutions that generate strong incentives for worker-firm relations of short duration—discriminate against human capital investment on the job and against labor productivity growth. This situation actually embodies a flexible employment relation in real life, despite the rigidities observed in the formal legal labor contract.

Furthermore, the relatively large difference between workers' basic wage and total labor costs to the employer—combined with an unemployment insurance program that creates incentives for the transformation of signed contract jobs into unsigned contract jobs—induces the growth of unsigned contract (informal) work relations. The importance and behavior of this informal segment of the Brazilian labor market will be analyzed in the following section.

Segmentation and Informality

High unemployment rates, large and stable wage differentials among sectors, and a low degree of labor mobility among sectors are all evidence that a labor market is not functioning as a single competitive market. The fact that such labor market situations exist in several world economies has led to the development of various models (such as efficiency wage models and insider-outsider models) to explain why certain labor markets are not competitive and how noncompetitive labor markets function.

One of the basic reasons for the noncompetitive behavior of a labor market is the existence of binding labor legislation that is neither universally required nor enforced. The objective of this section is to investigate the connection between labor legislation and labor market functioning in Brazil.

To conduct this research we divide the Brazilian labor market into three parts. We divide the occupied labor force into self-employed workers and employees.[5] Then we divide the hired employees into two groups according to whether they have a formal labor contract. Formal labor contracts are regulated by extensive legislation, and only workers with formal contracts have access to social programs such as unemployment insurance and social security pensions and benefits. To hire a permanent worker without a formal labor contract is illegal, but certainly this rule is not strictly enforced by Brazil's government. Employees with (without) a formal contract will be referred to as formal (informal) employees.

To avoid difficulties involved in analyzing a spatially heterogeneous market such as the Brazilian labor market, we restrict our analysis to the six major metropolitan areas: Recife, Salvador, Belo Horizonte, Rio de Janeiro, São Paulo, and Porto Alegre. For convenience, we are going to refer to these six metropolitan areas as a group called metropolitan Brazil. The labor force in metropolitan Brazil comprises 15 million workers, or 25 percent of the entire Brazilian labor force.

The Concept of Segmentation

A group of workers in a given economy is said to be homogeneous when these workers have the same preferences about job-related features (wages, vacations, work amenities) and when they can be used interchangeably in production (as perfect substitutes)—that is, when the level and composition of production are

---

[5] Public servants, nonpaid workers and employers were excluded from the analysis.

completely unaffected by interchanging jobs among workers in the group. The concept of homogeneous workers is central to the discussion of labor market segmentation and discrimination.

As long as the well-being of workers does not influence production but increases costs (since it requires higher wages, extra fringe benefits, or a workplace with more amenities), then profit-maximizing firms will choose to minimize the welfare of workers. In a competitive labor market without mobility costs, offers by given firms to workers will be bound by the offers made by the remaining firms in the market. As a result, in this economy all homogeneous workers will have the same level of welfare. Hence, all homogeneous workers will be indifferent to which jobs they perform among all jobs occupied by workers in the same group.

In summary, the combination of three facts—irrelevance of workers' welfare to production, perfectly competitive labor market, and absence of mobility cost—implies that all homogeneous workers will be indifferent to all jobs occupied by workers in the same group, irrespective of how diverse the product they produce, the technology being used, or the amount of capital or other inputs available. In other words, in an economy with these three characteristics, homogeneous workers will experience the same level of welfare despite any level of heterogeneity among firms with respect to technology, product line, or availability of other inputs.

Labor market segmentation has been used in the literature with at least two distinct meanings. First, segmentation for some analysts describes the situation in which there is no mobility among certain segments of the labor market; as a consequence of this lack of mobility, homogeneous workers do not necessarily receive identical offers from all segments of the labor market, and as a result, they will develop preferences for certain sectors. Second, since the lack of mobility is a sufficient but not necessary condition for homogeneous workers to prefer certain sectors, other analysts use the actual existence of these preferences themselves to define labor market segmentation. The first definition implies that in cases of labor market segmentation, workers are not indifferent vis-à-vis segments, and the second definition uses the existence of such preferences itself as the hallmark of segmentation.

Temporary disequilibria of the labor market can lead workers to have temporary preferences for certain sectors, so when using this second definition, it is important to consider the labor market as segmented only when the preferences of workers for certain sectors are persistent. In this study we use the second definition of segmentation. Therefore, here it is possible to have labor market segmentation and labor mobility at the same time. What defines segmentation is not the lack of labor mobility, but rather the existence of workers' preferences for certain segments of the labor market. This more general definition of segmentation is preferred because it covers important models of the functioning of the labor market such as the Harris-Todaro model and others based on the efficiency wage idea. In all of these models, workers have clear preferences for certain sectors, but mobility is not precluded.

Of course jobs have many attributes that directly affect the welfare of workers, but in this case only wages are considered. Therefore, labor market segmentation will exist when equally productive workers receive different wages in different segments of the labor market.

Institutional Segmentation

On the one hand, labor market segmentation may be generated by differences across firms with respect to technology and market power. On the other hand, it may be generated by labor market legislation and unions. In general, any specific form of segmentation is the result of a combination of all of these forces. For instance, unions can generate segmentation only if they happen to be in a sector in which firms have some market power; otherwise there would be no profits to be shared between union members and firms. Regarding segmentation between protected and unprotected sectors, in general firms in the protected sector pay higher wages than do firms in the unprotected sector, even in the absence of any labor legislation, since the two groups of firms probably differ with respect to the technology and organizational procedures used.

The present study is concerned primarily with labor market segmentation that arises as a result of labor legislation. Therefore, in studying segmentation we choose the form that is most likely to be directly and intimately related to labor legislation. Our discussion of Brazil's labor market segmentation is based on the three segments mentioned earlier: autonomous workers, employees with formal labor contracts, and hired employees without formal labor contracts.[6]

The Concept of Degree of Segmentation

There exist several wage differentials between the formal and informal sectors that we could either compute empirically or imagine conceptually. Here we shall

---

[6] Although this form of segmentation is likely to be intimately related to regulation of the labor market, there is no guarantee that the legislation is in fact the main cause of the segmentation. It could occur that the labor market would be segmented along similar lines even in the absence of any labor market regulation. For example, consider an economy in which because of technological reasons there exist "high-paying" jobs and "low-paying" jobs, even in the absence of regulation. Once regulation is introduced, the "high-paying" jobs will naturally obey the regulation but the "low-paying" jobs will not. In the end, workers will prefer the jobs obeying the legislation, but the difference between formal and informal jobs is certainly not a consequence of the introduction of legislation. In this case, legislation is only helping to identify the "high-paying" jobs and is not the cause of the segmentation.

discuss various conceptual wage differentials and try first to clarify the meaning of each and then identify which one is closely related to the notion of degree of segmentation.

The first wage differential one might consider is the difference in the average wage between formal and informal workers. This wage differential can be easily computed from information from a sample of workers. The computation, however, tends to overestimate the degree of segmentation for two reasons: first, because workers in the formal jobs tend to be, on average, more skilled than workers in informal jobs; and second, because formal jobs tend to be better than jobs in the informal sector with respect to characteristics unrelated to compliance with labor legislation.

Another wage differential that might be extensively examined is the one found between formal and informal workers with identical observable characteristics. This wage differential tends to be smaller than that with no control for workers' characteristics. Since we can control for only a few worker characteristics (typically including gender, education, age, race, and area of residence), we can observe that this controlled wage differential is not necessarily equal to the wage differential between equally productive workers in the formal and informal sectors. These would be the same only if the distribution of the nonobserved characteristics were the same among formal and informal workers. But since the distribution of the observed characteristics is not the same among formal and informal workers, and since workers were not randomly allocated among sectors, there is substantial reason to believe that the unobserved characteristics are also unequally distributed among formal and informal workers. Therefore, although the controlled wage differential among formal and informal workers constitutes an important empirical tool, there exists no guarantee that this controlled wage differential would be close to the wage differential between equally productive workers.

If we could observe all worker characteristics, we could compute the wage differential between equally productive workers in the formal and informal sectors. Although this wage differential between equally productive workers could be considered the degree of segmentation between formal and informal sectors, it could not be taken as the degree of segmentation induced by labor legislation. The reason is that jobs in the formal and informal sector differ not only because of compliance or noncompliance with labor legislation but also with respect to other attributes that could influence wages. In other words, the wage differential between equally productive workers certainly answers the question of how much higher the wage of an informal worker would be if that worker were employed in the formal sector.

Nevertheless, this wage differential does not answer the question of what would be the wage gain of an informal worker if his or her current employer decided (or were forced) to comply with the labor legislation. To the extent that formal and informal jobs are very distinct with respect to several other characteristics, it is possible that workers might experience considerable wage increases if they could get a formal job, but would experience a wage reduction if the current employer decided or were forced to comply with labor legislation. In other words, it is possible to have informal workers who would prefer formal jobs but, at the same time, would prefer that labor legislation not be enforced in their current jobs. In this case, workers prefer formal jobs not because such jobs comply with legislation but because such jobs are better with respect to other attributes. In summary, the wage differential between equally productive workers in the formal and informal sectors is a precise measure of the degree of segmentation between these sectors, which is the result of all factors that could make jobs in these two sectors different. Therefore, this wage differential does not necessarily measure the degree of segmentation induced by labor legislation.

If the formal and informal sectors differed only because one complies with the labor legislation and the other one does not, then the wage differential between equally productive workers in the formal and informal sectors would be a precise measure of the degree of segmentation induced by labor legislation. But even in this case, this wage differential would not answer the question of what is the gain to workers in the formal sectors because of the existence of the labor legislation.

To answer this question we have to compare the current wage of workers in the formal sector with the wages that they would have if the legislation were not enforced at all. The wages that workers currently in the formal sector would obtain in the absence of any labor legislation are not necessarily identical to the wages that equally productive workers are currently obtaining in the informal sector. The reason is that the elimination of the labor legislation is a nonatomistic labor market change. Hence, if it occurs, it would generate changes in the general equilibria of the labor market, affecting the allocation of labor across the formal and informal sectors and the level of wages in both. Only under very specialized assumptions would the new equilibrium wage structure equal the current wage structure in the informal sector. In general, the two structures will differ in that the wage gain of a worker in the formal sector, because of the existence of labor legislation, will not be equal to the current wage differential between equally productive workers in the formal and informal sectors.

Basic Characteristics of the Metropolitan Labor Markets in Brazil

Next we shall examine four basic empirical characteristics of the labor market related to the formal-informal segmentation: (i) the unemployment rate, (ii) the degree of informalization, (iii) the degree of segmentation, and (iv) the degree of labor mobility between formal and informal jobs.[7]

---

[7] Except for the measures of mobility, all estimates in this section refer to a standardized labor force. The methodology used to generate these standardized estimates is presented in the Appendix.

Unemployment Rate

One of the striking features of the Brazilian labor markets is a consistent low rate of unemployment. For the 1982-92 period, the unemployment rate for metropolitan Brazil was, on average, only 4 percent of the labor force (Table 2.4).

Another important characteristic of the unemployment rate in Brazil is its low sensitivity to economic shifts. The unemployment rate tends to be stable over time and to have very modest variations across areas and types of worker. It has been affected very little by the sharp fluctuations in the level of economic activity in Brazil since 1980. In fact, during the recession in the beginning of the 1980s, the unemployment rate increased to only 5.5 percent, and in the recession at the beginning of the 1990s the unemployment rate reached only 5 percent. During the period of growth in the middle of the 1980s, the unemployment rate declined to 3 percent.

Table 2.4 shows how the unemployment rate varies by area of residence, education, and gender of the worker. These estimates reveal small variations in the unemployment rate along all three dimensions. The rate varies by less than 2 percentage points, being higher in the Northeast and lower in the South and Southeast.

With respect to the variation of the unemployment rate across educational levels, there exists an inverted U-shaped curve. The rate increased from 4 percent among illiterate workers to 4.5 percent among workers having from five to eight years of schooling, and it decreased sharply from that point on to reach 2.2 percent among workers with a college education.

Moreover, men and women have similar levels of unemployment. Amadeo, *et al.* (1993) found similar results. They also claim that the unemployment rate for men is more sensitive to economic fluctuations. Moreover, they show that the low sensitivity of the unemployment rate among women is not the result of a greater sensitivity of their labor force participation rate—that is to say, it is not true that the female unemployment rate is low during recessions because women tend to drop out of the labor force during these times.

As for the age profile of the unemployment rate, there is a monotonic decline with age, indicating that unemployment hits younger workers the hardest. The unemployment rate is close to 10 percent among workers less than 25 years old and below 2 percent among workers more than 45 years old.

Degree of Informality

Just as striking as the low rate of unemployment is the high degree of informality of the Brazilian metropolitan labor markets. As Table 2.4 shows, on average for the 1982-92 period, only slightly more than one-half (55 percent) of the labor force was composed of employees with formal labor contracts. Over this period,

Table 2.4. Brazil: Unemployment Rate, Degree of Informalization, and Degree of Segmentation by Type of Worker, 1982-92

Type of worker	Unemploy-ment rate	Formal employees	Informal employees	Self-employed	Formal-informal	Formal self-employed
Gender						
Male	3.9	59.1	10.3	17.6	0.37	0.29
Female	4.0	48.8	18.8	23.8	0.49	0.62
Years of schooling						
0	3.9	44.2	22.9	29.2	0.42	0.46
1-4	4.3	52.1	16.2	25.3	0.41	0.42
5-8	4.5	57.7	10.1	21.2	0.36	0.37
9-11	3.4	61.1	9.6	12.3	0.41	0.46
12+	2.2	56.1	12.7	8.1	0.56	0.39
Area of residence						
Porto Alegre	3.5	57.8	11.8	18.2	0.32	0.35
São Paulo	3.6	60.7	13.8	15.5	0.42	0.35
Rio de Janeiro	3.3	53.3	15.8	20.1	0.39	0.37
Belo Horizonte	3.4	55.0	13.3	20.2	0.43	0.45
Salvador	4.4	54.4	11.6	22.7		
Recife	5.2	49.5	15.1	23.0		

Source: Ministry of Labor, Law 4.923.

employees without a formal labor contract represented 14 percent of the labor force, while self-employed workers represented 20 percent. The remaining 11 percent was made up of employers (4 percent) and public sector workers (7 percent). As opposed to the stability of the unemployment rate along all dimensions, the degree of informalization measured by either the proportion of employees without formal labor contracts or the proportion of self-employed workers tends to vary substantially over time, across areas, and by type of worker.

Table 2.4 reveals some reduction (2 percentage points) in the degree of formalization during the recession in the beginning of the 1980s. Except for this modest fluctuation, there is no other fluctuation or trend in the 1980s. In particular, there is no trend toward a greater degree of formalization of labor relations in metropolitan Brazil. The beginning of the 1990s, however, saw a dramatic change in the degree of formalization, with the proportion of employees with formal labor contracts declining by 6 percentage points in less than three years.

Over the period, the proportion of self-employed workers increased by almost 6 percentage points. Except for a small fluctuation in the first half of the 1980s, the proportion of self-employed workers experienced a continuous process of growth, which was particularly fast in the beginning of the 1990s. During this period, the proportion of self-employed workers increased 3 percentage points in two years.

The geographical disparities in the degree of formalization and informalization are presented in Table 2.4. Formalization tends to be lower in the Northeast and higher in the South and Southeast, being more than 10 percentage points higher in São Paulo than in Recife. Rio de Janeiro is an exception to this rule, being a metropolitan area located in the Southeast, yet with a degree of formalization similar to those observed in the Northeast.

The degree of formalization and informalization also varies substantially with the level of education of workers. The proportion of formal employees increases monotonically from 44 percent among illiterates to 61 percent among workers with secondary education (an increase of 17 percentage points), and the proportion of informal employees declines monotonically from 23 percent among illiterates to 10 percent among workers with secondary education (a decline of 13 percentage points). The decline in education in the proportion of self-employed workers is even more impressive; this proportion declines from 29 percent among illiterates to 12 percent among workers with secondary education (a decline of 17 percentage points).

Table 2.4 also reveals sharp gender-based differences in the degree of formality and informality. Some 59 percent of males in the labor force are employed with a formal labor contract, but only 49 percent of females in the labor force have the same status. The proportion of females employed without a formal contract is 9 percentage points higher than the proportion of females working as self-employed.

Degree of Segmentation

Table 2.4 presents estimates of the average wage differential between formal and informal employees and between formal employees and self-employed workers. In both cases, we are comparing workers with identical observed characteristics (age, education, gender, and area of residence). The overall average indicates that the (geometric) mean wage of formal employees is 52 percent higher than the corresponding mean among informal employees and 51 percent higher than the corresponding mean among self-employed workers with the same characteristics.[8] If we are willing to assume that omitted worker characteristics do not explain very much of this wage differential, then we are led to conclude that workers in the formal sector receive wages substantially greater than equally

---

[8] The 52 percent figure is obtained as $100(1-e^{-0.42})$, where 0.42 is the log-wage difference between formal and informal workers.

productive workers in the informal sector. Furthermore, if we are willing to assume that the main cause for the wage differential between equally productive workers in the formal and informal sectors is compliance with labor legislation, then we are led to conclude that this factor can increase wages by approximately 50 percent.

Both differentials declined sharply during the 1980s, mainly from 1984 to 1987. The decline was considerably greater for the log-wage differential between formal employees and self-employed workers than for the log-wage differential between formal and informal employees. In fact, while in 1984 the log-wage differential between formal and informal employees (self-employed workers) was above 0.5 (0.6), by the beginning of 1987 this log-wage differential declined to less than 0.35 (0.25). Since 1986, the log-wage differential has been oscillating around 0.35 without any clear trend.

Table 2.4 also shows that these wage differentials are considerably stable across groups of workers defined on the basis of area of residence, educational level and gender. In all cases the log-wage differential is between 0.30 and 0.60. Both wage differentials tend to be greater among females, with the log-wage differential between formal employees and self-employed workers being considerably larger for females than for males. With respect to the level of education, the wage differential between formal and informal workers has a U-shape, declining from illiterates to the category of five to eight years of schooling, and increasing sharply from that point on. The log-wage differential between formal employees and self-employed workers also has a U-shape, being smaller among workers with five to eight years of schooling. Finally, the log-wage differential between formal and informal employees is quite stable across metropolitan areas, being lower in Porto Alegre (0.32) and higher in Recife (0.50). Overall, the differential tends to be lower in the South and higher in the Northeast and in Belo Horizonte, reaching intermediate levels in the Southeast.

Degree of Mobility

We have not yet ascertained the extent to which the sizable segmentation is static or dynamic. This can also be expressed as the extent to which workers initially not allocated to formal jobs will have access to formal jobs in the future, or the degree of labor mobility between formal and informal jobs, or the extent to which the allocation of workers to formal or informal jobs is temporary or persistent.

Estimates of the degree of mobility among sectors is always a difficult empirical task since it necessarily requires longitudinal or retrospective data. Here we shall present evidence on labor mobility among formal jobs, informal jobs, and self-employed activities based on two previous studies: Barros, Sedlacek, and Varandas (1988) and Barros, Camargo, and Sedlacek (1990).

The first study examines only the mobility of employees in the metropolitan area of São Paulo, between jobs offering formal labor contracts and jobs not offering formal labor contracts. This study found what could be considered a large degree of mobility between these two segments. More specifically, this study found that over a period of one year, 9 percent of the employees moved between these segments in either direction. Since the mobility would be equal to 18 percent if the allocation of workers to segments in the two consecutive years were independent, the observed mobility (9 percent) is one-half of the mobility that would be observed if the allocation of workers to segments in the two consecutive years were independent. Moreover, this study shows that since each year 4.9 percent of the population moves from jobs not offering formal contracts to jobs offering formal contracts, and since the proportion of informal employees was 11 percent, then almost 50 percent of the informal employees in a given year will be formal employees in the next year.

The second study investigates mobility between self-employment and jobs not offering formal labor contracts. The study also expands the earlier analysis, considering both the metropolitan areas of São Paulo and Recife. It has three main conclusions: (i) the degree of mobility is higher in São Paulo than in Recife; (ii) the mobility between formal and informal employees is much greater than the mobility between self-employed activities and jobs offering formal contracts; and (iii) self-employed activities and jobs not offering formal contracts are more similar and have a greater degree of labor mobility in Recife than in São Paulo (in fact, in São Paulo, self-employed activities tend to be preferable to jobs without formal labor contracts, while in Recife, both of these work opportunities generate essentially the same level of earnings).

The Role of the Informal Sector in Brazil

Who Suffers the Most from Segmentation?

By definition, the existence of segmentation means that a given group of workers in the informal sector earns less than its counterpart group of workers in the formal sector. So for each type of worker group, segmentation means a gain for those in the formal sector and a loss for those in the informal sector. The absolute amount of gains and losses from segmentation is not equally divided among different types of worker groups. These gains and losses are greater for worker groups for which the degree of segmentation and the degree of informalization are greater. In other words, the degree of segmentation indicates the wage loss (gain) of each worker in the informal (formal) sector, while the degree of informalization (formalization) indicates the proportion of workers that will experience this loss (gain).

To provide an indication of how the aggregate measure of the wage loss of workers in the informal sector varies by type of worker, we multiply the degree of segmentation by the degree of informalization for each type of worker and compare the results. Since the degree of informalization and of segmentation both tend to be higher among workers with lower earning capacity, the loss from segmentation tends to be greater precisely among the workers with lower earning capacity, who are largely found in the informal sector. This is particularly true for women, younger and older workers, and the least educated. An important exception occurs with the most educated segment of the labor force, which has the largest proportion of informal employees and a larger wage differential between formal and informal employees than workers with nine to 11 years of schooling.

Structural Labor Absorption

Despite paying lower wages, the informal sector has been considered important because of its capacity to generate jobs for a large percentage of the labor force. But this property is relevant only if we consider the informal sector as competitive. In fact, if the fundamental characteristic of the informal sector is the payment of wages below marginal productivity thanks to an asymmetric capital-to-labor relationship biased against labor, then a formalization of the informal sector will increase wages without any impact on the demand for labor. In summary, the generation of jobs by the informal sector is not a valid argument against policies promoting the formalization of that sector, since in this case the informal sector can be formalized without destruction of jobs.

When the informal sector functions as a competitive segment of the labor market, there exists a serious conflict between formalization and labor absorption. In this case, policies biased against the informal sector may have important consequences on the overall level of employment.

Depending on the environment under consideration, different characteristics of the informal sector should be analyzed. The importance of the informal sector in the short run depends on its relative size (proportion of labor force in the informal sector) and on how sensitive the demand for labor in this sector is to changes in wages and other policies—that is, its importance depends on its current contribution to labor absorption and on the sensitivity of its demand for labor to policies devoted to formalization of the labor market.

During the process of adjustment it is crucial to analyze the extent to which the informal sector's demand for labor is insensitive (or at least, less sensitive than the formal sector's demand for labor) to the cyclical fluctuations typical of any adjustment process. In other words, if the demand for labor of the informal sector is very insensitive to macroeconomic fluctuations, then the informal sector may have an important role in absorbing labor during recessions despite having perhaps no relevance in absorbing labor during periods of steady growth.

Finally, the desirability and relevance of the informal sector in the long run depend on two factors: (i) the sector's ability to compete with the formal sector and to experience considerable growth in its demand for labor; and (ii) the sector's capacity to improve productivity and wage levels.

Policy Proposals

Based on the foregoing analysis, many policy proposals can be made regarding reforms to improve the behavior of the Brazilian labor market. Before beginning, it is important to note the extreme degree of flexibility of that market. The rate of open unemployment is very low, real wages vary quite freely, the average period of unemployment is very short, and the turnover rate is quite high—all of which are true for both the formal and the informal segments of the labor market. One important consequence of this is the near lack of incentive for firms and workers to invest in specific training. As a result, very little on-the-job training is provided in the Brazilian economy.

As suggested earlier, this high level of flexibility is, at least in part, the result of an institutional framework that creates incentives for greater flexibility, largely through the FGTS dismissal fund and fine and the FAT unemployment insurance scheme. These institutions motivate workers to precipitate their own firing by reducing productivity when the labor market is tight, and they motivate employers and workers alike to increase the informality of the labor sector.

If all of this is indeed so, then it would seem to be important to change these institutions in order to increase the efficiency of the labor market by providing incentives for firms and workers to invest in specific training and by tightening the relationship between unemployment insurance and employment retraining.

The FGTS system together with the low employer cost of worker dismissals encourages a very high degree of labor turnover. The present system should give way to another in which (i) the costs of dismissal would be lower for those firms that prefer to lay off workers instead of simply firing them without fair cause; (ii) the FGTS would be transformed into a pension fund, administered by workers, employers, and government representatives, that could be used only upon a worker's retirement; (iii) the FAT unemployment insurance fund, not the workers, would get the money from the fee paid by firms dismissing workers; and (iv) only those unemployed workers who participate in retraining programs would be eligible for unemployment insurance. The combination of these elements would certainly reduce the rate of turnover, with positive effects on labor's productivity.

In our discussion of institutional aspects of the labor market in Brazil, it became clear that the labor code is too detailed and all-encompassing and that the labor courts intervene too much in capital-labor relationships. The code was written in keeping with the principles that workers should be protected from employers' potential excessive exploitation and, at the same time, that organization at the plant level should be avoided, in order to reduce capital-labor conflict.

This approach has resulted in a union structure embodying a perverse corporatism in which the federations are not very representative of the rank and file. As noted, this institutional arrangement is also partly responsible for the high degree of labor turnover in Brazil and for the existence of the large Brazilian informal sector. Furthermore, it also tends to create "freeloading" behavior in collective and individual bargaining. The existence of the informal sector (as seen in the last half of the chapter) is associated with important wage differentials and differences in the capacity of the various labor groups to endure recessions and structural reforms.

The main policy proposal stemming from our analysis here would be to increase the role of direct negotiations between employers and employees and to reduce the role of the labor courts. In principle, the labor courts should not intervene in collective bargaining. This stance would imply a radical change in the role of unions and the system of worker representation. Of course, where unions are well organized, the law is not as essential and the courts by definition should not have to play a major role. But where unions are weak, the elimination of the labor code could have negative effects on the well-being of workers. Hence, the process of reducing the role of the labor code and the labor courts is very difficult and delicate.

The reform should also eliminate the union's monopoly of representation and the compulsory contribution by workers and employers to class association.

Two additional ideas deserve consideration. The first is the elimination of the "just cause" clause of dismissals. If workers are dismissed, they should be eligible for unemployment insurance benefits, provided they meet the conditions of retraining and reallocation to another job. Just cause is very difficult to define and, in general, is used by workers and employers to free-ride in the labor market. The second idea is to eliminate the provision that collective contracts should cover all workers, regardless of affiliation to the union. This provision creates incentives for workers to free-ride on the unions, and it reduces the incentive to affiliation, and therefore unions' bargaining power.

A new system in which negotiations replace the labor code should be implemented through a gradual transition process and should be accompanied by changes in the nature of the representation of workers. Incentives to represent workers more effectively could be created by increasing the power and responsibility of union and worker representatives within firms. At this level, the representative bodies could be responsible for negotiating specific working conditions, changes in working hours, and conditions of dismissals above those stipulated in law—in other words, everything directly related to the actual functioning of a given firm. Real wages and general working conditions could be negotiated at a more aggregate level—perhaps sectorial or even national—as minimum standards. As worker organization improves, the degree of legal protection can gradually be reduced.

One final aspect to be considered here is the definition of criteria for private or government arbitration. Arbitration should obey set rules and should be encouraged as a way of making the costs and benefits of strikes available to workers and employers, without the government having to play a pivotal role.

The debate on these issues has already started in Brazil. There is consensus on the part of both the employers and unions that the current degree of interference of the labor courts is too high. Nevertheless, the way is not yet perfectly clear for the establishment of more pragmatic measures for gradually moving into a new structure.

Bibliography

Abramo, L. 1986. O resgate da dignidade. Master's thesis, Applied Economics Department, University of São Paulo (FEA/USP).

Amadeo, E., R. Paes de Barros, J.M. Camargo, et al. 1993. *Human Resources in the Adjustment Process.* IDB Working Papers Series No. 137. Inter-American Development Bank.

Amadeo, E., and J.M. Camargo. Política salarial e negociação: perspectivas para o futuro. OIT/Ministério do Trabalho. Mimeo.

_____. 1990. *The Brazilian Labor Market in an Era of Adjustment.* Discussion Paper. Department of Economics, Pontíficia Universidade Católica do Rio de Janeiro (PUC/RJ).

Atkinson, A.B., and J. Micklewright. 1991. Unemployment Compensation and Labor Market Transitions: A Critical Review. *Journal of Economic Literature* 29 (December): 1679-1727.

Azeredo, B., and J.P. Chahad. 1992. O programa brasileiro de seguro-desemprego: diagnóstico e sugestões para o seu aperfeiçoamento. Série Seminários n. 01/02, IPEA. 01/92, IPEA.

Barros, R.P., J.M. Camargo, and G. Sedlacek. 1990. Os três mercados: segmentação, mobilidade e desigualdade. IPEA, Rio de Janeiro.

Barros, R.P., G. Sedlacek, and S. Varandas. 1988. Uma análise da mobilidade no mercado de trabalho brasileiro: perspectiva de segmentação. *Anais da ANPEC.*

Camargo, J.M. 1990. Salários e negociações coletivas. *Pesquisa e planejamento econômico* 20 (2): 305-324.

Castro, M. 1988. Participação ou controle: o dilema da atuação operária nos locais de trabalho. Instituto de Pesquisas Econômicas/USP.

Collier, R.B., and D. Collier. 1979. Inducement versus Constraints: Disaggregating "Corporatism." *The American Political Science Review* 73.

Consolidação das Leis do Trabalho. 1989. EDUSP.

Katz, C.H. 1993. The Decentralization of Collective Bargaining: A Literature Review and Comparative Analysis. *Industrial and Labor Relations Review* 4 (October): 3-22.

La Rocque, E. 1989. Sindicalismo brasileiro. Undergraduate monograph.

Pastore, J. 1993. A flexibilização como estratégia de competição. CNI. Mimeo.

Pastore, J., and H. Zylberstajn. 1988. *A administração do conflito trabalhista no Brasil.* São Paulo: Instituto de Pesquisas Econômicas/USP.

Simonsen, M.H. 1983. Indexation: Current Theory and the Brazilian Experience. In *Inflation, Debt, and Indexation,* eds. R. Dornbusch and M. H. Simonsen. Cambridge, Mass.: The MIT Press.

Soskice, D. 1990. Wage Determination: The Changing Role of Institutions in Advanced Industrialized Countries. *Oxford Review of Economic Policy* (4): 36-61.

Tavares, M.H. 1988. Difícil caminho: sindicatos e política na construção da democracia. In *A democracia no Brasil,* eds. F. W. Reis and G. O'Donnell. São Paulo: Vértice.

APPENDIX: HETEROGENEITY

The Degree of Segmentation

Let P be the universe of analysis and p a worker in this population. Let $W_i(p)$, $W_s(p)$ and $W_f(p)$ be three hypothetical log-wages associated with worker p. $W_i(p)$ is the log-wage that worker p would have if he has an informal labor contract. $W_s(p)$ is the log-wage that worker p would have if he has a self-employed activity. $W_f(p)$ is the log-wage that worker p would have if he had a job with a formal labor contract. So the labor market is segmented whenever these three log-wages are not the same, at least for a given group of workers. The average degree of segmentation is defined as

$$\Delta_i = E\,[W_f - W_i]$$

and

$$\Delta_s = E\,[W_f - W_s]$$

If we could observe for each worker all three log-wages, we could easily estimate the two expressions for the degree of segmentation. Unfortunately, for each worker p, only one of the three hypothetical log-wages can be observed. This is the major problem in estimating the degree of segmentation in a labor market with heterogeneous workers.

Let $C(p)$ be a set of observed characteristics of worker p and $F(p)$ an indicator of the segment of the labor market that worker p is currently in. $F(p)$ can assume three values: f, i, and s, indicating, respectively, the situations of formal employee, informal employee, and self-employed worker.

For workers with identical characteristics, $C(p) = c$, the degree of segmentation can be defined as the following:

$$\Delta_i = E\,[W_f - W_i \mid C = c]$$

and

$$\Delta_s = E\,[W_f - W_s \mid C = c]$$

Although these two expressions cannot be estimated (since we observe only one log-wage for each worker), the following two log-wage differentials could be easily estimated:

$$D_i = E\,[W_f \mid F = f,\ C = c] - E\,[W_i \mid F = i,\ C = c]$$

and

$$D_s = E\left[W_f \mid F = f,\, C = c\right] - E\left[W_s \mid F = s,\, C = c\right]$$

These two log-wage differentials are, respectively, (i) the log-wage differential between formal and informal employees with identical characteristics C, and (ii) the log-wage differential between formal employees and self-employed workers with identical characteristics C. In general, these log-wage differentials are not identical to their corresponding degree of segmentation. To better understand the relationship between these log-wage differentials and the degree of segmentation, note that the degree of segmentation can be written as

$$\Delta = E\left[W_f \mid C = c\right] - E\left[W_i \mid C = c\right]$$

and

$$\Delta_s = E\left[W_f \mid C = c\right] - E\left[W_s \mid C = c\right]$$

Therefore, the difference is that in the expression for the degree of segmentation, all expectations are taken among all workers with identical characteristics C, while in the expressions for the log-wage differentials, the expectations are also taken among workers with identical characteristics C but within segments of the labor force. In a labor market with heterogeneous workers, in general, the expectations taken for the overall population differ from the expectation taken for segments of the population.

Nevertheless, under certain circumstances, expectations taken for all workers with identical characteristics C will be the same if we take the same expectation for just one segment of the labor market. One case in which this will happen is when the characteristics C are the only source of heterogeneity among workers. In fact, in this case, all workers with identical characteristics C are perfect substitutes for each other and the log-wage differential among segments will be an appropriate measure of the degree of segmentation. Although sufficient, it is not necessary to have the characteristics C as the only source of heterogeneity in order for the log-wage differentials to be an appropriate measure of the degree of segmentation. The sufficient condition is to have all other sources of heterogeneity that are not captured by the characteristics C to be equally distributed within each segment of the labor market. Formally, this condition requires that the following be true:

Assumption 1 (A1): The joint distribution of (W_f, W_i, W_s, C, F) is such that, conditional on C, (W_f, W_i, W_s) and F are independently distributed. This assumption implies that for $k = f, i, s$,

$$E = [W_k \mid F = k, \, C = c] = E \, [W_k \mid C = c]$$

Therefore,

$$D_i = \Delta_i \ y \ D_s = \Delta_s$$

In this study, we only estimate log-wage differentials like D_i and D_s. These log-wage differentials refer, however, to measures of the degree of segmentation. It is important to keep in mind that this association is valid only if A1 is satisfied.

Basic Estimates

In this study we assume that the observed-characteristics element C has five components: (i) gender, G; (ii) age, A; (iii) level of education, E; (iv) area or region of residence, R; and (v) the time period, T, during which the worker is observed. Each group of workers homogeneous with respect to these five characteristics is referred to as a compartment of the labor market. The number of compartments is given by the product of the number of categories that each characteristic can attain.

Our first empirical step is to estimate seven indicators for each compartment: (i) the average wage of formal employees; (ii) the average wage of informal employees; (iii) the average wage of self-employed workers; (iv) the proportion of formal employees; (v) the proportion of informal employees; (vi) the proportion of self-employed workers; and (vii) the unemployment rate. To simplify the estimation procedure, we assume that all indicators vary with the age of the worker as a quadratic function. The parameters of this quadratic function, however, are allowed to vary freely with the remaining four components. Formally, we assume that for $k=f,i,s$,

$$E = [W_k \mid F = k, \, G = g, \, A = a, \, E = e, \, R = r, \, T = t] = \alpha \, (k, \, g, \, e, \, r, \, t) + \beta \, (k, \, g, \, e, \, r, \, t) \cdot a + \delta \, (k, \, g, \, e, \, r, \, t) \cdot a^2$$

$$P \, [F = k \mid G = g, \, A = a, \, E = e, \, R = r, \, T = t] = \varphi \, (k, \, g, \, e, \, r, \, t) + \gamma \, (k, \, g, \, e, \, r, \, t) \cdot a + \eta \, (k, \, g, \, e, \, r, \, t) \cdot a^2$$

and

$$P[U = 1 \mid G = g, \, A = a, \, E = e, \, R = r, \, T = t] = \lambda \, (g, \, e, \, r, \, t) + \mu \, (g, \, e, \, r, \, t) \cdot a + \nu \, (g, \, e, \, r, \, t) \cdot a^2$$

where $U(p)=1$ when worker p is unemployed. Based on these estimates for the average log-wages of formal and informal employees and self-employed workers, for each compartment we can compute, simply by taking differences, the log-wage differential between formal and informal workers, D_i, and the log-wage differential between formal employees and self-employed workers, D_s, for each compartment. Implicitly assuming that assumption A1 is satisfied, we refer to these log-wage differentials as alternative measures of the degree of segmentation. We use the proportion of formal employees in each compartment as an indicator of the degree of formalization in that compartment. Finally, the proportion of informal employees and the proportion of self-employed workers are used as two alternative measures of the degree of informalization in each compartment.

Based on these estimates of the unemployment rate and the degree of formalization (informalization) and the degree of segmentation by compartment, we can follow each of these indicators along any of the five dimensions that constitute our vector of observed characteristics. In other words, given the estimates by compartment, we can investigate how each indicator varies by gender, age, educational level, and area of residence of the worker, as well as how they vary over time.

From Multivariate Analysis to Standardized Univariate Analysis

The estimation procedure described allows free interactions among the five dimensions of the observed characteristics. On one hand, this procedure is preferable because it imposes little structure on the data. On the other hand, it creates a problem for analyses of individual dimensions. The problem is that if one chooses to study the variation of one indicator along one given dimension, there will be as many possible profiles along this dimension to be analyzed as there are possible values for the other four dimensions. For example, if one chooses to investigate the temporal variation in the degree of segmentation, there will be as many time profiles as there are choices for the gender, age, level of education, and area of residence of the worker—that is, for each choice of these four variables, the degree of segmentation will, in general, follow a different time profile.

Since we are not interested at this point in the peculiarity of each of the many possible analyses but only in the main features they have in common, we opted to investigate only the average of these many possible patterns. Next, we describe precisely how we average these many patterns.

In describing the procedure, we are going to restrict our attention, without any loss of generality, to the degree of segmentation as measured by log-wage differentials between formal and informal workers in the same compartment. All aspects of the methodology can immediately apply to all other indicators.

Since the objective is to compute the average of many profiles, all the discussion centers around which system of weights should be used. We denote by Λ_k the system of weights used to compute the average profile along dimension k,

$k=1,...,5$. Each Λ_k provides a weight for each compartment which should add to one when summed over all compartments with the same value for the dimension k. The following example is intended to clarify this notion. Consider again a study of the temporal variation in the degree of segmentation measured by the log-wage differential between formal and informal employees. In this case, D_i (g, a, e, r, t) denotes the degree of segmentation in the compartment (g, a, e, r, t), and there are as many possible temporal profiles for the degree of segmentation as possible choices for g, a, e, and r. Thus, the idea is to compute the average of these many temporal profiles using a system of weights. In other words, we compute the average temporal profile $D_{i,5}$ which for each time period t is given by

$$D_i, 5(t) = \sum_g \sum_a \sum_e \sum_r D_i(g, a, e, r, t) . \Lambda_5(g, a, e, r, t)$$

where L5 (g, a, e, r, t) are non-negative numbers which must satisfy

$$\sum_g \sum_a \sum_e \sum_r \Lambda_5(g, a, e, r; t) = 1$$

for all t, in order to be an appropriate system of weights. Besides these two conditions, the system of weights could, in principle, be arbitrary. But as we are going to show next, imposing certain restrictions on the weights has several methodological advantages.

The Advantages of Invariant Weights

Consider (without any loss of generality again) the expression for the average time profile of the degree of segmentation $D_{i,5}$ which for each time period t is given by

$$D_i, 5(t) = \sum_g \sum_a \sum_e \sum_r D_i(g, a, e, r, t) . \Lambda_5(g, a, e, r, t)$$

In this expression the weights $\Lambda_5 (g, a, e, r; t)$ are allowed to vary with t. There is, however, a strong inconvenience in this choice, derived from the fact that even if the degree of segmentation $D_i(g, a, e, r, t)$ does not vary over time, the average profile $D_{i,5}$ may still vary over time as long as the degree of segmentation $D_i(g, a, e, r, t)$ varies with either g, a, e, or r. This is certainly an undesirable feature and could easily be avoided by assuming that $\Lambda_5(g, a, e, r; t)$ does not vary with t.

Note that a natural choice for the weights $\Lambda_5(g, a, e, r; t)$ would be the conditional distribution of the population across compartments in each year—that is,

$$\Lambda_5(g, a, e, r; t) = P[G = g, A = a, E = e, R = r \backslash T = t]$$

Nevertheless, by imposing the restriction that $\Lambda5(g,a,e,r;t)$ must be time-invariant, we eliminate this very natural choice. Still valid, however, to be used as weights, is the marginal distribution of workers by gender, age, educational level, and area of residence. In other words, a valid choice for $\Lambda 5(g,a,e,r;t)$ is

$$\Lambda_5 (g, a, e, r; t) = P[G = g, A = a, E = e, R = r]$$

Nonetheless, in the next section, we are going to show that this choice also has its conveniences.

The Advantage of Product Weights

Consider (again, without any loss of generality) the case of the degree of segmentation. Assume the average degree of segmentation for each year, $D_{i,5}(t)$, has been computed. We now want to estimate an overall degree of segmentation, which we denote by $D_{i,5}$. We obtain $D_{i,5}$ as an average of the time-specific degree of segmentation, $D_{i,5}(t)$, via

$$\tilde{D}_{i,5} = \sum_t D_{i,5}(t) \cdot \lambda_5(t)$$

where $\lambda_5(t)$ are positive numbers that add up to one.

Since we are also computing average degrees of segmentation by gender $[D_{i,1}(g)]$, age $[D_{i,2}(a)]$, educational level, $[D_{i,3}(e)]$, and region $[D_{i,4}(r)]$, we could find estimates for the overall degree of segmentation from all four of these dimensions by taking appropriate weighted averages. Let these weighted averages be denoted by $D_{i,1}, D_{i,2}, D_{i,3}, D_{i,4}$ and defined as

$$\tilde{D}_{i,2} = \sum_a D_{i,2}(a) \cdot \lambda_2(a)$$

$$\tilde{D}_{i,3} = \sum_e D_{i,3}(e) \cdot \lambda_3(e)$$

$$\tilde{D}_{i,4} = \sum_r D_{i,4}(r) \cdot \lambda_4(r)$$

where $\lambda_1, \lambda_2, \lambda_3,$ and λ_4 are four systems of weights.

It would be natural to restrict all these systems of weights in such a way that all five estimates for the overall degree of segmentation must coincide—that is, a desirable property would be $D_{i,1} = D_{i,2} = D_{i,3} = D_{i,4} = D_{i,5}$.

Perhaps surprisingly, this requirement imposes no restrictions on the choices of the weights $\lambda_1, \lambda_2, \lambda_3, \lambda_4, \lambda_5$. But it does impose severe restrictions on the choice of the systems of weights used to generate the average profiles for the degree of segmentation $\Lambda_1, \Lambda_2, \Lambda_3, \Lambda_4, \Lambda_5$. Specifically, in order to have $D_{i,1} =$

$D_{i,2} = D_{i,3} = D_{i,4} = D_{i,5}$, it is necessary that the following restrictions on Λ_1, Λ_2, Λ_3, Λ_4, Λ_5 hold:

$$\Lambda 1 \ (a, e, r, t; g) = \lambda_2(a) . \lambda_3(e) . \lambda_4(r) . \lambda_5(t)$$
$$\Lambda 2 \ (g, e, r, t; a) = \lambda_1(g) . \lambda_3(e) . \lambda_4(r) . \lambda_5(t)$$
$$\Lambda 3 \ (g, a, r, t; e) = \lambda_1(g) . \lambda_2(a) . \lambda_4(r) . \lambda_5(t)$$
$$\Lambda 4 \ (g, a, e, t; r) = \lambda_1(g) . \lambda_2(a) . \lambda_3(e) . \lambda_5(t)$$
$$\Lambda 5 \ (g, a, e, r; t) = \lambda_1(g) . \lambda_2(a) . \lambda_3(e) . \lambda_4(r)$$

Therefore, all choices of weights are determined by the choice of the univariate weights λ_1, λ_2, λ_3, λ_4, λ_5. A natural choice for them, which is the one used in this study, is to let them be identical to the marginal distributions of G, A, E, R, and T—that is,

$$\lambda_1(g) = P \ [G = G]$$
$$\lambda_2(a) = P \ [A = a]$$
$$\lambda_3(e) = P \ [E = e]$$
$$\lambda_4(r) = P \ [R = r]$$
$$\lambda_5(t) = P \ [T = t].$$

CHAPTER THREE

CHILE

Pilar Romaguera
Cristián Echevarría
Pablo González[1]

The development strategies of the Latin American countries have undergone significant changes that have affected their productive structure and the operation of the labor market. In the first place, the powerful exogenous shocks of the mid-seventies and early eighties prompted important changes in the allocation of resources, both physical and human. These adjustments were carried out at different speeds and with varying degrees of success, but they were always associated with high rates of unemployment and prolonged periods of job-seeking. These social costs highlighted the difficulties Latin American labor markets have had in terms of operation and adaptation. In the second place, most of the countries of the region have begun to move toward liberalization and are opening themselves up to external competition. The need to compete successfully in the international marketplace calls for an efficient and flexible labor market.

This chapter examines Chilean labor law with special reference to the question of how well the labor market is working. It is divided into four sections. The first offers an overview and statistical description of the Chilean labor market as a framework for analyzing the country's labor law. The second section describes Chilean labor law, with particular attention to provisions governing individual and collective labor contracts. This section examines laws on hiring and firing, collective bargaining procedures, and strikes. The third section looks at labor institutions, including government agencies and unions, and also contains data on financial resources, number of members, etc. The last section presents final comments.

[1] The authors would especially like to thank Andrea Butelmann, who participated in the initial stages of designing this project and contributed valuable comments to its development. We would also like to thank the participants in seminars held at CIEPLAN as well as those from the preliminary meetings at the IDB of the Regional Network for Applied Economic Research.

The Chilean Labor Market: Overview and Statistical Description[2]

In the last two decades, Chile has changed its development strategy and applied adjustment policies to deal with economic imbalances and crises. Both factors profoundly affected the labor market. The economic crises of the mid-seventies and early eighties led to far-reaching adjustments in the labor market, with high rates of unemployment, falling real wages, and concentration of income. The changes in development strategy were also associated with changes in the role played by institutions, in the state's involvement in the economy, in the amount of regulation of the labor market, etc.

This section briefly describes the changes that have taken place in the labor market in recent decades. This will provide a frame of reference for the analysis of labor law presented in the subsequent sections.

Economic Cycles and the Labor Market

Analysis of the adjustment of the labor market in response to economic cycles is extremely important because the degree of flexibility with which that market is adjusted can be influenced by labor law and practice.

In the case of Chile, it has been argued that the labor market provided the main adjustment valve in the economic stabilization and restructuring processes of the seventies and eighties (Meller, 1992).

It is generally known that important economic reforms were put into practice in Chile during the 1970s: deregulation of domestic markets, liberalization of external trade, opening up of the capital account of the balance of payments, fiscal reforms, and liberalization of the domestic financial market. The country experienced two sharp recessions, in 1975 and 1982, with significant drops in production and rising unemployment (see the macroeconomic figures in Appendix 1). However, while employment recovered very slowly after 1975, the adjustment of the labor market was much faster after the crisis of 1982.

Below we shall examine the labor adjustment through employment and wages in the two recessive cycles and try to identify elements that might be affected by labor regulations. It will become evident that labor regulations were much more flexible in the 1980s than previously, with particular differences appearing in wage policy.

However, many factors influence the adjustment of the labor market. In particular, while the crisis of 1975 was connected with a structural shock—with an

---

[2] This section is based partially on Mizala and Romaguera (1993). For further references see González (1990, 1993b), Meller and Romaguera (1992), Raczynski and Romaguera (1993), and Vial, Butelmann, and Celedón (1990).

opening up to external forces and changing relative prices—the recession of 1982 was connected with an added shock associated with the external debt crisis and the bankruptcy of the domestic financial system. As has also been noted in other economies, the adjustment of the labor market is slower in dealing with sectoral shocks than with added shocks.

Employment and Unemployment

Until the mid-seventies, the unemployment rate in Chile historically stood at 5 to 6 percent. It tripled during the recession of 1975 and remained at high levels for the rest of the decade, despite the recovery of the GDP (Table 3.1).

An 8 percent drop in employment from 1973 to 1975, along with the growth of the labor supply, led to an increase of 10 percentage points in the unemployment rate. The figures show private employment responding clearly to declining production, and public employment to a declining role of the state. Public sector employment fell by 62,000 in that period,[3] while the private sector shed approximately 169,000 jobs.[4] The adjustment in employment was facilitated by the low level of compliance with labor laws—despite the restrictions on causes of dismissal set forth in the Labor Code—and repression of union activity.

Production began to recover gradually in 1976, and employment recovered slowly in its wake. In 1981, when the economic recovery peaked, the open unemployment rate was 10.8 percent, or 15.6 percent if emergency employment programs are included.

In 1982 the Chilean economy went into a new recession. From 1980 to 1982 the number of employed fell 13.3 percent. This indicated a nine point increase in the unemployment rate. The open unemployment rate rose to 19.6 percent in 1982, or 28 percent if the emergency employment programs are included.

It is interesting to note that not only did employment decrease more in this recession (13.3 percent in 1980-82, as against 8 percent in 1974-75), but this decrease primarily affected private employment.[5]

There were two reasons for the recession's swift impact on employment. From an institutional point of view, a new labor code in force at the time simplified lay-offs and reduced the cost of severance. In addition, a large number of businesses went bankrupt.[6]

---

[3] The sharpest reduction in public employment took place from 1973 to 1975, followed by a more gradual decline through 1979. In 1980 the process then accelerated again, shrunken though the public sector already was. See Marshall and Romaguera (1981) and Velásquez (1988).

[4] Figures based on ODEPLAN estimates based on INE data. See *Exposición de la Hacienda Pública* (Public Finance Report), 1989.

[5] Public employment fell by 31,000 from 1980 to 1982 (see Velásquez, 1988).

[6] Bankruptcies numbered 810, a huge increase over the 81 in 1975 (see Mizala, 1992).

Direct employment was used in both periods (through emergency job programs) as one of the principal methods of fighting unemployment. Furthermore, in the crisis of the 1970s the hiring of additional workers was subsidized as a way of stimulating employment.[7]

Emergency job programs were introduced in 1975—the first being the *Programa de Empleo Mínimo* (PEM) or Minimum Employment Program—with the aim of mitigating the effects of the recession that hit Chile that year. In 1982 these programs—most notably the *Programa Ocupacional para Jefes de Hogar* (POJH) or Job Program for Heads of Households—were extended to other segments of the population. In 1976, 5.4 percent of the labor force was enrolled in PEM, and that figure remained approximately the same until 1981, when it fell to 4.8 percent. The number of people signed up in emergency job programs reached its peak in 1983, with 13.5 percent of the work force; from 1986 it declined steadily until the programs were terminated in December 1988 (Table 3.2). The figures show that these programs were important in alleviating the unemployment problem. However, some observations concerning their impact on employment are in order. The easy access to these programs attracted the secondary labor force, and it may be assumed that a number of those signed up in emergency job programs became informal workers when the programs were discontinued. Apparently, participants in the emergency job programs found it difficult to enter the formal labor market even when the economy was recovering, since their low skill levels limited their ability to move from one sector to another.

Production began to recover in 1984, and starting in 1986 this upswing spurred employment significantly. In 1989 the economy returned to historic open unemployment rates of around 6 percent. From then on, the main problem gradually shifted from high unemployment to the quality of employment and then to a potential labor shortage.

Wages and Indexing Policy

Although unemployment rose substantially in both recessions, real wages were among the many other items that reacted differently in each one.

In the 1975 recession, real wages had been driven down by the strong inflation of 1972-73, which left them 40 percent lower in 1974 than in 1970. In the subsequent recovery they did not recover their 1970 level until 1981. Wages then held their ground in 1982 despite the new crisis, only to plunge in 1983 and remain in the doldrums until the 1987 recovery. Wages were strongly influenced by institutional wage-setting mechanisms throughout this period.

---

[7] There were other means of spurring employment by reducing labor costs. In particular, contributions to benefits diminished, significantly lowering the cost of hiring.

Table 3.1. Chile: Wage and Unemployment Indicators

Year	Minimum wage (April 1989 $)	Open	Plus PEM+POJH (Percentages)	General	Public sector (December M82=100)
		Unemployment rate		Real wage index	
1970	5.7	—	109.1	113.1	—
1971	3.8	—	135.1	139.8	—
1972	3.1	—	103.4	104.2	—
1973	4.8	—	51.3	46.9	—
1974	9.2	—	64.1	64.0	15,407
1975	14.9	17.2	62.3	64.7	15,424
1976	12.7	18.1	78.6	75.6	16,022
1977	11.8	17.7	79.6	78.8	16,968
1978	14.2	18.4	84.7	81.5	20,031
1979	13.6	17.5	91.7	87.3	19,393
1980	10.4	15.7	99.6	93.8	19,435
1981	10.8	15.4	108.5	102.2	22,520
1982	19.6	28.0	108.2	109.0	22,662
1983	16.8	30.1	96.7	93.8	18,255
1984	15.4	24.0	96.8	94.4	15,601
1985	13.0	21.1	92.7	89.0	14,797
1986	10.8	16.0	94.6	85.9	14,302
1987	9.3	12.1	94.4	83.2	13,424
1988	8.3	9.0	100.6	90.5	14,402
1989	6.3	—	102.5	92.0	15,999
1990	6.0	—	104.4	88.1	17,090
1991	6.5	—	109.5	93.9	18,625
1992	4.9	—	114.4	100.1	19,452
1993	4.6	—	—	—	20,420

Source: Based on data of the National Institute of Statistics (INE); deflated by the consumer price index (CPI) corrected by Cortázar and Marshall (1980) for the period 1970-78.
Notes: The average unemployment rate was calculated using as much available information as possible. It covers the following periods: 1970-74, annual National Planning Office (ODEPLAN) estimate; 1975: May-December; 1976-79 and 1982: October-December; 1981: April-June and October-December; 1983: May-December; 1984-1993: January-December. The PEM + POJH figures are annual averages. The compensation indicator was modified (discontinued) in May 1993. The taxable minimum income rose by 20 percent starting in March 1981 because of changes in the social security premiums (DL 3501).

In the 1974-79 period, wage negotiations were suspended and wages varied according to the mandatory readjustments set by the public sector. These readjustments arose from indexation based on past inflation (partial or total), which under conditions of declining inflation sharply drove up real wages. Under the 1979 Labor Plan, collective bargaining was reintroduced for a percentage of the labor force. However, public sector readjustments continued to cover the private

Table 3.2. Chile: Emergency Employment Programs
(Annual average)

	Emergency Employment Program			PEM	POJH
	PEM	POJH	Total as %		
	(In thousands)		of labor force	(1988 pesos)	
1975	72.7		2.3	12,920	
1976	172.0		5.4	11,746	
1977	187.7		5.9	8,397	
1978	145.8		4.2	6,333	
1979	133.9		3.9	5,775	
1980	190.7		5.2	5,494	
1981	175.6		4.8	4,680	
1982	226.8	81.2	8.4	5,403	13,099
1983	341.6	161.2	13.5	5,147	10,293
1984	167.6	168.7	9.0	4,294	8,588
1985	134.3	190.0	8.4	4,928	8,213
1986	81.0	140.4	5.2	4,125	6,874
1987	35.7	88.4	2.9	3,441	5,734
1988	9.0	24.9	0.8	3,000	5,000

Source: Economic and Social Indicators 1960-88, Central Bank of Chile, and Raczynski and Romaguera (1995).

sector as well, which did not engage in collective bargaining, while wages as a whole remained indexed to past inflation.[8]

Wage increases in 1982 came about partly because total indexation with respect to past inflation was applied in the private sector, and partly because rising wages in the public sector closed the gap with the private sector.

Indexation rules changed in 1982. Mandatory indexation of private collective contracts was abolished at the same time as the devaluation in June of that year, on the argument that indexation made adjustment of the economy in recessionary times difficult. Simultaneously, a special provision was introduced to reduce nominal wages by making the minimum level for real wages the same as it had been in 1979, before the application of the fixed nominal exchange rate policy. These measures brought down real wages by around 20 percent.

Several factors influenced the behavior of wages in the period under analysis and caused it to differ in the two recessions.

---

[8] The indexation mechanisms are different for workers who bargain collectively and for those who do not bargain. See Appendix 1 and Mizala and Romaguera (1991).

First, it is apparent that different models were used to determine wages in each period. In the first period, the absence of legislation (prohibition against collective bargaining) paradoxically led to a rigidity in the labor market imposed by the institutional determination of wages. In the second period, wages were clearly more influenced by market forces.[9]

Secondly, a change in the government's wage policy in the second crisis modified the institutional context referred to in the preceding paragraph and deliberately depressed the wages under its direct influence: the minimum wage and the wages of public sector workers.[10]

Thirdly, the effect of inflation was much smaller in the second period. Indexation therefore not only played a less important role from the institutional point of view, but obviously also had a smaller quantitative effect on real wages, since the sharp increases of the inflation of the second half of the 1970s were not repeated.

These reasons, among which reduced labor regulation played a role, largely explain the faster adjustment of the labor market in the eighties.

Recent Trends in the Labor Market

Unemployment became a less dominant topic among analysts of recession cycles once it was reduced to its historically common levels. Current discussion of the labor situation centers on two apparently contradictory issues: the potential scarcity of labor and the limitations such scarcity would place on growth, and the social problems associated with underemployment and unemployment in certain population groups. Labor regulations could have some influence on the first of those problems.

The informal sector accounted for 22.3 percent of those employed in 1990 and 21.5 percent in 1992, according to MIDEPLAN estimates based on the CASEN survey.[11] There are no time series to measure whether the informal sector acted as a shock absorber in business cycles, but the figures on nonsalaried

---

[9] In Mizala and Romaguera (1991) a structural change is shown to have occurred in the setting of wages from 1982 on. Until 1979, nominal wages closely followed the government's readjustment policies, along the lines of the "centralized" model developed by Cortázar (1983). From 1979 to 1982 there was a transition phase, and in 1982 the public sector ceased to lead the way in determining wages.

[10] From 1974 the minimum wage rose by 26 percent in real terms; from 1982 to 1988 minimum wages fell by 36 percent (Table 3.1).

[11] The estimate of 32 percent by the National Institute of Statistics for 1991 was considerably higher. The difference stems from the fact that MIDEPLAN's estimates consider employees of service and trade establishments of fewer than five persons who have a work contract as formal workers.

workers show that this population group has been relatively stable over the last decade.[12]

Another cause for concern is the youth unemployment rate, which is 2.3 to 2.6 times higher than the adult rate, depending on the period observed. This ratio ranges from 1.5 to 2 in developed countries. This is one of the reasons for the youth training programs that have been initiated in recent years.

Future economic growth will have to be based on the rising productivity of those currently employed and on the inclusion of new groups in the labor force. However, although information is scarce on this point, the movement of workers from the informal to the more modern sectors seems to have been very limited due to their limited skills and lack of work experience. In addition, the increase in the number of the employed may stem from three sources: the absorption of unemployed workers, an increase in the labor force through the growth of the population of working age, and the inclusion of individuals previously not economically active.

With unemployment at 5 percent, the unemployed have ceased to be a significant source of employment growth. Meanwhile, the working-age population has grown at a fairly stable rate in recent times, averaging 1.7 percent from 1986 to 1991. Therefore, future growth in employment will necessarily call for increased participation in the labor force.

The rates of participation in the Chilean labor force appear low by international standards. By way of example we offer some figures in Table 3.3 which highlight the low rate of participation by women (of all ages) and young people (male and female).

These comparisons can be evaluated differently: the high rates of participation in the secondary labor force can be positive or negative, depending on what they reveal. High rates of participation of young people are negative if they reflect low school enrollment, positive if they indicate that easy access to the labor market makes it easy for people to both study and work.

Comparisons with developed countries show a labor structure different from that of Chile. The developed countries have a market that offers greater entry opportunities to the secondary labor force, better transition from education to work, and more permanent jobs for women. Another example of these differences is the importance of part-time work for young people and women. In Canada, 67 percent of men working part-time are less than 25 years of age; the corresponding figure in Chile is below 20 percent.

However, analysis of labor law discloses no bias toward the secondary labor force, except for maternal protection. Nor are restrictions in evidence with regard to types of contracts or work days.

---

[12] See Infante and Klein (1992) and Leiva (1993).

Table 3.3. Chile: Participation Rates by Age Groups
(Percentages)

Age group	Chile 1991	Germany 1990	U.S. 1991	England 1990	Canada 1990
			Women		
15-19	10.2	37.3	39.8	57.9	55.9
20-24	39.3	75.6	68.4	75.0	76.5
25-44	43.1	69.1	74.8	72.9	77.7
45-64	30.4	46.6	60.7	56.3	53.5
65-plus	6.0	20.0	8.0	3.3	3.8
Total	31.3	45.7	55.6	52.0	58.4
			Men		
15-19	28.2	43.2	40.6	61.5	58.9
20-24	76.8	79.8	74.4	86.6	82.8
25-44	96.1	94.1	91.5	94.4	94.0
45-64	84.7	79.6	80.7	80.4	79.3
65-plus	30.3	5.2	15.5	8.6	11.4
Total	75.2	72.8	72.2	73.1	75.9

Source: International Labor Organization, *Labor Statistics Annual, 1992.*

It is a reasonable premise that many avenues should be pursued to modernize the labor market—and to ensure that this modernization is inclusive and not exclusionary. The transition from education to work, mobility, and the participation of the labor force all need to be improved. In some of these areas, labor law may have a part to play, such as encouraging nontraditional forms of contracting. It does not seem desirable to let the Chilean economy's current greater demand for labor spark widespread capital intensification as long as problems in absorbing the secondary labor force persist and a lagging sector with low-productivity jobs continues to exist.

Labor Law: Flexibility and Autonomy

The previously described transformations that have affected the Chilean economy and labor market have also led to significant changes in the regulatory framework of the labor market, both in actual labor laws and in the extent to which they are enforced, accepted and supported by the various social players.

In the sixties and early seventies, Chilean labor law was regarded as highly protective in character: it was difficult to lay off workers, severance costs were high, strikes dragged on indefinitely, rates were fixed for certain occupations, the state was involved in setting wages, etc. Special rules for some unions (such as the oil workers, copper miners, and railroad workers) also made labor law very complex.

This situation was altered by the military coup of 1973, but it changed more in practice than in law. Thus collective bargaining and labor union activity were banned in that year (and remained banned until 1979), so that lawful strikes and collective negotiation over compensation became impossible. However, most of the provisions of the individual labor contract (e.g., those pertaining to severance pay) were maintained. Still, the legal provisions that remained unchanged received little enforcement.

Labor law began to undergo actual change in 1978 and 1979. Layoffs without cause were reintroduced, with the employer required only to pay workers' severance pay at the rate of one month's wages for each year of employment, without a cap on the number of months.[13] The Labor Plan enacted in 1979 established a new regulatory framework for the labor market and collective bargaining, the right to strike, and union activity (among other things) were restored.[14] These provisions offered workers only a small measure of protection, however. The participation of labor unions and officers in political affairs and party activity was limited. Although collective bargaining encompassed the right to strike, workers were allowed to be separated from their jobs after the strike had lasted 30 days, and fired after 60 days. Previously (prior to 1973) the practice of *descuelgue* (disconnecting) did not exist and the strike could last indefinitely.

This period also saw the abolition of many of the prerogatives or special rules for workers' associations or groups. For example, the professional licenses that practitioners of certain occupations (barbers, actors, orchestra musicians, electricians, bakers, etc.) were required to possess were abolished by Decree Law 2.950 of 1979. Special provisions or exemptions (remuneration, minimum wage, permits, working hours, etc.) for certain occupations, such as waiters' tips, the minimum wage for pharmacy employees, and the special allowance to journalists, were eliminated by Decree Law 3.500 of 1980. This brought considerably more standardization in labor regulations.

---

[13] Appendix 5 contains a summary of the various legal provisions on dismissal and severance pay, since these are basic features of the type of legislation encountered in different periods.

[14] Four bodies of law stand out in this period: the Labor Plan, Decree Law 2.756 on union organizing, and Decree Law 2.758 on collective bargaining; Law No. 18.018 of 1981 amending Decree Law 2.200 on individual labor relations; laws 18.011 and 18.032 of 1981 subjecting shipboard and port workers to the general provisions of DL 2.200; and norms governing labor rights set forth in the Political Constitution of 1980 (see Alamos, 1986).

A new series of changes in labor regulations began in 1990, with amendments to the laws on labor contract terms, collective bargaining, labor unions and other labor organizations, and to some clauses of the individual labor contract.[15]

The Chilean labor market has evolved through four distinct regulatory frameworks: from 1931 to 1973, a highly protective and complex system with a wide range of special provisions; from 1974 to 1978, a combination of *de facto* deregulation and union repression in which regulations concerning layoffs, severance and wages were maintained; from 1979 to 1989, legislation designed to weaken regulation and limit the power of unions, which took effect with the Labor Plan of 1979 and took a further step with the deindexation of wages in 1982; and since 1990, changes that sought to enhance worker protection without reducing the flexibility of the labor market.

The Chilean economy has thus seen great transformations in labor law and worked its way toward a consensus concerning current labor law. Therefore, although some challenges remain, the law appears more solidly established than elsewhere in Latin America and fewer changes are expected.

In what follows we shall analyze Chilean labor law in depth, focusing on elements that either have a specific impact on labor operations or still hamper the enactment of laws governed by the principles of fairness, autonomy and efficacy.[16]

Labor Code

To understand Chilean labor laws one must be aware that the Labor Code governs the labor relations of all workers and employers with the exception of public sector employees, who fall under special statutes.[17] Meanwhile, the Administrative Statute (Law 18.834) governs relations between the state and personnel of ministries, local and provincial governments, and centralized and decentralized

---

[15] Law No. 19.019 on termination of labor contracts has been in effect since December 1990, Law No. 19.049 on labor unions since February 1991, Law No. 19.069 on labor organizations and collective bargaining since January 1991, and Law No. 19.250 on individual labor contracts, workers' protection and labor jurisdiction since November 1993. The new Labor Code covering these four laws was published in January 1994. This is the code analyzed in the tables and appendices of this work.

[16] See Cortázar (1993).

[17] The Labor Code does not apply to employees of the Civil Service (centralized and decentralized), the National Congress, and the Judicial Branch, nor to workers of enterprises or institutions wholly or partly owned by the state, provided that those workers are covered under the law by a special statute. The workers mentioned are, however, subject to the provisions of the Labor Code in matters not governed by their respective statutes.

public services, with a few exceptions made for bodies subject to special laws.[18]

The potential coverage of the Labor Code is therefore very broad: unless otherwise provided by law, any employer/employee relationship should fall under an individual or collective labor contract governed by the Labor Code.

As previously noted, Chilean labor law has attained a high degree of standardization, generally eliminating exceptions or special treatment aimed at certain workers. The remaining special regulations generally refer to specific groups of workers (dockworkers, drivers, domestic workers, etc.). However, there are differences between labor regulations affecting public and private workers, a subject we shall examine below.

The following section describes the norms governing individual labor contracts and the regulation of collective labor contracts. It goes on to examine compliance with those provisions and the nonwage costs that labor regulations impose on businesses.

Regulation of Individual Labor Contracts

The main characteristics of individual labor contracts are set forth in Table 3.4, which also allows a comparison between private and public sector legislation.

Chilean labor law provides for different types of contracts (indefinite, fixed term, etc.), which ensures considerable flexibility in labor relations. Nevertheless, contracts are subject to more restriction in the public sector. Moreover, workers are not offered a probation period (except for domestic workers), although in practice three-month fixed term contracts are used for that purpose.

The maximum work week is 48 hours long for the private sector and 44 for the public sector. Rules concerning work at night and on holidays are also more flexible in the private than the public sector, as shown in Table 3.4.

With respect to compensation, the only restriction in the private sector is the legal minimum wage, while compensation in the public sector is governed by a uniform pay scale that is adjusted by law.[19]

Table 3.5 provides data on layoffs in the private sector in terms of notice, cause, severance pay and unemployment benefits. Table 3.6 provides data pertaining to the public sector. This is one of the fields where there are major differ-

---

[18] Excepted agencies are the Office of the Comptroller General of the Republic, central bank, armed forces, public law enforcement and security forces, municipalities, National Television Council, and public enterprises created by law. These are governed by their respective charters, bylaws, and rules and regulations.

[19] In the past, compensation in the private sector was more highly regulated, as it was indexed to past inflation and subject to compulsory readjustment of wages (particularly sectors not subject to collective bargaining). These regulations were eliminated partially in 1979 and totally in 1982. See Mizala and Romaguera (1991).

ences between the laws governing the public and private sectors, and in which the private sector has experienced significant change.

In the private sector the main difference lies in the fact that cause for dismissal is attributed to either the worker or the employer, and this determines whether severance pay (IAS) and prior notice are required. The acceptance of "needs of the firm" as cause for dismissal provides considerable flexibility in the hiring and firing of workers. In addition, the specific grounds (failure to report for work, tardiness, etc., see Table 3.5) show that the laws make it possible to dismiss workers who do not discharge their duties satisfactorily.

The concept of "needs of the firm" as cause for dismissal distinguishes between different types of law (more protective or more flexible) and in the case of Chile has only existed since 1978. However, the legislation dealing with the question of whether dismissal can be unilateral (1978) or the cause for dismissal must be specified (1990) has been modified.

In the public sector the causes for dismissal are different. In the first place, fewer faults on the part of the worker are spelled out, and the process of employee performance evaluation is slow and cumbersome and subject to appeal, so that in practice it is very difficult to fire a public functionary. There is no cause for dismissal equivalent to the private sector's "needs of the firm."

Severance packages are more restricted in the public than in the private sector, but the issue of severance in the public sector is relatively unimportant given the near impossibility of dismissal. Of course this issue would be of interest should a change in the law introduce more labor flexibility into public administration.

The problems faced by the public sector in upgrading its personnel stem not only from the difficulty of dismissal but also from the manner in which staff vacancies are filled: the person in the next grade down is promoted.

The issue of modernizing human resources is part of the larger current problem of how to modernize public administration.[20] In this connection some provisions of labor law concerning the public sector ought to be revised with a view to developing a more flexible human resources policy. Such a policy might, for example, limit automatic promotion, institute more public competition to fill vacancies, and streamline dismissal procedures.

Coverage and Enforcement

The actual importance of labor laws lies not only in their potential coverage but also, obviously, in their actual coverage.

The first major exception to labor law involves, by definition, self-employed workers. According to INE estimates, self-employed workers in the period from

---

[20] See, for example, the interview of Mario Marcel, Deputy Director of Budgets, in *Estrategia*, May 1994.

Table 3.4. Chile: Individual Contracting Standards

	Dependent Private Sector (Labor Code)	Public Sector (Administrative Statute)
Probation period	Only for domestic workers: two-week probation	None
Types of contract		
• Indefinite	Law 19.010, especially Article 1 Yes	Worker hired for a staff position
• Contract	Not provided for in the private sector	Limit: 1 year, maximum 20 percent total of staff positions
• Fee	Services not entailing employment. Governed by the rules and regulations of the organization	Only professionals and technicians with higher education or experts; for non-routine tasks
• Fixed term	Contract may not exceed one year, or two for managers and professionals	Not available
• Piecework	Yes	Not available
• Other	Special contracts: trainees, farmworkers, seamen, dockworkers, casual workers, domestic workers	Positions of exclusive trust are governed by special rules
Work schedules	48 hours per week (some workers are subject to special work schedules)	44 hours per week
Special work schedules	Overtime: any time that exceeds the ordinary work schedule. Two hours a day maximum	The agency head may order overtime when it is necessary to complete unpostponable tasks
Compensation for specially scheduled work		
• Overtime	Time plus 50 percent	Compensatory free time equivalent to overtime worked plus 20 percent or, if that is not possible, payment based on time plus 20 percent

• Night work (9 p.m. to 7 a.m.)	None if those are the normal working hours	Compensatory free time equivalent to overtime worked plus 50 percent or, if that is not possible, payment based on time plus 50 percent
• Holidays	None if those are the normal working hours	Compensatory free time equivalent to overtime worked plus 50 percent or, if that is not possible, payment based on time plus 50 percent
Sick leave	No limit	Health problem incompatible with duties: more than six months in two years may result in dismissal
Compensation	Cannot be less than legal minimum wage or appropriate fraction thereof if time on the job is shorter than the legal norm	Standard pay scale, as readjusted by law
Annual leave	With more than one year of service, 15 days per year. With more than 10 years, with one or more employers, one additional day for every three years worked. No more than 10 years with other employers can be claimed. Minimum of 10 days' continuous leave	15 working days with less than 15 years as employee, 20 days with between 15 and 20 years, and 25 days with more than 20 years
Special leave	One day's paid leave in case of the birth or death of a child or death of spouse	Up to six working days with pay and three months without pay (may be denied)

Source: Prepared for this study on the basis of the Labor Code and Administrative Statute.

Table 3.5. Chile: Termination of Employment Under the Labor Code

Prior notice	30 days only if cause is Article 3 (see causes for dismissal)
Causes for dismissal:	
• Without right to severance pay for years of service (IAS):	Article 160 of the Labor Code. Ineligible for IAS: • Duly proven lack of integrity, actionable words or grossly immoral conduct • Business prohibited in writing in the labor contract conducted by the worker while on duty. • Failure of worker to report to work for two consecutive days, or two Mondays or a total of three days in one month • Unjustified or unannounced absence of a worker responsible for an activity, task or machine whose abandonment or idleness seriously disrupts business operations • Failure of worker to perform assigned work. • Acts, omissions or reckless carelessness affecting the firm's security or operation, worker safety or performance, or the health of the workers • Intentional material harm to facilities, machinery, tools, equipment or merchandise • Grave breach of contract
• With right to IAS:	Article 161 of the Labor Code: • Needs of the firm (including rationalization or modernization, attempts to remedy falling productivity, changing conditions in market or economy, and unsatisfactory job or technical performance of worker) • Written notice of dismissal from employer, only for domestic workers and administrative workers (managers, representatives, etc.)
Severance pay:	
• Voluntary separation	Only for indefinite contracts[1] From the seventh year of service the IAS for dismissal can be replaced by severance pay based on half a month per year
• Dismissal for cause	One month per year of service up to 11 if Article 3 was applied
• Dismissal without stated cause	Worker may require statement of cause. Labor Court may order payment of IAS plus 29 to 50 percent

• Other	Gives the right to IAS plus 20-50 percent from the employer as ordered by the labor tribunal under Article 2
Obligation to rehire	Only if the worker was exempted
Exemption	Article 3 cannot be invoked in cases of medical leave or maternal or union exemption
Unemployment insurance	Currently a severance allowance, funded totally by the state, exists for low-income workers. A bill providing for government unemployment insurance is pending

Severance allowance:

• Targeted	At public or private sector workers covered by the social welfare system who have lost their jobs for reasons beyond their control
• Description	Monthly economic assistance for up to 12 months paid by the *Instituto de Normalización Previsional* [Institute of Benefits Standardization] (INP) or the designated *Caja de Compensación* (compensation fund) as appropriate. In the case of public employees, the allowance is paid directly by the agency where the worker was employed, in the following amounts: • First three months: 13,922 pesos • 4th to 10th months: 9,282 pesos • 10th to 12th months: 6,961 pesos
• Other services	Medical care free of charge in the clinics and hospitals of the National Health Services System (SNSS) Family and maternal allowance for approved dependents
• Requirements	Must have paid into either benefits system (INP or AFP) for a total of at least 52 weeks or 12 months within the two years immediately preceding the date of separation Must be listed in the Municipal Register of Unemployment of the beneficiary's place of residence Must be listed in the Unemployment Register of the INP or AFP

Source: Prepared for this study on the basis of the Labor Code.
1 Domestic servants qualify for a special indemnity in all cases of half a month for each year of service. The employer is obligated to deposit 4.11 percent of the taxable compensation in a sub-account of the account of a Pension Fund Administration (AFP) office.

Table 3.6. Chile: Termination of Employment Under the Administrative Statute

Prior notice	Not required
Causes for dismissal:	
• Summary dismissal	Summary dismissal is decided by the hiring authority and must be based on one of the following: • Unjustified failure to report for work for more than three consecutive days • Conviction for a felony or misdemeanor • Organizing or belonging to unions connected with the administration of the state (eliminated in the proposed association of government employees); directing, promoting or participating in strikes; interrupting or preventing the conduct of business; improper possession of property; and other acts that disrupt the normal operations of state administration • Deliberate damage to agency property • Damage to public or private facilities
• Declaration of vacancy	Procedure applied in the following cases: • Incumbents in positions of trust will be asked to resign by means of a request prepared by the hiring authority • Health problem incompatible with duties (having taken sick leave for a total of six months in the last two years) or incurable • Loss of a civil service entry requirement • Repeated tardiness and absences • Unsatisfactory performance rating or conditional performance rating three times in a five-year period or twice consecutively[1]
• Redundancy	If a reduction in force occurs as a result of restructuring or merger, redundant employees who do not qualify for retirement will be offered severance pay equivalent to one month's compensation per year of service up to six years, tax-free
Severance pay:	Only for permanent employees
• Voluntary separation	No severance pay
• Dismissal for cause	Redundancy or incurable ill health qualify the worker for six months' compensation
• Dismissal without cause	May be appealed to higher authority
Mandatory reinstatement	Only if disciplinary action involving separation is overturned
Privilege	Proposed Government Employees' Associations Act would prevent the rating of managers (unless requested by them) and their transfer or reassignment

[1] Performance evaluation ratings are outstanding, satisfactory, conditional and unsatisfactory. Entered in personnel record (with merits and demerits) and performance evaluation (by immediate supervisor), which grade the following from one to seven: conduct, judgment, productivity, ability and dedication.
Source: Prepared for this study on the basis of the Administrative Statute.

July to September 1992 accounted for 27.5 percent of all employed workers, i.e., a significant percentage of the labor force.

Another measure of the "formalization" of labor relations is the percentage of wage-earners with labor contracts. MIDEPLAN's CASEN survey found that 81.8 percent of all employed persons had a labor contract in 1990 and 82.2 percent had one in 1992.

The figures also show that the percentage of workers without contracts is higher among younger (15 to 24 years of age) and older (age 65 and over) workers, and that firm size goes hand in hand with a marked difference. According to figures for 1990 cited by Chacón (1992), 31.9 percent of workers in businesses with one to five workers had no contract, compared with 5.8 percent in businesses with 200 or more workers.

Under these circumstances, although the code's application has expanded over time—and seems fairly high compared with other Latin American countries—coverage still needs improvement in certain sectors.

A final consideration associated with coverage is enforcement. The next section presents figures pertaining to the resources and personnel of the enforcement agencies. Those figures suggest that enforcement of the labor law has improved over time. The greater transparency and simplicity of current labor legislation must also have been helpful in this regard.

Job Protection Standards

Flexibility in hiring and firing, a topic already discussed, must be considered not only as a means of terminating contracts more easily but also in terms of its cost. As noted, IAS benefits amount to one month's pay per year of service, up to 11 months. Uncapped severance pay was eliminated in the late 1970s.

In many Latin American countries, including Chile, severance pay has become the worker's first line of protection against unemployment, owing to the lack of adequate unemployment benefits or insurance.

In Chile, the severance allowance was introduced in 1974 and its coverage has been limited, since it is intended only for low-income sectors. Table 3.7 contains information on the number of recipients.

The numbers of severance recipients obviously tend to reflect the unemployment rate, which explains their dwindling numbers in recent years. Nevertheless, their coverage continues to be very limited: only 37.5 percent of the potential beneficiaries are estimated to have used the system in 1991.[21]

---

[21] According to data from the Directorate of Labor, approximately 40 percent of all contract terminations stem from dismissals, and about 80,000 workers are estimated to have been eligible for an allowance in 1991 (Echeverría, 1993).

Table 3.7. Chile: Recipients of the Severance Allowance
(Annual average)

Years	Number of recipients
1980	74,277
1981	74,923
1982	130,799
1983	142,520
1984	97,822
1985	97,327
1986	84,410
1987	66,051
1988	51,750
1989	39,245
1990	33,845
1991	30,246
1992	23,432

Source: Ministry of Labor.

In addition to the coverage problems, the existing allowance system has the disadvantage of being funded almost entirely by the state and paying a very small income (Table 3.5) unrelated to the worker's previous earnings.[22]

The combination of a limited unemployment benefits program together with high severance pay is viewed as an obstacle to the creation of a more flexible Chilean labor market.

A consensus appears to exist on the need to change the existing severance allowance system by creating a more general system, i.e., unemployment insurance funded by businesses and workers and offering benefits directly commensurate with contributions. An unemployment insurance bill was introduced by the government in 1993 but not implemented by the last administration.[23] The need to replace the current allowance with an effective unemployment insurance system is one of the political challenges with which the labor laws appear to be confronted.

Regulation of Collective Labor Contracts

The regulations governing collective labor contracts include provisions covering labor unions and collective bargaining. The third section of this analysis will be

---

[22] See Mizala and Romaguera (1994).
[23] See Cortázar (1993) and Echeverría (1993).

completed with quantitative data on bargaining as it affects the dependent labor force and the unionized labor force.

Table 3.8 shows the general aspects of collective bargaining. The collective bargaining process establishes the working conditions and compensation for the parties concerned over a given period, which by law must be at least two years. This is one of the features with a potential for introducing rigidity into the labor market, since firms would be forced to respect preestablished conditions in a changing economic environment. However, it has the advantage of stabilizing labor relations and making conflicts less likely, thereby enhancing productivity.

The imposition of minimum terms on contracts would entail less rigidity if compensation were linked to the firm's performance. The labor law makes possible regular payments associated with various types of incentives, such as bonds or commissions, and includes the existence of participative wages and bonuses. The introduction of participative wages has been promoted by the ministerial authorities. Although their application seems to be limited, it is for reasons that appear unrelated to the legislation.[24]

Table 3.9 shows who may negotiate and other procedural matters. Chilean labor law allows not only unions but also groups of workers who may organize for that purpose to join in the bargaining process. This is a feature that lends considerable flexibility to bargaining but can at the same time weaken the pressure exerted by the union, even in cases where a single union exists in the firm.

Bargaining by area of activity is another matter that has been debated and changed. Current legislation permits bargaining by area of activity (the Labor Plan of 1979 prohibited it) but requires the prior assent of the parties involved in the process, i.e., workers and businesses. Therefore, even when unions cover more than one firm this does not automatically mean that negotiations will extend to all the firms, because the employers must be willing to initiate a bargaining process.

Labor unions do not need prior authorization to establish themselves, and the only conditions to which they are subject are that they abide by their statutes and represent at least a certain percentage of the firm's workers.[25] The unions are also allowed to set up, join, or leave federations, confederations, and the like.

---

[24] See Cortázar (1993) and Bravo (1990). According to a case study by Bravo, the incentive systems most frequently used are production bonds and negotiation; 42 percent of all the firms of his sample offered their workers some kind of incentive in 1988.

[25] In firms with more than 50 workers a minimum of 25 workers is required, and the membership must represent at least 10 percent of the total. If the firm has 50 or fewer workers, the minimum number is eight and the membership must represent more than 50 percent of the total. A group of 250 or more workers at the same firm may always form a union, regardless of the percentage they represent.

Table 3.8. Chile: Collective Bargaining

Bargaining parties	One or more employers and one or more labor unions or workers who have joined forces for this purpose, in private sector enterprises or enterprises in which the state has an interest or is represented
Who may not join in bargaining	• Workers with apprenticeship contracts • Workers hired on a temporary or seasonal basis • Managers, supervisors, agents or attorneys in fact (provided they have administrative responsibilities), persons authorized to hire and fire workers, and workers who, by arrangement with the firm, exercise supervisory or inspection functions within it
Minimum life of contracts	Two years
Maximum life of contracts	No legal limit
Parties bound by the contract	The firms whose workers initiate the formal collective bargaining process. However, prior agreement of the parties is required if the bargaining involves more than one firm
Scope of the negotiations	Any issue relating to compensation or other benefits in kind or in money, and in general common working conditions
Limits to the agreements	Any provision that restricts or limits the employer's ability to organize, direct and administer the firm, and any matter alien to the firm
Rules concerning special groups	Collective bargaining with seamen
Minimum clauses	• Precise determination of the parties affected by the contract • Provisions concerning compensation, benefits and working conditions that have been agreed upon • Term of contract, which may not be less than two years • If the parties so agree, the designation of an arbitrator charged with interpreting the contract and settling disputes
Intervention of the state	• Labor Office: may intervene throughout the entire collective bargaining process and during the life of a collective contract as authenticating officer and regulator • Labor courts: hear and process petitions of the parties involved in the bargaining or the collective contract • Executive Branch: periodically determines firms against which strikes are not permitted and which are therefore subject to binding arbitration; exceptionally orders resumption of work in firms where a legal strike may deprive the public of essential supplies or compromise national security; determines the National List of Labor Arbitrators
Bargaining by area of activity	Collective bargaining involving more than one firm, as would be the case with bargaining by area of activity, is permitted by law. However, prior agreement of the parties involved in the process is required so that the rules can be developed

Source: Prepared for this study on the basis of the Labor Code.

Membership in a labor union is voluntary and personal. The issues that have created controversy in the past are whether payment by workers of dues to the firm's union should be voluntary or not, and what should be the contribution of nonunion workers who benefit from collective contracts. The questions on these points are how far people who assume no burden at all should be allowed to benefit, what weakens union organization, and what practices undermine the workers' individual freedom. The challenge is how to balance the advantages and disadvantages of union organization with those of the workers' individual freedom.

Conflict Resolution Mechanisms

Two of the questions surrounding labor law are what conflict resolution mechanisms does it provide, and what sort of balance does it strike between state intervention and the freedom of action of the principals? Figure 3.1 consists of a flow chart of the various phases of collective bargaining and conflict resolution in Chilean labor law. As we shall see, although these phases are highly regulated in terms of time limits, alternative approaches, etc., they allow the actors (businesses and workers) considerable autonomy in direct negotiations and are intended to help resolve conflicts step by step.

The draft collective contract may be presented by a union of the firm or a group of workers of the firm, or by another labor organization (two or more unions, inter-firm union, federation or confederation). The deadlines for the firm's reply to the draft contract differ in these two modalities, but thereafter the process is similar. If the firm does not reply, the draft is deemed to have been accepted. The firm can reply by accepting the draft, putting forward new proposals, or objecting to the draft.

The possibility of conflict arises if workers do not accept the firm's new proposals or if the firm objects to the draft. After a negotiating period, the firm's final offer must be put to a vote.[26] The process is designed for the collective bargaining to conclude within 45 to 60 days, and if no positive settlement is reached, the process triggers a strike. If a strike is called, the bargaining process continues until an agreement is reached and the collective contract is signed.

Table 3.9 presents more information on the manner in which the conflict develops and the characteristics of the strike. The strike must be decided by an absolute majority of the workers of the firm involved in the bargaining.

---

[26] Voting on the final offer is subject to time limits. If the bargaining is conducted by company unions or groups of workers and the firm does not have a collective contract in effect, the vote must be held within the last five days of a total of 45 from the presentation of the draft; in firms with a collective contract in effect, the time limit is the last five days of the collective contract's life. When the organization is carried out by other labor organizations, the vote must be completed during the last five days of a total of 60 days from the presentation of the draft.

Table 3.9. Chile: Collective Labor Conflicts

Grounds for a legal strike	Refusal of the employer's final offer in the formal collective bargaining process
Conflict prevention and resolution mechanisms	• 45-day bargaining period when one firm is involved, and 60-day period when more than one firm is involved • Mediation: the parties may at any stage of the negotiations decide by common accord to appoint a mediator • Arbitration: the parties may at any time submit the negotiations to arbitration, which is moreover binding where a strike or lock-out is prohibited, or in the case of negotiations in which a back-to-work order is issued • Strike: the law establishes mechanisms that make it easier to end a conflict • Upon expiry of the legal term of the negotiations, the parties may extend the life of the previous contract and continue bargaining • The bargaining committee may require the employer during the negotiations to sign a new collective contract with provisions identical to those contained in the contracts in effect at the start of the negotiations, excluding clauses concerning readjustability • New votes may be called for at any time during the strike • Possibility of individual reinstatement of the workers involved
Who makes the decision to strike	The absolute majority of the workers involved in the collective bargaining process
Strike procedures in practice	• Legal strike • Illegal strike • Brief work stoppage (less than one day) • Slowdown
Strike deadlines	• Voting period: during the last five days of the life of the collective contract. Where no such contract exists, within the last five days of the period of 45 days counting from the presentation of the draft collective contract (or 60 days in the case of bargaining at a level higher than the firm) • Initiation period: the third working day following the date of approval • Maximum duration: indefinite
Replacement of striking workers	The employer may hire replacement workers on: • The first day of the strike, if the last offer has the quality, timeliness and characteristics specified under the law (contract plus readjustability) • The 15th day following presentation of the final offer, if it has the characteristics laid down by law but is presented after the deadline • The 15th day of the strike, if the employer's final offer does not have the timeliness or characteristics specified by law

Source: Prepared for this study on the basis of the Labor Code.

The process has been designed so as to further a settlement of the conflict, and several mechanisms help to bring that about, by means of bargaining committees and by allowing for new votes to be taken. Finally, individual workers can be reinstated from the 15th day after the beginning of the strike (if the employer's offer is the same as the former contract) or from the 30th day (if the offer is different). This feature—as well as others—implies a tendency to repeat the firm's final offer should difficult negotiations be anticipated.

During the strike, the workers are not required to report to work and the employer is not required to pay any compensation. The strike can continue indefinitely, and the employer may hire replacement workers while it remains in effect.

Once the strike has been called, the employer may declare a lockout or temporary shutdown of the plant, either partial or total. A lockout may be declared only if the strike affects more than 50 percent of the workers or if it halts activities that are essential to the firm's operation. It should be noted, however, that although this mechanism is provided for by law, it is not applied in practice in Chile.

Structure of Labor Costs for the Firm

Reference was made in the first section of this chapter to changes in the law that affected compensation (see also Appendix 1). In particular, there have been periods in which collective bargaining was allowed (or not allowed) to cover compensation and in which indexation or compulsory adjustments of compensation existed.

Tables 3.10 and 3.11 contain additional information on the structure of the costs imposed on firms by labor regulations and social security.

It will be seen that the employer's nonwage accounting costs are low and have declined as a result of the reforms made in the Chilean social benefits system in 1981. In the final analysis, to be sure, the problem is one of elasticities that determine who (worker or employer) will have to pay the economic cost of the taxes on work. It should also be noted that certain benefits, such as "travel" and "placement," which were provided for in earlier legislation (1970s), have been eliminated, although they are still offered in some firms.

Labor Organizations

This section identifies the agencies responsible for executing labor programs and intervening on behalf of the workers, including government agencies and labor unions.[27]

---

[27] No information is included on employers' associations, but these diminished in importance in an economy in which bargaining by area of business activity does not exist.

Figure 3.1. Chile: Collective Bargaining

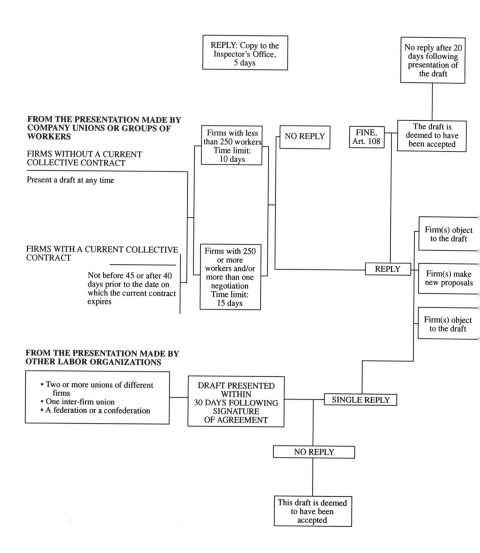

Source: Labor Office, Department of Collective Bargaining.

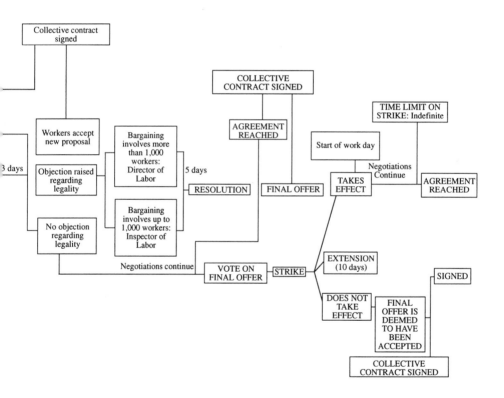

Collective contract signed

Workers accept new proposal

Objection raised regarding legality

No objection regarding legality

3 days

Bargaining involves more than 1,000 workers: Director of Labor

Bargaining involves up to 1,000 workers: Inspector of Labor

5 days

RESOLUTION

COLLECTIVE CONTRACT SIGNED

AGREEMENT REACHED

FINAL OFFER

Start of work day

TAKES EFFECT

TIME LIMIT ON STRIKE: Indefinite

Negotiations Continue

AGREEMENT REACHED

Negotiations continue

VOTE ON FINAL OFFER

STRIKE

EXTENSION (10 days)

DOES NOT TAKE EFFECT

FINAL OFFER IS DEEMED TO HAVE BEEN ACCEPTED

SIGNED

COLLECTIVE CONTRACT SIGNED

Table 3.10. Chile: Structure of Manpower Hiring Costs

Benefits:	
Annual leave	Employees with more than one year of service receive 15 days of paid leave per year. With more than 10 years of service (working for one or more employers), one additional day earned for each three years worked, up to a maximum of 10 years
Holiday bonuses	Not required by law in the private sector. In the public sector, bonuses are paid by law for Christmas and national holidays; the amount is decided for each particular occasion
Annual bonus	In firms that practice real accounting the annual bonus is not less than 30 percent of the cash profit of the current fiscal year, or alternatively 25 percent of accrued annual compensation, to a maximum of 4.75 monthly minimum incomes
Allowances:	
• Local travel	Not required by law
• Placement	Not required by law
Employer's contributions:	
• Work-related accidents	The employer pays a tax ranging from 0.85 percent and 6.4 percent of the employee's taxable compensation in order to finance social security coverage for work accidents and occupational illnesses
Severance fund:	
• Severance pay based on seniority	No legal requirements. The law mandates severance pay based on seniority in case of dismissal without just cause. However, there are no rules requiring that firms maintain a fund for that purpose
• Severance pay in place of prior notice	The law mandates payment of one month's compensation in cases of dismissal for reasons not attributable to the worker, when the employer does not give notice of termination of the contract at least 30 days in advance. However, there are no rules requiring that firms maintain a fund for that purpose

Source: Prepared for this study on the basis of the Labor Code.

Table 3.11. Chile: Contribution-to-Wage Ratios
(Percentages)

Types of contribution	Worker	Firm	Total
Pensions			
Pension fund administrations	12.84 - 13.7	—	12.84 - 13.7
Former pension system	12.24 - 34.35[a]	—	12.24 - 34.35
Health	7.0	—	7.0
Work-related accidents[1]	—	0.85 - 6.8	—
Local travel	—	—	—
Placement	—	—	—
Unemployment insurance	—	—	—

Source: Decree Law 3.500, Decree Law 3.501, Superintendency of Pension Fund Administrations, Domestic Taxes Service.

[a]The assessment rate applied to agencies of the former pensions system includes the assessment for pensions and for various systems of dismissal or indemnification based on length of service, death allowance, and assessments paid to solidarity funds for the financing or various other benefits.

[1]The assessment rate applied to the system of work accidents and occupational diseases differs by sector of economic activity and depends on the actual accident rate of each firm.

Ministry of Labor and Social Welfare

This ministry is responsible for the design and implementation of labor policy (enforcement, employment, and training), and also for social security policy and the regulation and operation of the various social security subsystems (except for health care), such as pensions, family allowances, work-related accidents and occupational diseases, disability (including maternity), and unemployment.

Changing emphasis in labor policy translates into institutional change in terms of numbers of people, resource allocation, and the creation of new programs.

Table 3.12 contains information on the relative importance of the Ministry of Labor's budget for the period 1980-94. The first column corresponds to the general national budget and the second to the sum of the fiscal contributions of all the ministries. The second and third columns trace the ministry's budget and the tax contribution the ministry receives. The important role of the Ministry of Labor, which accounts for almost 30 percent of total resources, stands out clearly even if, as we shall see, a large share of these resources are devoted to social security. The last two columns focus on the Labor Office *(Dirección del Trabajo),* which is the agency most closely concerned with enforcement. From 1990 to 1994 this agency's budget and staff were augmented significantly.

Table 3.13 itemizes this ministry's budget. The most important columns (Institute of Benefits Standardization and Benefit Funds, or *Cajas de Previsión*)

Table 3.12. Chile: Relative Importance of the Labor Administration. Budget of the Ministry of Labor and the Labor Office, 1980-94
(Billions of June 1993 pesos)

	National budget	Tax contribution	Ministry budget net tran.	Tax contribution	Labor Office budget	Labor Office complement
1980	4,008.3	2,074.9	1,059.6	264.3	2.3	771
1981	4,444.1	2,498.5	1,318.5	307.4	2.1	771
1982	5,058.1	2,800.3	1,101.6	422.5	2.4	463
1983	4,128.7	2,021.6	1,012.8	529.1	1.6	463
1984	2,267.5	1,637.4	814.7	417.5	1.3	463
1985	3,227.7	2,492.3	1,072.7	704.4	1.6	465
1986	3,139.9	2,441.9	961.3	665.8	1.6	465
1987	2,930.1	2,185.3	990.7	624.6	2.9	813
1988	3,096.1	2,320.3	1,032.3	681.1	3.0	779
1989	2,752.9	1,974.0	938.3	625.9	2.9	779
1990	2,736.8	2,017.1	971.8	668.8	2.7	813
1991	3,251.4	2,385.9	1,026.4	681.8	2.9	981
1992	3,587.6	2,680.5	1,187.7	836.2	3.7	1,088
1993	3,880.9	3,052.3	1,275.5	900.0	4.5	1,223
1994	4,103.6	3,266.4	1,333.1	935.7	5.6	1,263

Source: Law Concerning Public Sector Budgets, 1980-94.

trace social security outlays. There are also new programs: the third and fourth columns correspond to the financing of the Youth Training Program, or *Capacitación de Jóvenes*, both directly and through the National Training and Employment Service, or *Servicio Nacional de Capacitación y Empleo* (SENCE).

Outlays for supervision and training obviously represent a very low percentage of the budget in comparison with those for social security. Nevertheless they show a substantial increase in the last few years.

Other agencies also inspect and monitor businesses for compliance with safety standards and measures to prevent work-related accidents: the health services covering firms not affiliated with medical care funds check compliance with the law on work-related accidents and occupational diseases; the employers' medical care funds check the firms affiliated with them; and the National Geology and Mining Service performs the same function with respect to mining companies.

Another public agency that ought to have an important role in the labor market is the Municipal Placement Offices or *Oficinas Municipales de Colocación* (OMC). These offices are responsible for finding out about vacancies in businesses in their areas and alerting qualified job-seekers to them. Around 25 percent of the country's municipalities have an OMC.

The traditional functions of the OMCs are enrollment, listing of vacancies,

Table 3.13. Chile: Itemized Budget of Ministry of Labor
(Billions of June 1993 pesos)

Year	Under Secretariat of Labor	Labor Office	Training and technical education	Youth Training Program	National Training and Employment Service	Under Secretariat of Social Welfare	Super-intendency AFP	Super-intendency of Social Security	Institute of Benefits Standard-ization	Benefit funds, gross	General Directorate of Secured Credit	Transfers, net total
1980	252	2,297	0		2,539	76	0	459	0	1,046,450	7,572	1,059,645
1981	306	2,108	0		2,646	74	0	509	0	1,301,630	11,216	1,318,489
1982	375	2,354	0		3,642	95	963	615	201	1,081,581	11,764	1,101,591
1983	252	1,620	0		1,524	74	643	464	133	1,000,268	7,844	1,012,821
1984	183	1,282	0		1,207	61	519	353	80	999,555	6,537	814,720
1985	250	1,605	0		1,367	73	696	492	86	1,431,212	9,943	1,072,737
1986	259	1,553	0		1,168	70	724	465	80	1,306,938	9,322	961,305
1987	278	2,891	0		1,172	89	683	586	86	1,311,467	12,767	990,654
1988	474	3,038	0		1,215	127	825	630	86	1,401,018	11,249	1,032,343
1989	458	2,860	0		1,153	128	813	555	83	975,318	8,124	938,296
1990	401	2,736	0		759	122	757	533	697,461	1,007,482	7,338	971,782
1991	486	2,945	3,644	0	1,053	127	794	532	781,279	1,064,976	8,314	1,026,398
1992	639	3,697	11,950	110	1,264	138	897	576	889,090	1,218,963	8,317	1,187,828
1993	628	4,498	15,477	59	1,901	142	1,110	627	948,705	1,301,483	8,330	1,275,592
1994	773	5,648	15,416	65	2,183	149	1,223	654	991,155	1,360,582	9,408	1,333,272

Source: Law Concerning Public Sector Budgets, 1980-94.

Table 3.14. Chile: Municipal Placement Offices: Numbers of Enrollees, Vacancies and Placements

Year	Enrollees	Vacancies	Placements
1977	61,456	13,760	8,216
1978	71,035	24,474	15,211
1979	84,176	28,856	17,098
1980	96,234	31,528	20,473
1981	113,424	38,975	28,686
1982	194,466	31,531	26,091
1983	166,288	31,873	25,736
1984	113,089	34,078	27,731
1985	105,022	35,957	29,916
1986	113,566	49,959	39,701
1987	99,836	62,863	49,974
1988	104,528	80,351	59,555
1989	83,021	68,078	50,770
1990	80,221	49,715	35,781
1991	94,392	49,711	34,556
1992	105,785	62,065	37,195
1993	121,383	63,924	36,884

Source: Ministry of Labor.

job orientation, placement, and statistical record-keeping. In practice, many offices are so under-equipped and short-staffed that they keep their activities stripped down to the simplest essentials.

The functions of the OMCs have moreover changed as a result of their participation in the Ministry of Labor's Youth Training Program, in which they serve as points of entry.[28] The OMCs have to promote the program, enroll trainees, place them in accordance with vacancies, and conduct follow-up efforts.

Table 3.14 contains information on the number of individuals enrolled, the number of vacancies, and the number of OMC placements. The demand for this service (the number of enrollees) was evidently significant in the period of high unemployment, yet the number of vacancies and placements did not respond positively in the period 1980-86. In addition, recent years have seen the number of enrollees and vacancies rise without a correspondingly higher percentage of placements.

The OMCs face several problems in their role as brokers in the labor market,

---

[28] The training courses are given by private institutions, with public funding allocated through a bidding procedure. The courses include both theory and on-the-job training.

some of which stem from concrete problems such as serving two administrative masters (municipalities and SENCE), meager funding, and unqualified staff.

Attempts have been made through the Youth Training Program to encourage the professional upgrading of the OMCs, and a major endeavor has been made to improve their infrastructure by connecting them to a computer network at the national level. If this effort is carried through, the OMCs will probably be able to operate effectively sometime in the future as government agencies helping people to find employment and play a more important role as labor intermediaries.

Labor Unions

Table 3.15 sets forth the conditions that govern labor organizing (supplementing data in the second section of this chapter) and provides additional information on organizational categories and procedures for electing officers and financing unions. Subsequent tables present quantitative data tracing union activity.

The scale of union organization varies greatly from one economic sector to another. The highest rates are found in the mining sector, with 66.9 percent, while the rate for manufacturing is 22 percent. As usual, unions prove to be strongest in oligopsonic sectors dominated by large enterprises.

By and large, the figures tend to indicate an upswing in union activity during the period, as reflected in the number of federations and confederations, the percentage of workers covered by collective contracts, and other measures of union activity. Also, a significant percentage of workers belong to umbrella organizations such as federations and confederations.

In the last several years, therefore, the changes in labor policy and law have been accompanied by a surge in union organizing.

Final Comments

The foregoing review of the Chilean experience with labor law was intended to give some idea of the advances made in the direction of flexibility and less government intrusion in labor-related matters. These final comments and the recommendations growing out of them take that effort a step further.

The history of the labor market outlined in the first section shows how this market adjusted course in the face of the macroeconomic recessions that Chile has experienced in the last two decades. The labor market's adjustment—especially in terms of employment—was swifter in the seventies than in the eighties. Although many of these differences may stem from the fact that the shocks were different (sectoral rather than general), changes in labor law also appear to have played an important role.

Wage-setting was much more "flexible" in the eighties; paradoxically, the prohibition of collective bargaining introduced a certain rigidity into the labor

Table 3.15. Chile: Conditions Governing Labor Organizations

Membership	• Voluntary, personal and not subject to delegation. This applies to dropping as well as acquiring membership. Simultaneous membership in more than one union is not permitted • Company union: members drawn from workers of a single company • Inter-company union: members drawn from two or more companies • Union of self-employed workers: members do not work for any employer • Union of casual or transient workers: members work for employers on a cyclical or intermittent basis
Procedures for electing officers	• Secret balloting open to all members of the union with at least 90 days' prior notice • The election must be held in the presence of an authenticating officer. Candidates for election to the union's board of directors enjoy immunity from the time their candidacy is formally announced to the employer until the date of the election. The announcement must be made no more than 15 days in advance • If the union has fewer than 25 workers, one director is elected • If the union has 25 to 249 workers, three directors are elected • If the union has 250 to 999 workers, five directors are elected • If the union has 1,000 to 2,999 workers, seven directors are elected • If the union has 3,000 or more workers, nine directors are elected • If three directors are elected, each worker will be allowed two votes. If five directors are elected, each worker will be allowed three votes. If seven directors are elected, each worker will be allowed four votes. If nine directors are elected, each worker will have five votes • Candidates who win the highest relative majorities are elected as directors. A director's term of office is two years, and reelection is permitted

Funding of the union

- Regular or special dues or contributions which the assembly imposes on the members. Membership dues are obligatory. The union assembly sets the amount, which the employer must deduct from compensation as regular dues. Contribution of the members to a collective contract and of those members to whom the collective contract applies
- donations *inter vivos* or legacies. Proceeds from disposal of property. Sale of assets. Fines levied on members
- Any other source of financing established by the union bylaws

Categories of labor organization

- Basic union: union covering one company
- Federation: body combining three or more unions
- Confederation: body combining five or more federations or 20 or more unions
The combination of 20 or more unions can give rise to either a federation or a confederation
- Labor league (*central sindical*): any national organization representing the general interests of the workers who are its members, and who can be from different sectors that produce goods or services. A league can be made up of any combination of confederations, federations, unions, associations of employees of the civil service of municipalities, and trade associations composed of individuals, as determined by their own bylaws. Retiree organizations established as legal entities may also join labor leagues

Source: Labor Code.

market by imposing public sector regulations on the private sector. The adjustment of compensation has been—both in law and in the figures—more flexible since 1982, when the readjustments and the mandatory indexation were abolished.

In addition, rigid rules on hiring and firing and high severance pay kept employment from rising. The law that was on the books until 1978 seemed to follow those lines, although it was rather casually enforced. Did the uncertainty associated with this state of affairs discourage employment? This theory has also been put forward to explain sluggish job creation in the seventies. Although the 1979 Labor Plan lowered the cost of hiring and firing and simplified the law, it should also be recalled that it was very unpopular with the workers. One of the advantages of the current (1990) law is that it not only maintains flexibility with respect to wages and layoffs, but that it enjoys a greater degree of social consensus as it offers workers more protection by enabling them to exercise their rights more effectively.

The labor market's reaction to the crisis also shows that the Chilean economy needs an adequate mechanism to shield incomes from unemployment. The current unemployment allowance is inadequate and insufficient, and in practice the emergency job programs have been the main line of defense against unemployment. The institution of unemployment insurance is one of the policy recommendations reaffirmed in this study.

The second section presented current Chilean labor law in some detail. It demonstrates that significant strides have been made in flexibility and deregulation while maintaining and enhancing the protection of workers' rights. In this sense Chilean labor law is advanced enough to mute any calls for change.

Nevertheless, some aspects of labor law and practice are still in need of improvement. For example, although progress has been made in enforcement, coverage could still be improved for workers in some sectors.

Enlarging the universe of workers who can engage in collective bargaining is another goal to be considered for the future. This could be accomplished by creating better conditions in the hiring of casual, seasonal, fixed-term, and piecework workers.

Another point to pursue is the difference between labor standards in the private and public sectors, and the need to modernize the latter.

A comparison of the Labor Code with the Administrative Statute shows that the latter is considerably more rigid. Added to the inflexibility of the law in the area of human resources administration is the public sector's budgetary inflexibility. These are points to consider in connection with the requirements of modernization faced by government agencies in many countries (and Chile in particular). This greater "inflexibility" of the labor law of the public sector manifests itself in several ways: compensation is subject to a single pay scale; there are limitations on contractual and fee-based work; there are major limitations on transferring and dismissing personnel; and the work day is shorter. In practice it

Table 3.16. Chile: Union Membership by Sector of Economic Activity, 1992

Economic activity	Number of members	Labor force	Percentage unionized
Agriculture, hunting, forestry, fishery	70,492	885,570	8.0
Mining and quarrying	62,262	93,130	66.9
Manufacturing industries	185,366	844,380	22.0
Electric power	15,885	26,930	59.0
Construction	53,720	372,240	14.4
Trade	100,143	903,280	11.1
Transport, storage, communications	105,779	355,610	29.7
Financial services, insurance, real estate and technical social services	34,416	255,940	13.4
Community, social and personal services	95,592	1,259,110	7.4
Others[1]	3,410	560	—
First-time job seekers	—	35,540	—
Total	724,065	5,032,290	14.4

Source: Labor Union Statistics, 1992, Labor Office, Department of Labor Organizations; Employment Survey, National Institute of Statistics, November-January, 1993.
[1]The fact that this category has more union members than members of the labor force may be due to underrepresentation of the latter in the INE employment survey.

Table 3.17. Chile: Growth of Umbrella Organizations
(Combining two or more unions)

	Number of members			Number of organizations			Number of affiliated labor organizations		
	Federation	Confederation	Total	Federation	Confederation	Total	Federation	Confederation	Total
1982	26,617	59,110	85,727	41	21	62	223	407	630
1983	45,256	79,235	124,491	87	24	111	432	627	1,059
1984	59,997	90,135	149,141	102	26	128	575	795	1,730
1985	69,812	103,738	173,550	119	28	147	672	925	1,597
1986	79,659	110,108	189,767	131	31	162	804	1,110	1,914
1987	88,548	133,093	221,642	144	36	180	961	1,347	2,308
1988	99,783	139,326	239,109	171	39	210	1,106	1,431	2,537
1989	114,889	162,974	277,863	174	41	215	1,359	1,737	3,096
1990	157,568	216,728	374,296	232	45	277	1,759	2,313	4,072
1991	207,404	280,144	487,548	262	49	311	2,156	2,844	5,000
1992	266,369	251,991	518,360	287	49	336	2,391	2,966	5,357

Source: Labor Union Statistics 1992, Labor Office, Department of Labor Organizations.

Table 3.18. Chile: Collective Bargaining Coverage

	Labor force (Thousands)	Number of workers covered by collective contracts	Percentages
1986	4,354.4	308,641	7.1
1987	4,354.4	331,204	7.6
1988	4,551.6	367,846	8.1
1989	4,674.6	472,340	10.1
1990	4,728.6	524,648	11.1
1991	4,794.1	526,091	11.0
1992	4,990.4	496,380	9.9

Source: Labor Union Statistics, 1992, Labor Office, Department of Labor Organizations; Employment Survey, National Institute of Statistics, November-January, 1993.

is very difficult to dismiss a public sector worker exclusively on the employer's initiative, as is done in the private sector.

As already noted, the modernization of human resources forms part of the ongoing issue of how generally to modernize government services. This is sure to be one of the most important aspects of labor policy in the years ahead.

When rigidity makes for a system in which incentives to productivity, creativity and innovation are weak or nonexistent, the "public goods and services" component of the Chilean economy's total output is bound to be affected.

It is maintained that the challenges faced by the labor market include the raising of participation rates. However, it is not clear that this process is affected by problems with the law, although there may be a negative bias (i.e., a cost) regarding the hiring of women. The law itself does not contain discriminatory provisions. However, it does contain special provisions to protect mothers, as well as rules concerning retirement (retirement age and survivors' pension) and heavy work.[29] What does seem clear is that employers "discount" from their compensation the greater nonwage cost of hiring women. Various studies point out that in the case of semi-skilled workers women earn only 70 to 80 percent as much as men, a discount that corresponds at least in part to their greater nonwage cost.

The flexibility of labor resources depends not only on rules concerning compensation and employment but also on training and preparation that make workers better able to adapt to technological change. Although these topics lie outside

---

[29] The latest Labor Code (January 1994) eliminates many of the restrictions on the types of work women are permitted to do.

Table 3.19. Chile: Workers Covered by Collective Instruments

	Agreements			Contracts			Total collective instruments		
	No. of workers	No. of instruments	No. of workers covered	No. of workers	No. of instruments	No. of workers covered	No. of workers	No. of instruments	No. of workers covered
1986	28,257	122	60,783	106,255	1,134	247,858	134,512	1,356	308,641
1987	37,374	174	65,631	159,318	1,958	265,573	196,692	2,132	331,204
1988	46,906	187	84,280	124,248	1,385	283,566	171,154	1,572	367,846
1989	78,693	315	125,599	222,493	2,429	346,741	301,186	2,744	472,340
1990	44,236	752	122,929	179,226	1,885	401,719	223,462	2,637	524,648
1991	50,244	822	94,480	252,385	2,764	431,611	302,629	3,586	526,091
1992	52,557	741	102,801	141,194	1,578	393,579	193,751	2,319	496,380

Source: Labor Office, Department of Labor Organizations.

the scope of this study, it should be stressed that the private sector plays an ever-growing role in these processes because of decentralization and diminishing state involvement. In Chile a tax break is currently designed to encourage businesses to spend money on training their personnel (the SENCE program). In addition there is the youth training program previously referred to, which is also implemented by private entities.

A policy recommendation from an institutional perspective would be to strengthen the labor intermediation efforts of the OMCs, perhaps by enlisting the services of private agents.

Finally, with respect to reducing state involvement in the administration of labor, Chile has since 1990 relied primarily on a three-tiered approach in labor affairs at the national level and a two-tiered approach in dealings at the firm or sector level. At the national level, the Minister of Labor invites the representatives of CPC (business) and CUT (labor) to negotiate on such matters as minimum wages and social security benefits. This has given rise to the Tripartite Agreement, which since the beginning of the present government has been signed in April and May of each year. At the firm or sector level, the intention is that the state should not get involved in labor conflicts at the firm level, in either the private or the public sector. In this context the law has moved in the direction of greater autonomy on the part of the labor actors, leaving them responsible for pursuing their interests through individual negotiation of compensation and working conditions.

Bibliography

Alamos, R. 1986. La modernización laboral. *Estudios públicos* 26 (Autumn).

Banuri, T. and E. Amadeo. 1992. Worlds Within the Third World: Labor Market Institutions in Asia and Latin America. In *Economic Liberalization: No Panacea*, ed. T. Banuri. Oxford: Clarendon Press.

Bravo, D. 1990. Los salarios participativos y su efecto sobre la productividad del trabajador y la estabilidad en el empleo. *Colección Estudios CIEPLAN* (No. 29, September). CIEPLAN, Santiago.

Chacón, B. 1992. Situación y características del empleo en Chile 1990. In *Población, educación, vivienda, salud, empleo y pobreza*. MIDEPLAN.

Corbo, V. 1980. The Impact of Minimum Wages and Industrial Employment in Chile. *Serie de Investigación* (No. 48). University of Chile, Santiago.

Cortázar, R. 1993. *Política laboral en el Chile democrático: avances y desafíos en los noventa*. Santiago: Editorial Dolmen.

Cortázar, R., and J. Marshall. 1980. Indice de precios al consumidor en Chile: 1970-78. *Coleción Estudios CIEPLAN* (No. 4, November). CIEPLAN, Santiago.

Echeverría, C. 1993. Los seguros de desempleo: análisis y recomendaciones. *Papeles de Trabajo PEP 11*. Corporación Tiempo 2000.

Ffrench-Davis, R., and D. Raczynski. 1988. The Impact of Global Recession and National Policies on Living Standards: Chile 1973-87. *Notas Técnicas CIEPLAN* (No. 97, February).

Frías, P. 1985. Afiliación y representatividad del movimiento sindical bajo el régimen militar: 1973-84. *Materiales para Discusión* (No. 83). CED, Santiago.

García, N. 1991. El salario mínimo en Chile, 1990. *Serie Investigaciones sobre Empleo* (No. 34). PREALC, Santiago.

González, P. 1993a. Profit Sharing, Unemployment and Effort. Economic Letters. Forthcoming.

_____. 1993b. El mercado laboral y la educación en Chile. Paper presented at the Political Economy of Education Seminar, ECLAC/UNESCO.

_____. 1990. Determinación de salarios en la economía chilena: una aplicación de las técnicas de cointegración. *Colección de Estudios CIEPLAN* (No. 29, September).

_____. 1988. Formación de un patrimonio de los trabajadores: la experiencia europea. *Fondos de Inversión*. Instituto Interamericano de Mercados de Capital, Caracas.

Gordon, M. 1988. *Social Security Policies in Industrial Countries: A Comparative Analysis*. Cambridge University Press.

Infante, R., and E. Klein. 1992. *Chile: Transformaciones del mercado laboral y sus efectos sociales, 1965-90*. Working Paper No. 368. PREALC.

Jadresic, E. 1989. Salarios reales en Chile: 1960-88. *Nota Técnica CIEPLAN* (No. 134).

Leiva, A. 1993. El sector informal en Chile: análisis de sus componentes y mediciones posibles. *Revista Estadística y Economía* (5): 85-115. Instituto Nacional de Estadística (INE), Santiago.

Marshall, J., and P. Romaguera. 1981. La evolución del empleo público en Chile, 1970-78. *Nota Técnica CIEPLAN* (No. 26).

Maturana, V., and O. MacClure. 1992. La negociación colectiva en Chile. In *El sindicalismo latinoamericano en los 90,* eds. L. Abramo and L. Cuevas.

Meller, P. 1992. *Adjustment and Equity in Chile*. Development Centre Studies, OECD, France.

_____. 1990. Revisión del proceso de ajuste chileno de la década del 80. *Colección Estudios CIEPLAN* (No. 30, December).

Meller, P., and P. Romaguera. 1992. Crisis, ajuste con éxito y costo social. In *Chile: Evolución macroeconómica, financiación externa y cambio político en la década de los 80*. Madrid: Fundación CEDEAL.

Mizala, A. 1992. Las reformas económicas de los años 70 y la industria manufacturera chilena. *Colección Estudios CIEPLAN* (No. 35).

Mizala, A., and P. Romaguera. 1994. Seguros de desempleo y flexibilidad del mercado laboral: evaluación de la experiencia chilena y análisis de sistemas alternativos. FONDECYT. Mimeo.

_____. 1993. Mercado del trabajo en Chile: ajuste, transición y desafíos futuros. Paper presented at the seminar, Instituciones Laborales frente a los Cambios en América Latina, IIEL-PREALC, May.

_____. 1991. ¿Es el sector público un sector líder en la determinación de los salarios?. Evidencia para la economía chilena. *Colección Estudios CIEPLAN* (No. 33, December).

Montero, C. 1990. La evolución del empresariado chileno: ¿Surge un nuevo actor social? *Colección Estudios CIEPLAN* (No. 30, December).

Raczynski, D., and P. Romaguera. 1995. Chile: Poverty, Adjustment and Social Policies in the 80s. In *Confronting the Challenge of Poverty and Inequality in Latin America,* ed. Nora Lustig. Washington, D.C.: The Brookings Institution and Inter-American Dialogue. Forthcoming.

Ramos, J., and D. Bravo. 1991. Hacia una institucionalidad laboral justa y moderna. Ministry of Labor, Santiago. Mimeo.

Regini, M. 1988. *La spida de la flessibilita.* Milan: Franco Angeli.

Romaguera, P. 1990. Dispersión salarial: modelos y evidencias para el caso chileno. *Colección Estudios CIEPLAN* (No. 29, September).

_____. 1989. Diagnóstico del desempleo en Chile y orientaciones de política. Working Document No. 66 (September). Labor Economy Program (PET).

Sáez, R. E. 1982. Evolución de la indexación en Chile. *Notas Técnicas CIEPLAN* (No. 49). Santiago.

Velásquez, M. 1988. Evolución del empleo público en Chile: 1974-85. Working Document No. 59. Labor Economy Program (PET).

Vial, J., A. Butelmann, and C. Celedón. 1990. Fundamentos de las políticas macroeconómicas del gobierno democrático chileno (1990-93). *Colección Estudios CIEPLAN* (No. 30, December).

APPENDIX 1. CHILE: OUTPUT AND INFLATION

| | Gross domestic product | | |
	Millions of 1986 pesos	Annual variation (%)	Inflation (%)
1970		2.1	34.9
1971		9.0	22.1
1972		-1.2	163.4
1973		-5.6	508.1
1974	2,745,563	1.0	375.9
1975	2,381,115	-13.3	340.7
1976	2,457,650	3.2	174.3
1977	2,660,813	8.3	63.5
1978	2,867,069	7.8	30.3
1979	3,071,463	7.1	38.9
1980	3,308,910	7.7	31.2
1981	3,529,836	6.7	9.5
1982	3,056,065	-13.4	20.7
1983	2,949,437	-3.5	23.1
1984	3,129,112	6.1	23.0
1985	3,238,003	3.5	26.4
1986	3,419,209	5.6	17.4
1987	3,644,681	6.6	21.5
1988	3,911,154	7.3	12.7
1989	4,308,306	10.2	21.4
1990	4,436,043	3.0	27.3
1991	4,705,074	6.1	18.7
1992	5,188,708	10.3	12.7
1993			12.2

Source: National Institute of Statistics and Central Bank.
Notes: Output reflects GDP according to the figures, expressed in 1986 pesos, of the new national accounts. These figures differ slightly from the previous version of the national accounts (in 1977 pesos). The rates for the period 1970-74 correspond to the old version, since no figures in 1986 pesos exist. Inflation reflects the variation from December to December according to official INE figures.

APPENDIX 2. CHILE: WAGE-SETTING REGULATIONS*

Until September 1973, wages were generally set according to the following rules: (i) compensation in the private sector was agreed to through collective bargaining or directly with the employer, subject to minimum wage regulations; (ii) the readjustment of compensation in the public sector was determined by law, and generally allowed for indexation of 100 percent with respect to past inflation; (iii) the readjustment of compensation in the public sector also applied to private sector workers, who did not take part in collective bargaining; and (iv) collective bargaining in the private sector was not subject to mandatory indexation, but general indexation (100 percent with respect to past inflation) existed in practice.

Following the military coup of September 1973, collective bargaining was suspended and union activity was prohibited. Between that date and July 1979 the rules for determining compensation in the private sector were modified. Wage readjustments for the private sector were decreed by the government and carried out by means of general readjustments of compensation (for both public and private sectors). A single pay scale (EUR) was established for the public sector.

General wage readjustments were based on partial indexation with respect to past inflation in 1974-75, and on total indexation from 1976 to 1978. However, the official CPI underestimated actual inflation during this period (see Cortázar and Marshall, 1980).

The Labor Plan of July 1979 (Decree Law No. 2758) brought back collective bargaining in the private sector and imposed a floor on it through mandatory indexation of 100 percent with respect to past inflation. Public sector compensation continued to be governed by the EUR and the readjustments decreed under the law; these readjustments were also applied to that part of the private sector which did not engage in collective bargaining.

The last change came about in June 1982, when the Labor Plan was changed by the abolition of mandatory indexation of private collective contracts. At the same time the laws providing for readjustments in the public sector ceased to apply to the private sector.

From the middle of 1982 the only government regulations refer to the minimum wage and readjustments of the EUR.

Minimum Wages

Minimum wage legislation was first passed in Chile in 1937. Initially the term was "living wage" and there were differences between blue collar and white

---

*The source for this appendix is Mizala and Romaguera (1993), Annex A. For further details see Mizala and Romaguera (1991) and Sáez (1982).

collar workers, and between different types of work: there were minimum wages for agriculture and for the industrial and trade sectors. For a while there were also differences by province.[1]

At the end of 1973 the various rates were unified and the minimum compensation that could be paid to a worker for his or her services was called "monthly minimum income" (Decree Laws No. 97 and No. 245 of October 24, 1973, and January 18, 1974). The monthly minimum wage was established by the government through decree law, and there was no set schedule for changing it.

The readjustability of the minimum wage has changed over time, and constitutes a distinct item of the government's wage policy.

In the last two decades the minimum wage trend has generally followed the period's economic and political cycles. But in the crisis of 1982 the minimum wage was deliberately allowed to lag behind other wages, in order to spur employment and cut inflation.

Minimum wage policy took an opposite tack in 1990, when the minimum wage was raised faster than the average growth rate of the economy, so that the poorest sectors of the population could regain the ground they had lost.

---

[1] See Corbo (1980) and García (1991).

APPENDIX 3. CHILE: REGULATION OF THE INDIVIDUAL LABOR CONTRACT*

The Labor Code governs the labor relations of workers and employers, but does not apply to state employees working in centralized and decentralized agencies, the National Congress, and the judicial branch, or to workers of state enterprises (or enterprises in which the state has a share), provided that those workers are covered under the law by a special statute.

However, the workers of those entities are subject to the norms of the Labor Code in matters not regulated by their respective statutes.

Civil servants are in general covered by the Administrative Statute, Law 18.834, which is described in Appendix 4. Appendix 4 presents information on the workers, public and private, subject to special regulations.

The main differences between the workers protected by the Labor Code (private sector) and those governed by the Administrative Statute (public sector) or other special statutes are that the latter are normally defined as "career civil servants," have tenure—i.e., to be dismissed they must be guilty of gross negligence as established by an appropriate inquiry—and receive compensation whose rates and readjustment are defined by law (except in some universities).

Finally, the following types of work do not call for a labor contract:

- Services rendered directly to the public, or performed in noncontinuous fashion or sporadically for home delivery.
- Labor practice.
- Services usually performed at home or in at a location freely chosen by the worker, without supervision or immediate direction from an employer.

Hiring Standards

Employers who do not produce a written labor contract within 15 days of hiring a worker—which is reduced to five days in the case of contracts covering a period of less than 30 days—may be assessed a fine.

The contents of a labor contract and the conditions under which it can be modified are specified in the Labor Code.

Types of Contracts

Contracts fall into four general categories and a number of special types. The general categories are:

---

*Promulgated January 7, 1994 by the Ministry of Labor and Social Welfare and published in the Official Journal on January 24, 1994.

- Indefinite.
- Fixed term. These may be signed for up to one year, or up to two years for managers and professionals. Workers who perform noncontinuous services under two term contracts during 12 months or more over a period of 15 months (counting from the initial hiring), or workers who continue working after the contract has expired with the knowledge of the employer, or workers whose contract is renewed for the second time, will be presumed to have been hired for an indefinite duration.
- Limited to a specific project or task.
- Probation.

The following special contracts exist:

- Apprenticeship. Applies only to persons under 21, overseen by SENCE. Two years maximum. Apprentices may total no more than 10 percent of the firm's total number of full-time workers.
- Farm workers employed directly in agricultural tasks. Working hours may be counted on a daily or weekly basis, depending on usual practice in the area. The regulations stipulate that average annual working hours may not exceed eight hours a day. Up to 50 percent of compensation may be in noncash form.
- Shipboard workers and seamen (by the week).
- Casual dockworkers. Working hours are counted over shifts and may total not more than eight and not less than four per day.
- Domestic workers. The minimum wage is 75 percent of the general figure.

Working Hours

Regular working hours may not in general exceed 48 hours a week, except for workers subject to special rules and the following:

- Workers employed by different employers.
- Managers, administrators, attorneys in fact with administrative responsibilities, and all persons working without immediate supervision.
- Persons working at home or in a place freely chosen by them.
- Agents, commission agents, insurance workers, traveling salespersons, bus conductors, and other workers who do not work on the employer's premises.

Working hours may not be spread over more than six or fewer than five hours, and may not exceed 10 hours per day. Regular working hours may be exceeded in order to prevent disruption to the firm's smooth operation or in other special cases. The excess must be paid as overtime.

Certain occupations are governed by special rules concerning working hours, e.g., drivers, tradespeople, and fishermen (see Appendix 5 for further details).

Overtime. May be agreed upon for up to two hours per day on tasks that by their nature do not injure the worker's health (as determined by the Office of the Labor Inspector or *Inspección de Trabajo*, whose decision may be appealed to the Labor Court or *Juzgado de Letras del Trabajo*). Overtime pay must include a 50 percent surcharge over the regular rate of compensation.

Rest periods. Except for continuous-process tasks (as determined by the Office of the Labor Inspector, whose decision may be appealed to the Labor Court), the workday is divided into two parts, with at least half an hour between them for lunch that is not counted as time on the job. Sundays are days of rest (from Saturday 9 p.m. to Monday 6 a.m.).

Sunday may be switched with a weekday as a day of rest under certain circumstances, such as in the case of workers in trade and services or work performed outside urban centers.

Compensation

Compensation is the monetary consideration the employer must pay to the worker under the terms of the labor contract.

Compensation consists of the base pay and overtime pay, commissions computed as a percentage of sales, purchases, or the like, shares of profits, and bonuses. The last-named are obligatory for all for-profit enterprises and cooperatives and are determined in accordance with any of the following mechanisms: a minimum of 30 percent of the year's profits, in proportional form or what was earned by each worker in the course of the year; or 25 percent of the monthly compensation earned in the course of the year. In this case, the maximum individual bonus will be 4.75 times the minimum monthly income.

Express authorization is in place for additional benefits—such as housing, lighting, fuel, food, or other payments in kind or services—to be provided by the employer. These must be specified in writing in the labor contract.

For the same reasons that collective bargaining does not take place by branch, there are also no mandatory rates by occupation or activity.

There is a minimum wage which generally applies to all workers over 18 and less than 65 years of age. For part-time workers it is prorated on the basis of their actual working hours. Workers bound by apprenticeship contracts are excepted from the minimum wage.

Compensation must be paid at intervals of not longer than one month. If the contract does not mention this point, advance payments must be made every 15 days on piecework and seasonal tasks.

Leave

Any worker with more than one year of service will be eligible for 15 paid workdays of annual leave (with Saturdays considered a non-workday). Any worker with 10 years of service, with one or more employers, continuous or noncontinuous, will be entitled to an additional day of leave for every additional three years of service, which will be susceptible to individual or collective bargaining. Not more than 10 years of employment by former employers may be claimed. At least 10 consecutive workdays must be allowed to be taken as leave; the rest may be spread out by mutual agreement.

Causes for Termination of the Contract

There are different types of cause:

- Article 159 (formerly Art. 1, Law 19.010)

1. Mutual agreement between the parties.
2. Resignation by the worker (30 days' notice).
3. Death of the worker.
4. Expiry of the time limit (fixed-term contract).
5. Conclusion of the work or service performed under the contract (performance contract).
6. Act of God or force majeure.

- Termination without right to severance pay. Art. 160 (formerly Art. 2, Law 19.010).

1. Lack of integrity, assault and battery, actionable words, or duly proven moral turpitude.
2. Business conducted by the worker that overlaps with his duties and was prohibited in writing in the labor contract.
3.1 Unauthorized absence from work for two consecutive days, two Mondays in one month, or a total of three days during the same time period.
3.2 Unjustified or unannounced absence from an activity, task or machine whose abandonment or idleness significantly disrupts the firm's operation.
4. Abandonment of the job by the worker.
5. Acts, omissions, or reckless conduct affecting the safety or operation of the firm, or the safety, activity, or health of the workers.
6. Intentional material harm done to facilities, equipment, tools, work implements, products, or merchandise.
7. Gross breach of contract.

- Grounds for termination. Article 161 (formerly Art. 3, Law 19.010).

1. Needs of the firm (includes the rationalization or modernization of the firm, reversal of falling productivity, response to changes in market or economic conditions, and inadequate performance or technical skill on the part of the worker).
2. Written notice of dismissal from the employer, only for domestic workers and workers with administrative responsibilities (managers, attorneys in fact, etc.).

The last two grounds cannot be invoked in the case of workers taking leave because of illness, an accident in the work place, or occupational disease. They furthermore require severance pay for time in service (one month per year of service and fractions over six months, with a maximum of 11 months' severance pay) and 30 days' notice, which can be exchanged for one month's compensation.

Special rule for domestic workers. Employers must deposit monthly, during the first 11 years of the labor relationship, 4.11 percent of compensation in an individual severance account whenever one is created in the AFP system in the worker's name. The balance of this account can be withdrawn by the worker regardless of the cause for which the contract was terminated.

Alternative severance package. At the start of the seventh year of the labor relationship, the parties may replace severance for years of service with general severance for which the employer must pay into an individual account opened in the AFP in each worker's name, on a monthly basis, at least 4.11 percent of taxable compensation (with a maximum of 90 Units of Development or *Unidades de Fomento* [UF]).

Workers who believe they were dismissed on improper grounds, or without lawful cause, may appeal their dismissal within 60 business days from separation to the labor court in whose jurisdiction the firm is located. The court may order the severance pay to be increased by 20 to 50 percent.

There is a ceiling of 90 UF on the compensation on which the severance package is based. This includes the deductions for benefits or social security and cash allowances, and excludes the legal family allowance, overtime payments and benefits paid occasionally or only once a year, such as bonuses. Variable compensation will be averaged over the last three calendar months.

Protection

Employers may terminate contracts only with the prior permission of the court, which may grant it only on the grounds listed as items 4 and 5 in Article 1 and those in Article 2.

Maternity Leave

Workers will be eligible for six weeks' of maternity leave preceding and 12 weeks following childbirth. Their jobs must be kept for them during that time. During that period they will receive an allowance equivalent to their full compensation and benefits, with only social security taxes and other appropriate items deducted. Should the woman die in childbirth or during the period of leave following it, the remaining portion of the leave intended for care of the child will be given to the father, who will not enjoy protection. Leave is also available for workers to look after a seriously ill child less than one year old. Pregnant workers normally engaged in tasks deemed by the authority to be harmful to their health (including night work, strenuous activity, overtime) must be transferred, without reduction in pay, to tasks suited to their condition. Firms employing 20 or more female workers must provide, at their expense, a day care center for children under two years of age. The mothers will be allowed to spend two periods of time, which together must not exceed one hour, feeding their children, and such time will be counted as time spent working for purposes of compensation. Fines of 14 to 70 UTM will be levied for violations; fines for repeated violations will be doubled.

APPENDIX 4. CHILE: SUMMARY OF THE ADMINISTRATIVE STATUTE (Law 18.834)

Civil Service Career

Starts with a regular staff appointment (the staff is composed of supervisors, professionals, technicians, administrators and auxiliaries) and continues up to senior posts immediately below those of exclusive trust. In order to qualify one must, among other things, be Chilean, not have been dismissed from public employment for poor performance or for disciplinary reasons within the past five years, not be charged with a felony or misdemeanor, and have completed basic education.[1]

Types of Contract

- Indefinite, staff.
- Contract positions. A maximum of 20 percent of total staff positions. May be part-time.
- Payment by fee. May be used to hire professionals and technicians with advanced training or experts (including foreigners) in certain fields, for occasional tasks not normally carried out by the agency.

Compensation

Determined by a uniform pay scale, except for agencies that have special scales (Central Bank, inspection agencies, etc.).

Any public office must carry a grade reflecting the importance of the functions with which it is charged, and its holder is entitled to the salary and other compensation appropriate to it.

Allowances are available for the following purposes:
- Loss of cash. Only if the employee handles cash as a primary function, in which case the agency should take out insurance accordingly.
- Local travel. Only if duties require visits to other locations or inspection away from the office where the employee usually works, but in the same city, unless the agency provides the necessary means.
- Overtime.
- Moving. If the position or new duties oblige the employee to move from his normal place of residence, and when he returns to what was his place

---

[1]Initial appointment following public examination is to the lowest staff grade, unless there are vacancies in higher grades that could not be filled by promotion (a rare circumstance).

of residence before his appointment. This does not apply to transfers requested by the employee.

- Travel and subsistence expenses when appropriate.
- Other, as specified by law.

Training

The agency receives a training budget that it must allocate in accordance to training for promotion, staff development and voluntary training. Training results are included in the employee's performance record.

Performance Evaluation

A performance evaluation system determines the employee's advancement in his service career. Performance is rated as outstanding, satisfactory, conditional or unsatisfactory. The rating is entered in the personnel record (with merits and demerits) and performance evaluation (by immediate supervisor), which grade the following on a scale of one to seven: conduct, judgment, productivity, ability and dedication. Employees may file appeals with the Qualifying Board or other authority, as appropriate.

If an employee receives an unsatisfactory performance rating, or a conditional performance rating three times in a five-year period or twice consecutively, the position will be declared vacant.

Work Week

The regular work week is 44 hours, Monday to Friday, with a maximum of nine hours per day. Some staff positions may be part-time. The supervisor may order overtime immediately following regular hours, at night or on Saturdays, Sundays, or holidays when unpostponable tasks have to be completed. Overtime earns compensatory leave (time worked plus 25 percent if immediately following regular hours; time worked plus 50 percent at night or on Saturday or Sunday). If compensatory leave is not possible, overtime pay is earned at the rate of normal pay plus 25 percent for work immediately following regular hours, or normal pay plus 50 percent for work at night or on Saturday or Sunday. "Night" refers to the hours between 9 p.m. and 7 a.m.

Transfers

Transfers apply only to functions appropriate to the position, and require at least 30 days prior notice. If both spouses are public employees and residing in the same locality, one may refuse the transfer unless both are transferred to the other station. Temporary duty: no more than three months in a calendar year, except for special studies.

Leave

Fifteen business days for employees with less than 15 years of service (even in the private sector); 20 days between 15 and 20 years; and 25 business days for employees with 20 or more years of service.

Days off for study or training: up to six business days paid and up to three months unpaid, except in the case of study grants.

Disciplinary Measures

- Censure. Written reprimand, two negative marks on personnel record.
- Fine. Monthly paycheck docked 5 to 20 percent. Two to four negative marks on personnel record.
- Summary dismissal. The following constitute just cause: (i) unjustified absence from the work place for more than three consecutive days; (ii) conviction for a felony or misdemeanor; (iii) organizing or belonging to unions connected with the administration of the state (eliminated in the proposed association of government employees), including directing, promoting or participating in strikes, interrupting or preventing the conduct of business, improper possession of property, and other acts that disrupt the normal operations of state administration; and deliberate damage to agency property or to public or private facilities.

An inquiry must be held, to last not more than five days. The employee has two days following notification to respond to the charges, as well as three days to submit evidence. Two days are given to issue a report. Decision of the authority requesting the inquiry takes two days. Reinstatement or appeal takes place in two days. Decision two days. If it is more serious than had been thought, then administrative proceedings and so forth come into play (Art. 121 ff.).

Causes for Separation

- Acceptance of resignation.
- Retirement under a pension or annuity scheme applicable to the position.
- Declaration of vacancy.
- Dismissal.
- Elimination of the position.
- Completion of contractual term.
- Death.

With respect to positions of trust, dismissal takes the form of a request for resignation prepared by the authority responsible for the appointment. If the resignation is not submitted within 48 hours, the post will be declared vacant. Other grounds for declaring a vacancy (Art. 144) include:

- Incurable ill health (the employee receives six months' pay without having to work for it) or ill health incompatible with the demands of the position.
- Unexpected loss of some of the requirements for entry into the civil service.
- Unsatisfactory or conditional performance rating.

Management may deem taking sick leave for a continuous six-month period, or noncontinuously for a total of six months over a period of two years, to indicate ill health incompatible with the demands of the position. The six-month total may not include leave granted on the basis of work-related accidents or illness, or maternity.

If a reduction in staff occurs as a result of restructuring or merger, redundant employees who do not qualify for retirement will be offered severance pay equivalent to one month's compensation per year of service up to six years, tax-free.

APPENDIX 5. SUMMARY OF CHILEAN LAW ON DISMISSAL AND SEVERANCE

Law No. 16.455 of 1976

This was called the tenure law, since it barred the employer from terminating the labor contract without just cause. If the dismissal was deemed unfair by the courts, the worker had to be reinstated or the employer had to pay severance consisting of one month's compensation for each year of service, with no limit on the number of years. The norm was to consider every dismissal as without just cause unless gross misconduct could be imputed to the worker (e.g., theft).

Decree Law No. 2.200 of 1978

This decree law reintroduced summary dismissal as a way of terminating the labor contract. The employer could dismiss employees without cause upon payment of severance consisting of one month's compensation per year of service, for an unlimited number of years. It was applicable only to workers hired after the date of the decree.

Law No. 18.018 of 1981

This law retained unilateral summary dismissal by the employer, without any statement of cause or appeal procedure, and it reduced severance pay to one month per year of service with a maximum of five years. This package applied to workers hired after the date of the law.

Law No. 19.010 of 1990

This law establishes that any dismissal must be justified and at the same time reestablishes needs of the firm as grounds for dismissal. Severance pay for dismissal consists of one month's compensation per year, up to 11 years, for workers hired after 1981. There is no right to severance pay when dismissal arises from an act or omission on the part of the worker under the Labor Code. The option of general severance is created.

CHAPTER FOUR

URUGUAY

Adriana Cassoni
Gastón J. Labadie
Steve Allen[1]

Uruguay is one of the four countries that will make up the Southern Cone Common Market (MERCOSUR). Preparation for MERCOSUR has focused on lowering tariffs and further liberalizing trade. This new international framework, which is bringing about changes in the sectoral distribution of production and employment, urgently requires an assessment of the labor market. Such an assessment must stress the flexibility that the labor market will need to adapt to those changes as well as the role played by certain institutions and regulations. The capacity of the players and the legal framework to respond can be measured by analyzing recent experiences in Uruguay. The country already has undergone structural adjustment in the form of financial liberalization and price deregulation (since the mid-seventies), as well as relatively gradual trade reforms. In addition, the two two politically and institutionally contrasting periods of the nation's recent past—the military regime from 1973 to 1985 and the restored democratic system in power ever since—invites us to examine the labor market's response to very dissimilar circumstances, particularly as regards the role of unions and judicial practices concerning compensation for dismissal.

At present, although the labor market is apparently in reasonable balance, the trend in unemployment suggests that it is not operating as it should. At the beginning of the eighties the economic recession brought high unemployment rates. In recent years these have come down considerably more slowly than one would expect, given the performance of the economy. This experience was accompanied in the eighties by changes in the coverage and financing of the unemployment insurance system, which had been in place since the 1950s. Mean-

[1] Marisa Bucheli and Eduardo Ameglio helped prepare this paper. We also thank Carlos Mendivil, Jorge Rosenbaum, and Joaquín Serra for their contributions.

while, the public sector's role in the general dynamics of the labor market cannot be underestimated: unemployment in this sector has amounted to between 20 and 25 percent of total unemployment. In addition, it shows differences in the regulations on hiring and firing, in union membership figures, and in wage policy. And finally, there have been some changes in labor supply: the level of participation has risen substantially in the last 20 years and youth unemployment has been high, despite the rising average age of the labor force. Even with increasing school enrollment, there are still gaps in specific job training (Bucheli, *et al.,* 1993).

In that context, insight into labor practices and institutions that regulate the labor market, and into the ability to respond of the active players—businesses, workers and government—should help frame policy that will facilitate adaptation to future changes.

Macroeconomic Trends and Formal Analysis of Labor Market
Economic Trends, 1973-92

As the Uruguayan economy is small and very open, a constant stream of external shocks, especially regional ones, have largely determined its evolution over the course of time. From the mid-1950s to 1973 it went through a period of relative stagnation. During the military regime from 1973-85, policies were adopted to liberalize the economy. Finance and trade were opened up to the outside world and exports were promoted vigorously. Trade agreements with Argentina and Brazil were signed in support of those developments. The growth that took place in that period basically resulted from the rise in exports and productive investment; manufacturing was the most dynamic sector and registered the greatest increase in average productivity. Exports reflected a shift to nontraditional goods, as well as items destined for Argentina and Brazil. In 1978, a policy of advance posting of exchange rates (adopted to reduce inflation) slowed the growth of exports and manufacturing in general. Trade liberalization, which had basically focused on the elimination of nontariff restrictions, was extended to reduce tariffs, so that their average level dropped from 101 percent that year to 47 percent in 1981 (Macadar, 1988).

The course of the exchange rate in Argentina spurred tourism and invited an inflow of capital, which financed the high trade deficits. In 1982, however, the devaluation of the exchange rate in Argentina reversed this trend and raised expectations of devaluation which were realized in November of that year. These developments, in conjunction with the worldwide recession and the external debt crisis, plunged the country into a crisis that was to last until 1984. From 1985 to 1987, favorable external conditions, as well as the recovery of real wages brought about by the government in response to social demands following the restoration of democracy, sparked a new round of growth. Exports climbed, especially exports to the Southern Cone countries. In 1987 growth stopped, basically as a result of the reversal of the regional situation. Steady lowering of tariffs continued, so that the average duty stood at 28 percent in 1990 and at 18 percent in 1992. Inflation rose again from 1989 until 1992, when a slowing trend set in, aided by a stable exchange rate and favorable external conditions. Growth in 1992 soared to 7.4 percent, with a sharp increase in traditional exports, although manufacturing remained flat (Figures 4.1 and 4.2).

The Labor Market

The open unemployment rate varied considerably during the period (Figure 4.3). Until 1975, average annual unemployment was 7.9 percent in Montevideo. In 1976-78 it went into double digits despite growing GDP, probably because of changes in the composition of the GDP (increased production of exported goods and flat domestic consumption). This was a transitory phenomenon: the rate went down immediately afterwards and dropped to 6.7 percent in 1981, its lowest level since 1965. Real wages recovered slightly in 1980-81 after falling in the seventies. Average productivity followed a rising trend. The unemployment rate rose again in the recession of 1982-84, peaking at 15.3 percent in Montevideo, after which it declined. However, in the last few years its decline has been slow in comparison with the rate of GDP growth. Since 1985, real wages have recovered strongly, especially in the private sector, and average productivity has also generally grown.

Analysis shows the unemployment rate to have been greater in the eighties in terms of its variations as well as its level: the standard deviation, which was below one percentage point in the early seventies, rose to 2.2 percent in 1975-79 and to 3.9 percent in 1980-84, and then dropped to 1.8 percent in 1985-89, though without reaching the initial levels (Allen and Labadie, 1994).

Private sector performance in employment has been similar to that of GDP in general, although there was a slowdown after the crisis of the early eighties (Figure 4.4). At the same time, the stagnation of the manufacturing sector caused participation in services to rise in relation to overall employment. Job growth in the public sector slowed, however, and has even been negative in recent years.

Although explicit policies were in place to curb wages in the mid-seventies and to bring them back up from 1985 to 1989, they did not affect all workers equally (Figure 4.5). The national minimum wage fell continuously between 1975 and 1992, for a total loss of 58 percent in real terms. Wages in the public and private sectors followed similar trends until 1986. After keeping step with each other in the seventies, in 1979-85 the variations of public wages were greater. The situation changed in 1986, with real compensation in the private sector recovering while in the public sector it was flat or even decreased, falling in 1992 below the 1985 level.

Figure 4.1. Uruguay-Argentina: Gross Domestic Product and Real Exchange Rate, (RER) 1975-92
(Index 1983=100)

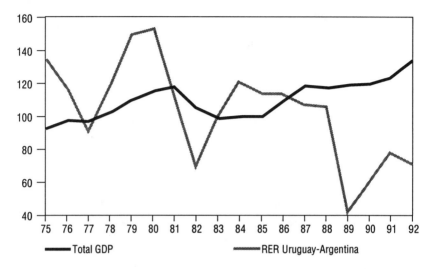

Source: Statistical Bulletin of the Central Bank.

Figure 4.2. Uruguay: Export Destinations, 1985-92
(Index 1975=100)

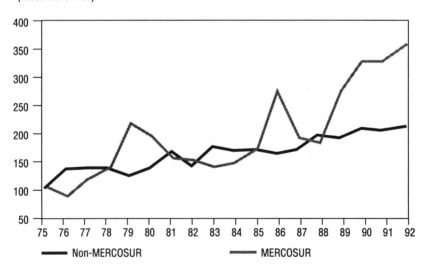

Source: Statistical Bulletin of the Central Bank.

Figure 4.3. Uruguay: Gross Domestic Product and Unemployment Rate, 1975-82
(Index 1975=100)

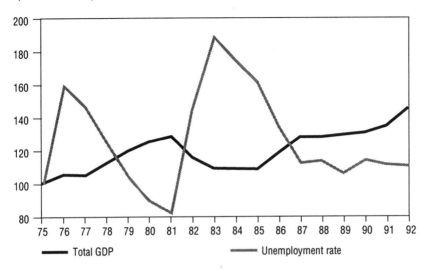

Source: Statistical Bulletin of the Central Bank, Continuing Household Survey, and the National Institute of Statistics.

Figure 4.4. Uruguay: Rates of Growth in Total Employment and Gross Domestic Product, 1975-92
(Index 1975=100)

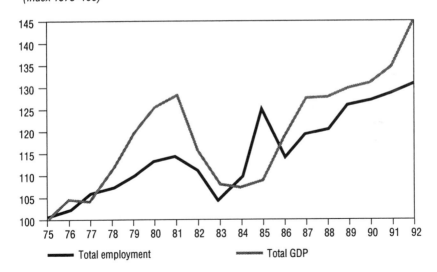

Source: Statistical Bulletin of the Central Bank, Continuing Household Survey, and the National Institute of Statistics.

Figure 4.5. Uruguay: Real Wages, 1975-92
(Index 1975=100)

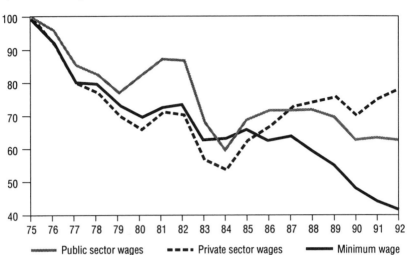

Source: Wage Survey and the National Institute of Statistics.

Changes in trade policy during the period especially affected the manufacturing sector. In the seventies this sector was the most buoyant and the one with the best potential to create jobs, but it was largely dependent on external economic conditions, and its participation in total employment and production has waned since the late eighties. Moreover, changes in the way its human resources are used have been underway since the recession of the early eighties. After sustained growth with substantial productivity gains in the seventies, and even rising real wages in 1979, signs of stagnation began to appear in 1980. Employment and wages responded almost immediately by falling until 1984 (Figure 4.6). Although employment rallied in the next period of growth, 1986-87, the greatest adjustment came about in man-hours of work, with the ratio of overtime to regular hours rising to 46 percent (Figure 4.7).

This could be linked to several phenomena, including the cost of seeking and selecting personnel, the lack of specific training noted in other studies, and union activity. However, this behavior can also be linked to uncertainty about how long stability and growth will continue, as well as changes in payroll taxes, which particularly affect the more formal sectors. From 1988 until 1991, during which time manufacturing activity was flat, employment fell (though less than in the past), so hiring would tend to appear stable.

Changes in the composition and level of the labor supply tended to keep the

Figure 4.6. Uruguay: Real Wages and Productivity, Manufacturing Sector, 1975-92
(Index 1975=100)

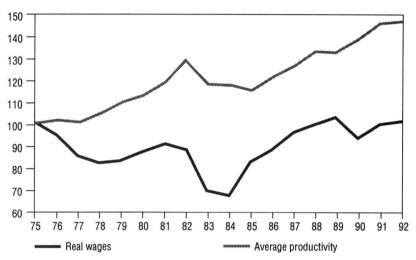

Real wages ▬▬▬   Average productivity ▬▬▬

Source: Wage Survey, Quarterly Industrial Survey, and the National Institute of Statistics.

Figure 4.7. Uruguay: Employment and Hours Worked Per Worker in the Manufacturing Sector, 1982-92
(Index 1982=100)

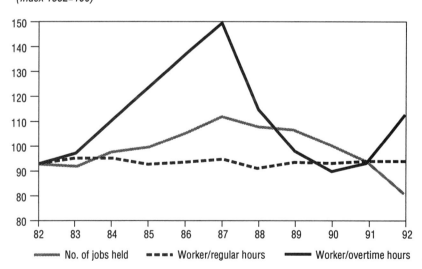

▬▬ No. of jobs held   ▬ ▬ Worker/regular hours   ▬▬ Worker/overtime hours

Source: Quarterly Industrial Survey and the National Institute of Statistics.

unemployment rate stuck at high levels. During this period the participation rate of women increased by 12 percentage points, and their massive entry into the labor force was largely responsible for the increase of approximately 7 percentage points in the overall rate of activity (Table 4.1).

Women, together with those under 25 years of age, have encountered the greatest employment problems. The reasons are to be found primarily in their lack of work experience and the higher costs which entails that difference in terms of training, absenteeism and part-time employment. Nevertheless, these changes only explain 10 percent of the rise in the mean unemployment rate if one carries out an Oaxaca-Blinder breakdown, leaving the increase in the duration of unemployment to explain the remaining 90 percent. The increasing duration of unemployment may stem from several causes. One may be high minimum wages set through collective bargaining, which impair the sectoral mobility of labor. Another may be discouragement experienced by the unemployed as the job-seeking process erodes their employability and their motivation.

Retraining and Segmentation

To study the impact of different institutional frameworks on the structure of the labor market, retraining is examined for various groups in the period 1981-91. Efforts are made to establish differences between the periods with and without unionization[2]. The importance of the proportion of public employment in the total and its institutional differences with the private sector makes the possible difference in retraining important, hence its analysis will receive special emphasis. In addition, although some indicators suggest that the informal sector has expanded in the last 15 years, the lack of systematized data prevents the completion of a proper econometric analysis. A preliminary definition of the informal sector would include unpaid workers and self-employed workers with no work place. However, given the size of the Uruguayan market, an appreciable percentage of such workers actually belongs to the formal market.[3] In any event, the evolution of this category in the period shows a continuous increase until 1986, along with the increase of the economically active population (EAP), so that it

---

[2] The figures are drawn from the Continuing Household Survey in the second half of 1981 and 1991. They refer to Montevideo and the urban areas of 10,000 or more inhabitants in the interior of the country. Mincer equations were calculated by sex for persons 14 years of age and older. The measure used for determining income is the logarithm of the monthly income of the respondent's principal occupation, including monetary compensation and payment in kind. The education variable is continuous, a result of the scalar product of the level for the last year of education completed. The experience variable is the age minus the years of education, minus six. The logarithm of the hours worked per week was included as a control variable.

[3] The National Institute of Statistics is planning a study designed to estimate the proportion of this group of workers that belongs to the informal sector, thus creating an appropriate informal sector definition.

Table 4.1. Montevideo: Economically Active Population and Unemployment for Selected Years, 1976-92
(Percentages)

	Specific rate of participation				Unemployment			
	Men	Women	Adults	Youth	Men	Women	Adults	Youth
1976	73.70	35.90	42.47	54.21	9.80	17.80	8.90	26.44
1981	76.08	39.50	56.67	48.28	5.05	8.96	5.03	15.26
1983	74.94	43.30	57.01	57.80	12.22	19.79	10.58	31.54
1985	75.10	45.20	60.63	54.86	10.15	17.05	8.39	29.12
1987	76.86	46.79	62.01	53.94	6.83	12.51	5.68	23.55
1989	75.17	47.08	60.98	54.86	6.55	11.15	4.80	24.14
1990	74.52	47.41	61.21	53.59	7.31	11.82	5.26	16.65
1991	74.30	47.50	61.06	56.11	7.10	11.30	4.92	25.29
1992	73.32	48.43	60.45	55.75	6.68	11.86	5.24	24.41

Source: Continuing Household Survey, National Institute of Statistics.
Notes: Adults: persons over 25 years of age. Youth: persons under 25 years of age. The amounts do not add up to 100 because specific rates are used (e.g., unemployed youths as a percentage of total youths, employed men as a percentage of total men, etc.).

represents between 7 percent and 8 percent of EAP. Currently its volume is equal to that of the unemployed. The (estimated) incomes earned by informal sector workers, though significantly smaller than those of the formal sector, present no differences in their change over time.

The trend in 1981-91. Using Mincer equations, and in spite of some noise in year-to-year estimates, the tendency among men to retrain is unequivocally low, both in Montevideo and in the interior, where the pattern is even more pronounced (Table 4.2). Moreover, the income differential between men with and without work experience does not produce a clear trend in either region. For women of the interior the back-to-school trend resembles the men's trend, while their re-turn-to-work experience follows a rather erratic pattern. In Montevideo, retraining diminished until 1989 but grew in 1991, while returns-to-work presents a clear downward trend. The wage differential between men and women shrank considerably in the interior and to a lesser degree in Montevideo throughout the period, while the wage differential between the capital and the interior diminished for both men and women. When a correction is applied by selection bias in accordance with standard procedure (Heckman, 1979; Greene, 1990)[4], the re-

---

[4] The procedure entails a two-step estimation. In the first step a probit model is estimated for persons who work and declare income. In the second, the estimation of the Mincer equation is performed, which contains the inverse of the "Mills reason" of the probit estimation. The results presented here include the full-information errors obtained from the use of the Heckman in Stata procedure, version 3.1.

Table 4.2. Uruguay: Retraining and Return to Work Experience by Sex, 1981-91

| | Retraining | | | | Return-to-work experiences | | | |
| | Montevideo | | Interior | | Montevideo | | Interior | |
	Men	Women	Men	Women	Men	Women	Men	Women
1981	0.096	0.080	0.099	0.119	0.119	1.044	0.551	0.721
1982	0.095	0.070	n.a.	n.a.	n.a.	1.051	0.430	n.a.
1983	0.093	0.072	n.a.	n.a.	n.a.	1 019	0.514	n.a.
1984	0.091	0.077	0.084	0.084	0.110	1.030	0.525	0.685
1985	0.096	0.077	n.a.	n.a.	n.a.	1.086	0.573	n.a.
1986	0.091	0.077	0.083	0.083	0.111	1.085	0.520	0.791
1987	0.097	0.067	0.074	0.074	0.101	1.049	0.630	0.763
1988	0.087	0.074	0.067	0.067	0.093	1.042	0.550	0.688
1989	0.086	0.074	0.070	0.070	0.096	1.017	0.575	0.754
1990	0.084	0.077	0.079	0.079	0.090	1.057	0.576	0.715
1991	0.088	0.083	n.a.	n.a.	n.a.	1.104	0.604	n.a.

Source: Prepared for this study on the basis of the Continuing Household Survey, National Institute of Statistics.
Note: Retraining figures are the coefficients of the "years of education" variable in a Mincer equation. The return-to-work experiences are the difference between the expected incomes of a worker with 30 years of experience and one without experience.
n.a. Not available

turns obtained are smaller than the results of using ordinary squared minimums, as was to be expected.[5] In this way, retraining declines for men from 0.102 to 0.085 in 1981 and from 0.097 to 0.077 in 1991. A similar, if smaller, pattern is present in the case of the women.

All these results are consistent with the role that unions and collective bargaining could have played in Uruguay since 1985. Normally one associates unionization with wage compression between and within groups. In our case this has occurred in the wage differentials by education, sex and geographic location. The decade of the eighties, which is when this reduction took place, coincides with the return of union activity and collective bargaining.

Differences between the public and the private sector. In 1981, 28.7 percent of employed men and 28.4 percent of employed women worked in the public sector. These figures were lower in the early nineties. The wages do not reflect

---

[5] The sample used in the Mincer estimations includes only public and private sector blue and white collar workers, since the income of self-employed workers and employers also includes returns on capital. Nevertheless, in order not to arbitrarily exclude these categories in an estimation with selection bias, use was made of an expanded sample of all persons from 14 to 64 years of age. The theoretical identification of this model requires the use of at least one variable more than in the Mincer model, hence a dichotomic variable of the marital state was included (1 = married).

market prices, since the amount allocated for them has been tied to cost-cutting and anti-inflationary policy and used as a redistribution mechanism. Since 1985, moreover, the sector's workers have been highly unionized. There should therefore be many forms of powerful pressure to curb wage increases and compress differentials. In 1981 the average wage for men was almost 5 percent higher in the public than in the private sector, and by 1991 it was 3 percent lower. In the case of women this differential was always in favor of the public sector (42 percent higher in 1981 and 14 percent higher in 1991). However, when education and experience are factored in one finds that men working in the public sector in 1981 actually faced a negative differential of 5 percent, which widened to 14 percent by 1991. Meanwhile, the wages of women working in the public sector dropped from 19 percent above those in the private sector in 1981 to 3 percent below them in 1991.

With respect to retraining, the estimations yield four major results (Table 4.3). First, in 1981 these were considerably higher for men in the private sector, with the gap widening by 1991. In the case of women, the difference was small in 1981 but increased considerably by 1991. In the second place, the decline in retraining on the part of men, described in the preceding section, was concentrated in the public sector, where it was 2.3 percentage points as opposed to 0.6 points (statistically insignificant) in the private sector. Third, retraining on the part of women increased in the private sector and diminished in the public sector. It is probable that retraining would have increased in Uruguay without this drop in the public sector, as it has in most countries. Finally, return-to-work experiences are much greater in the private sector, just like retraining, and they have in fact increased for men.

This analysis of the labor market in the period 1975-92 clearly shows that an examination of the institutional issues that might affect flexibility in adjustment must focus on matters relating to hiring and firing in the public and private sectors and to wage-setting, as well as on the system of labor relations and collective bargaining.

General Description of Labor Regulations and Institutions

Labor Standards[6]

Labor law in Uruguay encompasses many constitutionally derived standards pertaining to individual rights as well as general laws on labor and social security. The right of labor unions to strike is recognized, for example, as is the legal need for a special statute covering public employees. Labor law is not codified, how-

---

[6] This section is based on Ameglio (1994).

Table 4.3. Montevideo: Retraining and Work Experience, 1981 and 1991

	Men		Women	
	1981	1991	1981	1991
Private sector				
Education	0.108	0.102	0.075	0.096
Experience	0.078	0.088	0.037	0.044
Experience^2	-1.151	-1.269	-0.623	-0.674
Constant	6.580	4.469	6.815	4.537
R^2	0.374	0.363	0.156	0.182
N	2.086	3.904	1.431	3.186
Public sector				
Education	0.091	0.068	0.069	0.047
Experience	0.063	0.059	0.052	0.038
Experience^2	-0.941	-0.817	-0.759	-0.551
Constant	6.875	4.988	6.831	5.107
R^2	0.410	0.273	0.312	0.132
N	841	1.456	566	1.122

Source: Prepared for this study on the basis of the Continuing Household Survey, National Institute of Statistics.
Note: Retraining figures are the coefficients of the "years of education" variable in a Mincer equation. The return-to-work experiences are the difference between the expected incomes of a worker with 30 years of experience and one without experience.

ever, and the relevant legislation basically covers issues relating to workers' individual rights, which are highly regulated. By contrast, there is a conspicuous legislative vacuum as regards collective rights, which are practically unregulated. For this reason a great many decrees regulate the laws, especially in the area of individual law.

In addition, administrative decisions issued by the Ministry of Labor are designed to set forth the agency's legal position concerning the interpretation of specific matters, such as layoffs. Although they are not generally binding on employers, workers, or judges, the agency assumes this interpretive role seldom enough that, when it does, its rulings are usually accepted by the principals.

Finally, the collective agreement as a mechanism for generating standards of professional origin exists in those sectors where the union presence is strongest. There are also collective company agreements which generally supplement the agreements by industry. This method is used in the public sector when bargaining with certain public enterprises in the industrial or service sectors.

Labor: Actors and Institutions

The first section of Article 57 of the Uruguayan Constitution states, "The law shall promote the formation of trade unions by granting them exemptions and providing for their recognition as legal entities." However, no such provision exists to date. Against this unstructured background, the principle of union plurality is upheld in general terms. A single nationwide central labor union, the *Plenario Intersindical de Trabajadores* (Interunion Plenary of Workers), known by the initials PIT-CNT, encompasses the entire movement.

The situation in which employers find themselves is similar to that of the unions in that the state lays down no rules for them to follow in dealing with labor. Employers' organizations are governed by the law of association, which the Constitution recognizes in general terms. Their present structure has three organizations of national scope at its summit: the *Cámara de Industrias del Uruguay* (Chamber of Industries of Uruguay), the *Cámara Nacional de Comercio* (National Chamber of Commerce), and the *Cámara Mercantil de Productos del País* (Mercantile Chamber of Uruguayan Products). These organizations are divided by sector (textiles, metallurgy, construction, etc.), with each division focusing on its industry's particular interests.

The state performs three labor-related functions: it is the country's largest employer; it regulates, mediates, and oversees labor relations through the Ministry of Labor and Social Security (MTSS); and it exercises judicial authority by adjudicating individual disputes through the labor justice system under the judicial branch for private employees, and through the *Tribunal de lo Contencioso Administrativo* (Administrative Disputes Tribunal) for public employees. In its capacity as employer, the state is divided into a central administration (consisting mainly of ministries) and decentralized agencies, which engage in industrial and service activities. With respect to its central administration, the state must follow extremely rigid rules in hiring as well as in firing. The rules for the decentralized agencies are less rigid but still far more restrictive than what private employers have to contend with. One of MTSS's main functions is to ensure that labor rules are adhered to. Unlike other countries, there is no real enforcement agency that systematically enforces those rules.

The labor justice system, which has specialized courts (though not a special procedure) deals exclusively with individual work disputes. This means that it has no jurisdiction in collective disputes, whether these involve a matter of legal principle or a material controversy between parties. The foregoing notwithstanding, collective disputes over legal principle that cannot be resolved by agreement between the parties, despite mediation by MTSS, frequently turn into individual disputes in which the workers bring a multiparty action against a single employer. The case law which over time makes up specialized labor law is heavily relied upon by both sides in developing their arguments in actual litigation. In this sense precedent—which is not enshrined in the Uruguayan legal system—takes on importance in innumerable areas where the rules are unclear or simply do not exist.

Mechanisms for Setting Wages and Labor Costs

Four wage-setting methods have generally existed side by side: individual negotiation between workers and employers at the company level; government mandates, through which the executive branch sets the national minimum wage and the minimum compensation of domestic and rural workers; collective bargaining between businesses and unions; and negotiation through the *Consejos de Salarios* (Wage Councils), composed of government, business and labor representatives.

The simplest procedure is that of setting wages through a labor contract signed by the employer and the worker. By this method the worker negotiates working conditions and wages above the existing minimums, in compliance with the compulsory standards prevailing in a given sector. The executive branch, through the Ministry of Economy and Finance and, if appropriate, the MLSS, can further issue standards pertaining to compensation and, in particular, formulate labor categories and regulate the compensation of workers in private businesses (Decree Law No. 14.791 of June 8, 1978, Art. 1(e)). Every four months, MTSS sets the minimum wages for the private sector (the national minimum wage), thus determining that no one working in Uruguay, regardless of occupation, may be paid less than a stated amount. Also set every four months is the minimum compensation of domestic and rural workers. Finally, no minimum wage is mandated in the public sector. In each public agency, office, or enterprise the pay scale establishes a minimum entry-level salary.

The national minimum wage has almost no impact on the private labor market, for other wage-setting methods by which higher levels of compensation are determined limit its relevance. Furthermore, it has lost so much of its real value over time that it has become somewhat meaningless. Nevertheless, it is legally required that it be set because it operates as a variable in the adjustment of various social security benefits: the minimum and maximum amounts paid under several pension and retirement schemes are pegged to the national minimum wage. In addition, it serves as the benchmark for the caps on social security benefits: unemployment benefits may not under any circumstances exceed eight times the national minimum wage, the allowance for illness may not exceed three times the national minimum wage, and family allowances are fixed by law at 8 percent of the national minimum wage.

The third instrument available to the parties for negotiating and deciding on wage levels is the collective agreement. This is a very entrenched method used in those sectors where the labor movement is best organized (banking, tobacco, textiles, metallurgy, and construction).

The fourth method, which sets the most characteristic stamp on the country's labor relations system, is that of fixing wages through the Wage Councils. These were created in 1943 as tripartite bodies for the primary purpose of setting national minimum wages for the different sectors of economic activity. However, they soon evolved into forums for negotiating a very wide range of labor benefits (Law 10.442 of November 12, 1943). They developed a negotiating style from their inception and functioned very smoothly, becoming instrumental in strengthening the labor movement, especially in sectors where union membership was low. At present, and particularly since 1991-92, the government has withdrawn from the negotiations, leaving the negotiating field to employers and workers.

In 1968, when prices and wages were frozen, the executive branch stopped convening the Wage Councils and created the *Comisión de Precios e Ingresos* (Commission on Prices and Incomes), which was charged with setting wage and price increases. This mechanism proved effective only until the mid-seventies, when the market began showing increases in excess of the authorized levels, thus effectively transforming into legal minimums. Collective bargaining, for its part, was not in effect in that period because the unions were disbanded from 1973 to 1984.

With the return of democracy came strong pressures to restore the purchasing power of wages, and substantial pay hikes ensued. While the new government continued to set the national minimum wage, the Wage Councils were reinstated with the job of channeling the increases at the sectoral level. A *Consejo Superior de Salarios* (Superior Wage Council) established at the same time and composed of business and labor representatives, arbitrated in the bargaining process. Bargaining was carried out every four months and the government, in cases when unanimous or majority decisions supported the wage increase, legally validated the agreements by means of decrees establishing the minimum that the firms covered by each resolution could pay. When the three parties could not agree among themselves, the government determined the amount of the increase. Until 1986 the bargaining resulted in wage adjustments based on the inflation of the previous period. The government, however, with the aim of deindexing the economy, set percentage caps on the transfer of wage cost increases to prices, refusing to validate collective agreements that did not conform to this guideline. Because of the difficulty of enforcing this norm, it based the adjustment on half the sum of past and projected inflation, a procedure that prevailed until 1988. At the same time, without abandoning the practice of bargaining every four months but seeking to avert periodic labor disputes, it encouraged the signing of the so-called "long agreements." These had a life of one year or longer, and gradually the great majority of the negotiating groups fell into line with this approach.

The government that took office in 1990 partly blamed the indexation clauses for the inflationary surge of 1988-90 and therefore sought to modify the wage adjustment formula. It began in June 1990 with an attempt to deindex wages totally by decreeing an increase equal to the inflation target, which was considerably smaller than accumulated inflation. This did not affect those who had agreements in effect from the preceding period. Since the inflation rate accelerated in the months immediately following, the indexation clauses were reintroduced in the course of the talks between unions, businesses and the government. In September of that year, similar wage agreements, with trigger clauses of rather complex design, were adopted for all branches of business (but not included in the existing agreements already mentioned). In early 1992 these new agreements ran out and the executive branch withdrew from the negotiations, except where agreements were signed providing for a maximum increase of 35 percent (appreciably lower than anticipated inflation). In actual fact, the bargaining between labor and management did not comply with that condition and in most cases led to renewed agreements with trigger clauses. Partly because of the foregoing, bargaining became widespread at the company level. At the same time the spread widened between the minimum and average wages, and between public and private sector wages, since the minimum wage and public sector compensation are set by the government.

Labor Costs

As wage-setting mechanisms changed, so did charges assessed to fund government agencies. Employer contributions tended to increase the total wage bill until 1992; in 1993 they fell, but not to the levels of the early eighties (Table 4.4). The charges are based on annual wages, including the year-end bonus (one twelfth of annual compensation). Retirement and pension contributions and health insurance premiums are paid to the *Banco de Previsión Social* (BPS, Social Welfare Bank), which also withholds income tax (which then becomes part of general revenue). There is no specific levy for unemployment insurance, which is funded from general revenue. Although public sector workers are not covered by health insurance and the public sector is therefore not required to pay premiums for it, the payroll tax for social security is actually equal to the sum of private assessments for both. Civil service wages are not subject to the payroll tax, but the employer must contribute the same percentage to the *Fondo Nacional de Vivienda* (National Housing Fund). The autonomous agencies contribute to both.

Finally, the public sector pays a household allowance and offers employees a further allowance for each child. Both allowances are a percentage of the minimum wage, the first calculated on a sliding scale based on the minimum wage equivalence of compensation received. Private sector workers are entitled to the latter benefit, but it is paid by the state through BPS. Table 4.5 details the composition of the direct employment cost in 1985, 1992, and 1993, differentiating between public and private minimum wages. Thus the amount charged in the private sector for the year-end bonus, leave, payroll tax, and social security and

Table 4.4. Uruguay: Tax Rates on Private Wages, 1982-93
(Percentages)

Period	Social security Payroll tax	Social security Worker tax	Health insurance Payroll tax	Health insurance Worker tax	Tax on wages Payroll	Worker tax (Minimum wage multiple) up to 3	Worker tax (Minimum wage multiple) 3 to 6	Worker tax (Minimum wage multiple) more than 6
Jan. 1982 - Oct. 1982	8	10	4	3	1	1	2	2
Nov. 1982 - Sept. 1984	10	13	4	3	1	1	2	2
Oct. 1984 - Sept. 1989	12	13	4	3	1	1	2	2
Oct. 1989 - Feb. 1990	13	13	4	3	1	1	2	2
Mar. 1990 - Dec. 1990	16.5	13	4	3	1	3.5	5.5	7.5
Jan. 1991 - June 1991	16.5	13	5	3	1	2.5	2.5	7.5
July 1991 - Dec. 1991	16.5	13	5	3	1	2	2	7
Jan. 1992 - Dec. 1992	16.5	13	5	3	1	1.5	1.5	7
Jan. 1993 to the present	14.5	13	5[a]	3	1	1	1	2

Source: Bulletin, Social Welfare Bank.
[a] Only if the wage is higher than 1.25 times the minimum wage.

health insurance rose from 30 pesos in 1985 for every 100 pesos of gross compensation to 38 pesos in 1992. In the public sector the corresponding figures are 39 and 41 pesos, while for public sector workers earning the minimum wage in 1992 they are 77 and 83 pesos. In 1993 these figures were slightly lower.

When the real wage and tax trends are examined side by side, the gap in real terms between private, public, and minimum wages is seen to widen. If the three are supposed to have been identical in 1985, the real direct wage cost for the private sector increased 42 percentage points in the period, while for the public sector it fell by 13 percentage points for an average wage and 62 points for the minimum wage (Table 4.6).

With respect to legal personal contributions, those for social security and health insurance have remained the same over the period. The payroll tax, on the other hand, has been revised several times: after originally being 1 percent for those earning up to three times as much as the minimum wage and 2 percent for the rest, its spectrum was increased and enlarged on four occasions in the last 10 years before it finally returned to the original rates in 1993 (Table 4.4). In that year the employer's contribution to social security was lowered two percentage points, and the employer's and personal contributions to health insurance were eliminated on private sector wages below 1.25 times the minimum wage. These workers were no longer entitled to this benefit unless it was agreed upon with the employer, with the two parties paying the entire premium between them.

Table 4.5. Uruguay: Structure of Wage Costs, 1985, 1992 and 1993
(Percentage of annualized monthly compensation)

	Average wage Private sector 1985	1992	1993	Average wage Public sector 1985	1992	1993	Minimum wage Public sector 1985	1992	1993
Annual compensation plus allowances for	100.0	100.0	100.0	100.0	100.0	100.0	100.0	100.0	100.0
Vacations	3.0	5.6	6.0	0.0	8.3	8.3	0.0	8.3	8.3
Year-end bonus	8.3	8.3	8.3	8.3	0.5	0.5	8.3	2.0	2.0
Seniority bonus	0.0	0.0	0.0	0.7	6.0	6.0	2.0	40.0	40.0
Household allowance	0.0	0.0	0.0	8.5	2.0	2.0	40.0	8.0	8.0
Child allowance	0.0	0.0	0.0	2.8			8.0		
Net wage plus employer's contribution to	111.3	113.9	114.3	120.3	116.8	116.8	158.3	158.3	158.3
Social security	12.0	17.9	15.7	17.3	23.3	21.1	17.3	23.3	21.1
Health insurance	4.3	5.0	5.0	0.0	0.0	0.0	0.0	0.0	0.0
Payroll tax	1.1	1.1	1.1	1.1	1.1	1.1	0.0	0.0	0.0
National Housing Fund	0.0	0.0	0.0	0.0	0.0	0.0	1.1	1.1	1.1
Direct wage cost	129.8	137.8	136.1	138.8	141.2	139.0	176.8	182.7	180.5

Source: Bulletin, Social Welfare Bank.
Notes: Until 1992 there is no difference between private sector contributions over minimum and average wages.
The percentages refer to December 1985 and 1992 and January 1993.

Table 4.6. Uruguay: Real Wage Cost in Selected Years, 1985-93
(Real gross wage index 1985=100)

Year	Public wage	Private wage	Minimum wage
1985	139	130	177
1989	141	162	148
1992	128	175	117
1993	126	172	115

Source: Prepared for this study on the basis of data from the Bulletin, Social Welfare Bank, and the Wage Survey, National Institute of Statistics.
Notes: It is assumed that the three types of wages are at the same level in 1985 (100 1985 pesos). The real wage cost is calculated by applying the percentages of contributions and other payments to the real wage index with 1985 base = 100. The values refer to December of each year, except in 1993 (January).

In summary, real wage costs increased during the period 1985-89 as wages rebounded thanks to indexation and collective bargaining. In 1990 the growth of real compensation slowed, but private sector wage costs continued to rise as employers' contributions to social security increased in 1990-92. The minimum wage, meanwhile, followed a downward trend throughout the period and the public sector wage declined from 1990 on.

Hiring and Firing Procedures and Unemployment Insurance

Individual Hiring

In the private sector, entry into the labor market is unregulated and no rules limit hiring. Even though no law exists to establish hiring procedures, doctrine and jurisprudence in certain cases allow atypical forms of hiring. The public sector presents a diametrically opposite picture. The appointment of an employee is surrounded by formalities and must be completed by means of a public procedure if it is to be valid.

Although hiring procedures do not require formalities, work under the Uruguayan labor system is strictly scheduled pursuant to the first labor law of 1915 concerning the limitation of working hours. This law provides for an eight-hour work day and a work week of 44 hours in trade and 48 hours in industry. In addition, the law on overtime that went into effect in late 1988 introduced another rigidity into the system by defining as overtime any time worked in excess of each worker's work day. This defeats the weekly limit and means that the hours of each individual worker must be taken into account to determine when overtime, which requires extra compensation, has been triggered. As an example, a part-time employee working four hours a day will be working overtime as soon as the fourth hour is exceeded, even if the employee does not work longer than the legal eight-hour limit. The law also establishes a weekly limit of eight hours of overtime for each worker. Overtime is compensated with a surcharge of 100 percent on business days and 150 percent on days of rest or holidays. The law further regulates work on the worker's days off by establishing that the worker is not obligated to work. If the worker decides to do so, he receives twice his usual compensation, unless the worker opts for compensatory time off during the week. Night work (i.e., work between 10 p.m. and 6 a.m.) has not been generally regulated by any law, but on the basis of collective agreements or awards it is normally compensated with 20 to 25 percent extra pay.

Termination of the Labor Relationship, Dismissal Costs and Unemployment Insurance

Resignation from work is one procedure for terminating a labor relationship. The law requires no formality of any kind for this action, but as it has to be the result of a free individual choice, it is very commonly communicated in writing. The worker can also leave the job. In this case the employer must actively summon the employee to return to the job. If the employee does not do so, the labor relationship is formally terminated. The law also allows employers to lay off workers, requiring only that severance payment be made, at least in the private sector. In cases of demonstrable "blatant misconduct," a term lacking clear legal definition, the employer is exempted from the severance requirement. The completely different system of the public sector will be examined below.

Dismissal and Severance Pay in the Private Sector

No rule requiring prior notice of dismissal exists in the private sector. Although dismissal without notice has in some opinions been deemed an abusive exercise of the right to dismiss, this principle has not become part of the jurisprudence (Ameglio and Francés, 1994). In practice, prior notice is given in fixed-term contracts or when a collective agreement has been concluded. By contrast, prior notice is not given when a worker's misconduct provides a serious reason for immediate dismissal. There is also no requirement under law to justify the dismissal, rules such as the ILO's CIT 158 not having been ratified (Ameglio and Francés, 1994), but in practice a motive has to be established since consequences follow with respect to unemployment insurance and in some cases to proving that severance payment was made.

Severance to workers in industry and trade has been required since 1944. It consists of one month's wage for each year or fraction thereof worked in the firm, up to a maximum of six years. Day laborers receive 25 days' wages for every 240 days worked in a year, to a maximum of 150 days. Where the total is less than 240 days, the so-called "partial indemnity" applies, which provides two days' pay for every 25 days worked. Although this would not apply in theory, practice has established that the worker must also have worked a minimum of 100 days. No severance payment or compensation exists for voluntary resignation. Severance payments established by law can be increased when a powerful union capable of negotiating more generous terms or imposing its will makes that its objective (as illustrated by the case study involving the banking industry, which is presented below).

The Uruguayan legal system distinguishes four categories of dismissal: direct, indirect, abusive and fictitious (Ameglio, 1993). Indirect dismissal occurs when the employer violates the labor contract by injuring the worker (through delays in payment of wages, changes of schedule, and the like), and the worker resists. Partial dismissal takes place when benefits or wages are reduced and a compensation (not provided for under law) is offered. Abusive dismissal is a legal term connoting infringement of a right and moral damage (Art. 1321 of the CC), which is applicable when the employer exercises the right to dismiss in an illegal manner, by invoking false grounds or reasons. This term was admitted for the first time in 1978, and it is frequently applied when union officers or workers are dismissed for the legitimate exercise of their rights (Barbagelata, 1978). The result is that the *Tribunales de Apelación del Trabajo* (Labor Appeal Tribunals), which usually are slightly "pro-labor," have rendered awards of three to nine times the legally mandated six months' wages (Mangarelli, 1992). Consequently, even though a free system exists in theory, in practice this system has been limited and subject to certain situations involving "just cause" by this jurisprudential movement, which has nonetheless lost strength in more recent years (Ameglio, 1993). Fictitious dismissal entered the literature in 1981, with the law creating unemployment insurance (Law 15.180). It takes place when the employee qualifies for unemployment insurance because of a lack of jobs in the firm. The employee continues to receive insurance benefits for six months if the employer does not comply with his obligation to restore the worker to his position when requested to do so. In such cases the worker is eligible for severance pay. The same applies when workers have drawn unemployment insurance following a partial reduction in their work. If the worker requests total reinstatement after three months and the request is denied, he can apply for severance pay. Severance pay and unemployment insurance thus complement each other in the Uruguayan system. In practice, the worker will receive severance pay in monthly installments to supplement his unemployment insurance payments. In highly unionized sectors, part of the bargaining usually includes the rotation of personnel on unemployment insurance while downsizing measures are being negotiated. In these cases the employer normally covers the difference between the insurance payments and the worker's former wage.

Although no formalities are required for dismissal, standard practice is to give notice in writing of the date on which the labor relationship is to end. Such notice can take various forms, depending on the position held and the circumstances surrounding the dismissal. The former most notably includes union officers, who are protected by CIT 87 and 98 of the ILO, regulated by Decree 93 of 1968, which nevertheless does not constitute a "labor privilege." Current regulations provide that the labor inspection office of the MLSS should impose fines on businesses that engage in unfair practices or violate the stability of union activists (as specified in Agreement 98). For these cases the jurisprudence has used the concept of abusive dismissal as a way of establishing special compensation.

In addition to special compensation, the law provides for a number of cases that call for severance pay by virtue of special dismissal. Dual compensation is provided for ordinary sick workers while they are ill and up to 30 days following their return to work (Decree Law 14.407 of 1975), unless it is found that the dismissal had no direct or indirect connection with the illness—e.g., in cases of pregnancy—with three months' back pay, if necessary, following the three months of legal leave. Triple compensation and as much as 180 days' back pay following medical discharge is provided for workers suffering a work-related accident or an occupational disease (Art. 69, Law 16.074). Triple compensation is also granted to persons dismissed as reprisal for reporting a worker for evasion of social security contributions. Finally, traveling representatives and salespersons receive 25 percent added to their severance pay for their list of customers (Law 14.000).

Unemployment Insurance[7]

Organization, coverage and financing. The current system of unemployment insurance was created by law in 1981, and regulated beginning in early 1982. Changes made to the system under the reorganization of the social security system by the military government included the elimination of all special regulations for different groups. The current system was preceded by general insurance created in 1958 (Law 12.570) and other special systems, such as the labor exchanges. Earlier financing came from a 1 percent payroll tax and a 1 percent contribution charged to the worker, as well as a series of excise taxes on lotteries, alcoholic beverages, etc. Current funding is obtained from the general social security contributions and 4 percent of the value-added tax. This percentage also covers family allowances and the special contributions of social security to the health insurance of private sector employees (DISSE).

All private sector workers (except domestic workers) are covered by the

---

[7] This section is based on the paper prepared by Allen and Labadie for the project on Labor Market Flexibility in Uruguay and Chile sponsored by the Tinker Foundation. The papers commissioned for that project are summarized in Alfie (1994) and in CERES (1995).

system. Although rural workers are included in theory, no regulations have been issued to collect from them in practice. Professionals, even if working as employees, are not entitled to the benefit because they contribute to their own social security system, the *Caja de Profesionales* (Professionals' Fund). All persons receiving another social security benefit are similarly excluded. Ultimately, around 40 percent of the labor force was covered by unemployment insurance in 1991. Unemployment benefits are paid to all workers who have lost their job for any reason other than misconduct. Those furloughed for lack of work may also qualify, even though they are not actively looking for work and are not considered to be unemployed under the statistical definition used in Uruguay. In order to qualify for unemployment insurance, the worker must have paid into social security for at least six months of the previous year. Day laborers or workers paid by the piece must have recorded at least 150 days of work. Once a worker has collected insurance for the maximum period of six months, he is not eligible to collect again until he has paid into social security for six more months and at least a year has passed since the last time he collected.

The amount of the unemployment benefit is 50 percent of the average wage over the last six months. Persons who are married or have dependents collect an additional 20 percent. The amount paid cannot be less than 50 percent of the minimum wage on the date the worker begins to collect, nor can it be more than eight times the minimum wage, with the benefits being constant during the period in which they are collected. The average benefit has diminished in real terms since 1981 and stands at a very low level, close to the minimum wage and below 50 percent of the average industrial wage (Table 4.7). *The Dirección de Seguros de Desempleo* (DISEDE, Office of Unemployment Insurance) of the Bank of Social Welfare is the agency that handles applications for insurance benefits. Applicants must submit a form from the firm with the pertinent personal and work-related data within 30 days of losing their job. DISEDE has an inspection division that requests firms to complete the forms. If the applicant is found eligible, he or she begins to collect benefits two months later. In the past few years the number of recipients has fluctuated between 11,821 in 1989 and 14,560 in 1992.

The effect of the changes in unemployment insurance. The consequences of the changes that took place in 1981 cannot be evaluated in detail with the available data (the series of microdata used start in the second half of 1981). From a theoretical point of view, however, it is obvious that the new funding mechanism entailed the creation of a neutral tax with respect to resource allocation, while the old system constituted a tax on labor (like some other specific taxes). In this sense, the real question is to what extent this neutral tax would be subsidizing specific sectors or firms.

The possible effects of the insurance on the unemployment level depend on how generous or lasting the benefit is. The amount of the benefit has declined in

Table 4.7. Uruguay: Average Unemployment Benefits for Selected Years, 1981-91
(1981 Uruguayan pesos)

	Average amount (1)	Minimum wage (2)	Average industrial wage (3)	(1)/(2)	(1)/(3)
1981	2.06	1.33	2.92	1.54	0.71
1982	2.02	1.34	2.83	1.51	0.72
1983	1.48	1.20	2.24	1.23	0.66
1984	1.13	1.24	2.19	0.91	0.52
1985	0.92	1.11	2.66	0.83	0.35
1989	1.52	1.15	3.30	1.32	0.46
1990	1.44	1.44	3.03	1.00	0.46
1991	1.44	0.92	3.19	1.57	0.45

Sources: Office of Unemployment Insurance; Wage Survey, National Institute of Statistics.

real terms and, moreover, the new system has been more restrictive, requiring a pay-in period of six months and one year without collecting, while the former system required applicants to have paid in for only one of the preceding six months. In addition, eligibility requirements were tightened for partial benefits based on reduced schedules. Only 2 percent of those insured in 1989 and 1990 and 0.5 percent of those in 1991 met these conditions. In this sense, then, the insurance is not broader and could not explain the rise in unemployment in the 1980s. The baseline for calculating the amount paid out has not increased either, since the benefit is based on the average of the preceding six months and not solely on the last month. Only the duration has increased, from four to six months. However, the four months used to be routinely extended to six, by virtue of a provision in the law whereby the new time period was held only to have legalized a previous actual situation. Hence it does not seem likely that the changes in unemployment insurance were instrumental in raising unemployment. The true problem would seem to lie in the system's actual coverage, the small proportion of unemployed workers protected by it, and the profile of those recipients.

Unemployment insurance recipients. The highest percentage of unemployed covered by insurance was around 20 percent of the total (for men in the second half of 1981), while the average percentage is slightly over 15 percent (Table 4.8). On average, more than 60 percent of recipients were from the manufacturing sector, 15 percent from construction, and the rest—between 20 and 25 percent—from the wholesale trade, services and transport sectors. When the unemployed workers are broken down by sector, the manufacturing sector proves to be significantly overrepresented, with 32 percent of its unemployed collecting

Table 4.8. Uruguay: Breakdown of the Unemployment Rate for Men and Women
(Percentages)

| | Male unemployment rate | | | | |
	Overall rate (1)	Proportion of above (2)	First-time job-seekers (3)	On unemployment insurance (4)	(4)/(2)
1981	5.9	69.9	14.9	15.3	21.9
1983	12.0	73.8	13.9	12.3	16.7
1987	6.9	60.4	28.8	10.8	17.9
1989	6.6	60.4	29.5	10.1	16.7
1990	8.0	64.2	25.5	10.3	16.0
1991	7.2	65.7	22.4	11.9	18.1
	Female unemployment rate				
1981	5.9	61.3	28.5	10.2	16.6
1983	18.1	75.4	20.7	3.9	5.2
1987	12.1	65.2	30.2	4.5	6.9
1989	11.1	62.8	31.4	5.8	9.2
1990	11.9	64.1	30.9	5.1	8.0
1991	10.5	61.9	32.4	4.8	7.8

Source: Prepared for this study on the basis of the Continuing Household Survey, National Institute of Statistics.

unemployment insurance in 1982 and an average of more than 20 percent in the late eighties. Comparing the distribution by size of the firms sending unemployed workers to collect unemployment insurance with the distribution by size of firms in the Economic Census of 1988, one also finds that the largest firms are the ones that send proportionately more unemployed to collect insurance (Allen and Labadie, 1995; Alfie, 1994). The large manufacturing firms, which concentrate more than 50 percent of their employment in firms with 50 or more workers, ultimately tend to be the major users of unemployment insurance.

In fact, most of the recipients in 1989 and 1991 (almost 60 percent) were furloughed workers waiting to return to their jobs when the harvest began or business revived, or helping to use fictitious dismissal as a means of cutting job restructuring costs. These workers are not even statistically defined as unemployed, which makes the system's coverage even smaller. It would therefore be interesting to ascertain the magnitude of the transfers that these sectors are receiving. An estimate done for 1990 shows that the manufacturing industry and its workers received a net transfer of 12.5 million pesos, as compared with 2.6 million for construction and 1.7 million for trade. The redistribution comes from the workers in the banking and services sectors. The total balance indicates that the workers received from the rest of the society almost 14 million pesos in 1990, or some $12 million. Of this amount, the manufacturing industry received close to 86 percent (Alfie, 1994).

The Public Sector and Permanent Tenure[8]

The legal rule governing the hiring and firing of public sector workers is extremely rigid. This has made it very difficult to introduce changes in the structure and level of staffing in the sector. The principle of permanent tenure prevails in the public sector (Arts. 60 ff. of the Constitution). Workers cannot be laid off, and can in principle be dismissed only for negligence, incompetence, or criminal offense (Art. 168 of the Constitution) after an administrative hearing with right to defense and the opportunity for appeal to an independent tribunal (Administrative Disputes Tribunal). These rules require much more than prior notice, and failure to follow them invalidates the dismissal.

The law distinguishes four types of public sector workers: established officials, workers of autonomous entities and decentralized agencies, civil service employees, and workers under contract for a specific task. Hiring standards are relatively uniform for all categories, and all applicants must take a competitive examination except in cases of demonstrable "eminence or urgency." The relevant selection authorities differ according to the type of hiring and the agency involved. An established official can be dismissed only if incompetence, negligence or a criminal offense is proven through an inquiry legally overseen by the *Fiscal Nacional de Gobierno* (National Director of Public Prosecutions), and dismissal by the executive branch is then authorized by the Senate. In 1984 this rule was also made applicable to civil servants with a current contract, so that both categories enjoyed permanent tenure. With respect to workers of autonomous entities and decentralized agencies, some additional causes are included in their statutes. Contracts for a particular work or service, or civil service contracts starting in 1986, can be revoked with an indemnity of two-thirds of the compensation remaining until the end of the contract. In all cases the worker may appeal the decision to the Administrative Disputes Tribunal.

Against this legal background there were not many means available to the government for trimming the public sector, inasmuch as it is politically impossible to change the law regulating the dismissal of public employees. The implicit and explicit strategies adopted fall under three headings: the policy of increasing public sector wages through administrative action; the amendment of rules for new hires; and retirement incentives. Although 1985 saw wages rise substantially as part of the upturn throughout the economy, they remained flat in 1986, followed by a drop in 1989-90 and further stagnation since then. Thus the

---

[8] This section is based on a case study conducted for this project by Bucheli (1994).

private sector began to look more attractive in terms of compensation (Figure 4.5). However, the level of employment remained stable from 1986 to 1989, with efforts to boost income reflected by a 4 percent rise in the number of workers holding more than one job (Table 4.9). The public sector thus remained an attractive option for some groups of workers, since its wage structure is such that categories near the base of the pyramid are better paid than in the private sector (CERES, 1990b; Trylesinski, 1991). Retraining and work experience are greater in the latter sector, while women are more discriminated against and are paid a lower basic wage. Individuals with poorer prospects in the private sector would therefore find employment in the public sector advantageous. The changes in the composition of public employees by sex, age, and qualifications between 1986 and 1989 leads one to conclude that the decline in real wages encouraged the departure of male and younger workers, with only minor differences in terms of qualifications. A slight increase in the proportion of employees with primary education and incomplete university training is evident, however, along with a decrease in the proportion of those with incomplete secondary education and a university background.

The trend in employment by age and qualifications shows rising participation by younger workers who have some university training but no degrees, which may be explained by the facilities that the sector offers this group of workers (Table 4.10).[9] Another point to consider in evaluating the stability of the breakdown by education is that the data from the Continuing Household Survey refers only to employees whose primary employment (determined by earnings) is in the sector, so that the results might differ if all employed persons were included.

Curbs on the inflow of personnel into the public sector began in 1986 with the approval of the first standards. In particular, these standards restricted the filling of vacancies in the administrative and service sections. They were applied to the entire public sector except for the departmental governments, and their effect seems to have been positive: while the flow of workers to the autonomous entities and decentralized agencies shrank from 2,441 in 1987 to 1,273 in 1988 (and in the executive branch from 4,058 to 3,233), hiring in the departmental governments, not under the new regulations, increased significantly. In addition, a new law enacted in 1990 (Law 16127) froze the hiring of permanent staff and civil servants, even in the case of posts falling vacant subsequent to that date. Applications for the approval of works or services contracts increased at the same time; in the latter case, hiring was limited to professionals and technicians and/or to specific areas (judiciary, police, public health, etc.).

---

[9] Given the laws on working hours, leave and holidays, individuals who are studying would work on the average almost 60 percent more hours in the private than in the public sector.

Table 4.9. Uruguay: Characteristics of Public Sector Workers, 1986, 1989 and 1992
(Percentage of total)

	Montevideo			Interior		
	1986	1989	1992	1986	1989	1992
Men	62.2	59.9	54.6	70.9	67.4	62.0
Women	37.8	40.1	45.4	29.1	32.6	38.0
Up to complete primary	26.7	23.7	30.5	38.0	39.8	40.6
Incomplete secondary	28.4	27.6	22.2	26.1	25.7	21.2
Complete secondary	8.6	11.1	7.9	7.7	8.3	7.6
Incomplete and complete UTU[1]	11.6	11.0	8.0	12.2	10.9	9.6
Incomplete and complete teacher training	5.6	6.5	10.6	12.7	11.2	17.5
Up to 4 years university	7.2	9.5	12.9	1.7	2.3	2.5
More than 4 years university	11.9	10.7	8.0	1.6	1.8	1.0
30 years and less	31.6	24.2	12.7	30.1	22.8	13.4
Between 31 and 50 years	47.1	53.1	38.1	54.2	54.8	44.6
50 years plus	21.3	22.7	49.2	15.7	22.4	42.0
Employed in more than one job	17.8	22.1	14.2	8.6	12.7	8.8

Source: Continuing Household Survey, National Institute of Statistics.
[1]Universidad del Trabajo del Uruguay.

Finally, in 1990, incentives were offered to encourage retirement under three options: those not qualifying for retirement could elect to resign in exchange for a premium equivalent to 12 months' pay (twice the severance pay legally required of private employers) or monthly payments of 75 percent of their regular salary for two years. Employees legally eligible for retirement would receive 25 percent of accrued monthly retirement pay for two years. A system for redistributing employees in order to meet staffing needs was established at the same time. These employees would come from departments that had declared them redundant because of restructuring or reductions in staff (in which case the consent of the worker is not required) or because of any request submitted with the worker's agreement. It was moreover specified that employees with a university degree who could not apply their expertise in the positions they held could make use of the redistribution scheme. Retirement incentives were accepted by 11,280 employees (approximately 5 percent of the total). About the same number opted for 12 months' pay, as did those who chose 25 percent of accrued retirement pay, and they were evenly distributed between central government and decentralized agency workers.

The consequences for the different categories of workers in the sector can be partially analyzed by comparing the 1989 and 1992 data in Tables 4.9 and 4.10: while the effects on the breakdown by sex are similar to those for the period

Table 4.10. Montevideo: Educational Characteristics of Public Sector Workers, 1986, 1989 and 1992
(Percentage of total)

Educational segment	1986			1989			1992		
	Up to 30 years	From 30 to 50 years	50 years plus	Up to 30 years	From 30 to 50 years	50 years plus	Up to 30 years	From 30 to 50 years	50 years plus
Incomplete and complete primary	14.5	25.1	48.1	9.6	21.6	43.1	5.9	16.7	47.6
Incomplete secondary	32.2	27.3	24.6	29.8	28.2	24.0	20.7	26.9	18.9
Complete secondary	12.3	7.8	5.2	16.6	10.4	6.8	12.1	10.1	5.2
Incomplete and complete UTU[1]	15.9	11.4	5.5	10.9	11.7	9.5	13.1	9.8	5.3
Incomplete and complete teacher training	4.1	8.5	1.7	4.8	8.5	3.7	10.4	11.4	10.2
Up to four years of university training	9.5	6.8	4.8	18.0	7.5	4.8	28.4	14.3	8.2
More than four years of university training	11.4	13.1	10.0	10.2	12.0	8.1	9.4	10.9	4.6
Total	100.0	100.0	100.0	100.0	100.0	100.0	100.0	100.0	100.0

Source: Prepared for this study on the basis of data from the Continuing Household Survey, National Institute of Statistics.
[1]Universidad del Trabajo del Uruguay.

1986-89, the participation of younger workers is reduced by half, the proportion of those over 50 years of age doubles, and the percentage of workers with average education declines. With respect to movements by age and education in the younger group, most of the retirees were those with secondary schooling, while among those over 50 the proportion of workers who had completed secondary and university education diminished. The only categories whose numbers rose significantly were workers with teacher training and up to four years of university training. In the 30 to 50-year-old group the proportion of employees with incomplete university training also increased, although the percentage of university graduates did not fall commensurately. It further seems clear that of all public employees, those with more than one job were more inclined to accept the incentives. These were probably already working in the private sector, as is suggested by the approximately 35 percent reduction in the number of workers with more than one job.

The developments summarized in this section show that, despite the political constraints on substantially trimming the public sector, effective mechanisms can be devised to control the size of the state. Between 1989 and 1992, when the three mechanisms were all in operation, the number of employees was cut by approximately 20 percent. In particular, limiting the inflow of new employees does not seem to have given rise to major political problems, although it may have contributed to the high levels of youth unemployment. Indiscriminate wage cuts, by contrast, may result in an inappropriate breakdown of employment in the sector, encouraging older workers to stay on and fostering secondary employment. The incentives scheme encouraged the retirement of those eligible for retirement (around 20 percent) and probably of those who already had an entry into the private sector. The evidence that the proportion of employees with more than four years of university training may have declined suggests that an incentives system must be carefully designed, taking care not to significantly lower the quality of the public sector's human capital. In this case it would seem feasible to achieve a substantial reduction of employment in the sector.

Unions and Collective Bargaining

Legal Issues and Standard Practices

The history of the Uruguayan labor movement goes back to the closing years of the last century. Even before any laws had been passed on collective rights, certain groups obtained significant improvements in working conditions by means of the agreements signed following disputes. The first labor union was founded in 1905, by which time the labor movement can be regarded as permanently established. The movement took on certain features that have remained to the present: autonomy from the state, resistance to legislative attempts at regulating its activity, nonbureaucratic leadership, freedom to join the union, and a highly ideological attitude on the part of its members.

Most of the industrial unions were formed in the 1940s, at a time when the movement was reaching out not only to laborers but also to other workers and to employers. This process culminated in the unionization of public employees. One of the major impulses to the development of the labor movement came from the creation by industry of the Wage Councils in 1943 for the primary purpose of setting minimum wages but also of monitoring the application of their resolutions and acting as a conciliating body. The councils were formed by representatives of government, business and labor. Their resolutions applied to all firms of the sector, strengthening the labor movement and furthering organization by firms and industry. Once the unions were consolidated, collective bargaining moved into the private sector, so that the conclusion of private agreements that were later approved in the Wage Councils became standard practice in the late fifties and during the sixties (the first union to follow this course was that of the bank employees, AEBU).

The efforts to unify the movement finally crystallized in 1964 with the creation of the *Convención Nacional de Trabajadores* (CNT, National Convention of Workers), which began operations in 1966 as an umbrella for all wage-earners' unions. In 1973, immediately following the military coup, the CNT mounted a general strike that ran for 15 days. In the middle of the strike the CNT was declared illegal, and all collective bargaining was abolished for years. In 1981 a law was enacted permitting labor associations by firm, and the labor movement began to revive. Even before the restoration of democracy, it coalesced rapidly in the Interunion Plenary of Workers (PIT-CNT), an organization which was tolerated (though not legal) and whose demands were as much economic as political. From 1985 onward, the issue of wages was back at the center of the union debate and bargaining was carried on again through the 48 tripartite Wage Councils, which have been in the process of being subdivided.

Currently, unions are organized by industry but there are also company unions in both the private and public sectors, as well as some representing particular categories of worker (traveling salespersons and market vendors, for example). Membership is not obligatory and union dues are voluntary, although some unions have succeeded in turning dues into a payroll deduction. Officers are elected by secret ballot, except for the leadership of the central union organization, because of its federal agency status. In 1933, unions reported a total membership of some 188,000 workers belonging to 17 federations and 359 unions. Membership has dwindled by almost 50,000 in only five years. In 1993 the public sector accounted for 54 percent of members, heavily concentrated in the central administration, which has had the smallest drop in membership.

The collective contract, whose life is not legally restricted and generally runs for one or two years, is binding upon the contracting unit, i.e., the workers represented, whether or not they are members of the union, and upon the firms of the bargaining group and of industry. Sometimes, however, the agreement also covers third parties that are not directly involved. This was the case, for instance, with the agreements that came out of the Wage Councils, whose provisions were subsequently officially endorsed by the executive branch and therefore governed all firms of the sector, even those not directly represented by the employers' organization that had participated in the negotiations.

There are no legal restrictions on the issues submitted to collective bargaining, although the most frequent clauses vary little in the private sector. These include such areas as minimum wages by job category, wage adjustment procedure (mechanisms and terms), and working conditions. More detailed matters include the length of work day; holidays; job rotation and stability; additional social security benefits; recognition of union officers; and granting of facilities to the union leadership. They also include peace clauses, bargaining conditions in disputes, and payroll deduction of union dues. More recently, several agreements have included clauses pertaining to safety in the work place and accident prevention, the adoption of new technologies, worker training and downsizing. In the public sector, reflecting the differences in rules on hiring and firing, the most usual clauses concern minimum wage levels, although in the enterprises and the autonomous entities in general some matters of the type treated in the private sector are also covered.

The intervention of the government in collective bargaining is legally provided for only in the case of the Wage Councils. Their function is to set minimum wages and define professional categories by industry. However, they normally also participate in the voluntary wage negotiation committees formed for the purpose of renewing agreements. Once the agreement is signed, it must be registered with the MLSS, which verifies its legality.

The workers' unrestricted right to strike is enshrined in Article 57 of the Constitution and, in practice, issues relating to it are decided (as are other union matters) by the union in assembly meetings, generally through a nonsecret vote. The law requires seven days' prior notice (Law 13.270 of 1968, superseded by Decree Law 14.791 of 1978) for the strike to be legal, but no penalty is provided for noncompliance. In line with the regulations to prevent conflicts, some collective agreements have included clauses that provide for conciliation procedures preceding a walkout. In practice in both the private and public sectors, the parties often request that the MLSS arrange for bargaining through the *Dirección Nacional del Trabajo* (DINATRA, National Labor Office). The legislative branch is often also involved in the proceedings, through special committees. Employers' representatives, union delegates and MTSS officials all take part in the negotiations. On occasion, especially when lengthy agreements or wage-related topics are discussed, the participants also include officials of the *Oficina de Planeamiento y Presupuesto* (OPP, Planning and Budget Office) and the Ministry of Economy and Finance.

The law does not list any grounds for ruling out a strike. Some agreements, however, include "peace clauses" that preclude strikes in certain situations. Strike procedures are not regulated either, so that any procedure is permitted provided it does not violate civil or criminal law. Although the most frequently observed approach is the collective and concerted work stoppage, other forms have been adopted, such as *perlado* strikes (which affect a strategic part of the firm) in the private sector and rulebook slowdowns or partial strikes in the public sector. Although sit-in strikes are also permitted insofar as they entail no criminal offense, the Ministry of the Interior may authorize the intervention by law enforcement personnel (Decree 512 of 1966). Finally, in the case of services deemed essential the public authority may (under Law 13.720 of 1968 and Decree Law 14.791 of 1978) take measures necessary to maintain them. The authorities may go as far as requisitioning property and hiring persons to ensure the continuity of such services. However, the standards do not spell out essential services, so that it falls to the executive branch to make the final determination in that regard within five days from the communication of the conflict.

During a strike the labor contract is considered to be suspended but not dissolved, so that, although there is no work and no wages are paid, seniority is maintained, leave accrues (Law 12.590 of 1958), and strikers are not entitled to unemployment benefits. Even though there is no right to permanent tenure (except as it derives from general labor law, as in the case of public employees), the dismissal of a striking worker is deemed abusive by the jurisprudence. No standards governing conflict resolution procedure are on the books. The judicial branch has jurisdiction only in individual labor disputes and is excluded from intervention in any collective dispute. MTSS, meanwhile, may intervene as a mediator, but lacks the authority to issue decisions that bind the parties. Basically, settlements arise from the final agreement between the parties (self-resolution). The foregoing notwithstanding, voluntary intervention (which is not provided for under any rule) has taken place in disputes of major scope in the form of mediation extended by the *Comisión de Legislación del Trabajo* (Committee on Labor Legislation) of the Chamber of Deputies. Furthermore, binding arbitration is not provided for in the legal system, and voluntary arbitration is seldom used. In recent times, however, clauses regulating arbitration procedures have been included in agreements.

The Role of the Ministry of Labor and Social Security

In its capacity as mediator-conciliator, the MLSS acts in two spheres: collective labor relations and individual disputes. The former, the ministry's traditional area of negotiation, has furnished a reliable setting for discussing collective disputes. Employers and unions have both spontaneously sought its mediation when they considered direct dialogue between the parties to be at an impasse. Indeed, in

many cases both sides prefer to bring MLSS into the discussion of their differences from the outset and welcome its intervention. In recent years the ministry
has modified its policy concerning the regulation of wages in the private sector,
no longer convening the Wage Councils except in a few sectors. In spite of this
change, the National Labor Office of the MLSS continues to offer labor and
management a neutral setting in which to discuss their collective interests.

Trends and Impact on Employment and Wages

The impact of union activity has varied greatly over the last 20 years: extremely
intense from 1968 to 1972, when it was linked to the political situation, and then
nonexistent from 1973 to 1982 when unions were illegal. During 1983-84 they
began to reorganize and in 1985 they were back in full operation. They enjoyed a
very active period immediately following the restoration of democracy but then
saw participation wane in practically all sectors. The extent and history of unionization differ in the private and public sectors; it has been much more strongly
associated with the latter (Table 4.11). Considerable differences are also evident
among the various economic sectors: the labor movement has made few inroads
in the trade sector, but one finds highly unionized work forces in the electric
power, gas and water, and oil refining industries in the public sector, and the
banking and glass industries in the private sector. There are generally fewer union
members among self-employed workers—found mainly in trade and services—
than among wage-earners.

In order to determine the possible impact of union activity on wages, a standard Phillips-curve equation was used, in which the exchange rate of the private
nominal wage is a function of inflation and the unemployment rate. Additionally,
an indicator of the real cost of labor for the employer was included, on the assumption that the high costs in the immediately preceding period exert downward pressure on the current wage increase. Finally, a mute variable that takes
account of the presence or absence of unions was included to introduce the union
activity. It must be borne in mind, however, that its coefficient also captures the
effect of other changes which occurred simultaneously. That variable appears in
two forms: altering the ordinate at the origin and affecting the semielasticity of
unemployment, with the aim of ascertaining whether union activity moves the
curve or modifies the impact of unemployment on the wage rate.

The results obtained for the private sector indicate that the reemergence of
the unions in 1985 kindled inflation throughout the economy, increasing the growth
rate or diminishing the negative impact of the unemployment rate. For manufacturing the foregoing effects are somewhat less (Table 4.12). Since information
exists on the degree of unionization (i.e., the percentage of members) for the
various manufacturing industries, the foregoing analysis was supplemented with
the estimation of a panel model of fixed effects. Its results (See Appendix Table

Table 4.11. Uruguay: Membership by Sector, 1987, 1990 and 1993
(Percentages)

	1987	1990	1993
Agriculture, forestry, fishery	14.29	13.66	6.42
Manufacturing	27.33	23.00	17.61
Foodstuffs	51.53	32.10	30.08
Beverages	73.14	97.69	57.97
Tobacco	70.31	77.63	67.93
Textiles	49.51	44.49	47.84
Clothing	65.88	11.41	16.46
Leather	59.73	42.46	22.20
Paper	51.55	35.12	5.94
Graphics	31.32	23.99	22.48
Chemicals and medications	52.14	31.93	26.20
Oil	100.00	100.00	100.00
Rubber	72.83	77.76	75.87
Glass	65.28	67.89	84.44
Portland cement	32.73	30.30	24.23
Metals, machinery, electric appliances	40.99	29.60	34.54
Electric power, gas and water	85.44	91.12	91.57
Construction	16.36	17.09	10.04
Trade, restaurants, hotels	6.10	4.74	3.09
Transport, communications	35.34	32.88	19.88
Banking, insurance, business services	32.36	28.91	30.32
Social, personal and community services	22.29	21.66	20.85
Private sector	16.70	14.23	9.91
Public sector	41.98	42.31	48.72
Total	22.56	20.38	17.28

Source: Prepared for this study on the basis of employment data obtained from the National Institute of Statistics and the number of members of the First Special Congress (5/1987), the Fourth Congress (5/1990), and the Fifth Congress (11/1993).
Note: Calculated as the quotient between the members and the total number of persons employed for the major divisions (one digit) and between blue-collar and white-collar workers for the sub-branches of the manufacturing industries.

4.A.3) show that even using as a control variable the characteristics of the industry—such as the percentage of its sales in the local marketplace, the percentage of low-skilled workers, and the capital intensity of its technology—the degree of unionization continues to be an important variable in wage inflation. In this way the industries with a larger share of unionized workers show larger wage increase rates (1 percent more for every additional 10 percentage points of that share, on average).

In addition, an error-correction model was specified to model employment demand by analyzing the impact of the unions as an independent effect that moves the curve and by modifying the costs of adjusting the employment level to the

Table 4.12. Uruguay: Impact of Union Activity on Wages and Employment

	Until 1985	Since 1985
Effects on wages		
1. Economy		
Mute variable	0	0.09
Unemployment rate	1.95	-1.16
2. Manufacturing		
Mute variable	0	0.07
Unemployment rate	-1.85	-1.18
Degree of unionization		0.11
Effects on employment		
1. Economy		
Mute variable	0	0.11
GDP growth	0.40	0.09
2. Manufacturing		
Mute variable	0	0.36
Degree of unionization		0.04

Source: Appendix Tables 4.A.1 to 4.A.6.

variations in the demand for goods. The adjustment costs are associated not only with those generated by the hiring and firing of workers, but also with the costs stemming from the changes in the composition of the working group. The adjustment costs therefore involve the severance pay disbursed and the personnel search and selection costs, and also the variations in productivity. The direct consequence of the foregoing phenomenon is that, in terms of employment and hours worked, costs are adjusted to the changes in GDP. Thus the model includes a mute variable that affects the coefficients of the constant and of the rate of change in GDP. The results of the estimations (Appendix Tables 4.A.4 and 4.A.5) indicate that the general employment level, throughout the economy as well as the manufacturing sector, increased for each level of GDP from 1985 on. In the first case, there is a slower adjustment with respect to the GDP variations, which means reduced elasticity in the short term. This implies that although the employment growth rate is higher (other things being equal), the response to the changes in the demand for goods is substantially smaller. Two factors may possibly explain this behavior: one is that although the employment level was boosted for political reasons, union activity and the implementation of job security legislation drove up hiring and firing costs; the other is that adjustments are generally slower after a major crisis because of uncertainty about future macroeconomic trends.

No similar trend is evident in the manufacturing sector. Although employment rose in 1985, it dropped rather steadily through the period as a whole, while adjustment to fluctuations in output remained constant. This last result is not altogether surprising: since industry in general has undergone substantial transformation since the seventies, stemming from the greater productivity demanded by the international market, the sector may have developed mechanisms to keep payrolls and average productivity fairly stable. In this way, the labor market's new look following the restoration of democracy would have no major effects on the employment-output dynamic. The trend regarding regular and overtime hours, described earlier, supports this interpretation. Finally, the rising level of employment in manufacturing is partly associated with the reemergence of the unions, as indicated by the industrial subsector data (Appendix Table 4.A.6). This table shows that, if the characteristics of the branches are taken into account, union activity in the eighties can be credited with an average increase of half a percentage point in the employment level for every 10 points of difference in the percentage of membership.

A Case Study of Large Union Membership: The Banking Sector[10]

The Uruguayan financial system can be viewed as a sector with special characteristics in the marketplace: a large union membership of workers and employers in very strong, long-established unions, above-average wages, substantial worker benefits, its own welfare system, and no unemployment insurance. The state's participation in the sector is usually negligible, and financial institutions are subject to the banks' deposit insurance rules. Workers belong to the *Asociación de Empleados Bancarios del Uruguay* (AEBU, Association of Bank Employees of Uruguay), created in 1942 and operating with two councils: one working with the public banking system (four institutions) and the other with the private sector (22 banks and 24 other financial entities). Meanwhile, the private employers belong to the *Asociación de Bancos del Uruguay* (ABU, Association of Banks of Uruguay). Both organizations are directed by the banking sector: 80 percent of the employees belong to the AEBU, while all the private banks except one (which withdrew in 1993) belong to the ABU.

With respect to wage negotiations, the AEBU and ABU have a long tradition that was resumed in 1985 in a number of agreements. Since 1988 they have signed collective labor agreements of at least one year's duration that stipulate the minimum wage to be paid in each category and the months and rules for its adjustments, other minimum benefits, and some working conditions connected with leave and disciplinary measures. The adjustment rules followed the spirit of the officially adopted agreements, but the increases obtained were always greater. In 1988-89, for example, a higher real wage was provided in addition to a read-

---

[10] This section is based on a case study performed for this project by Bucheli and Dominioni (1994).

justment every four months based on past inflation. What was provided in 1990-92 was not real recovery but simply indexation based on the inflation of each preceding three-month period, with a trigger clause activated whenever accumulated price rises reached 15 percent, at which point an adjustment would have to be made on account. The state bank, for its part, also negotiated certain matters related to public sector wage policy (travel expenses and noncash benefits), whereby compensation was raised in 1985-89. In 1990 the financial systems organizations further succeeded in holding negotiations separately from the rest of the public sector, and in 1991 an agreement between the AEBU and the board of directors of the banks set wages at the minimum levels specified in agreements between the AEBU and ABU.[11] The agreed wage entails a six-and-a-half-hour work day. The agreements cover other matters in addition to wages, several of them not referred to in the general law. These include length-of-service bonuses and special family allowances (which in 1993 accounted for 11 and 3 percent of payroll, respectively), health care for the worker and his/her family, travel expenses amounting to 30 percent of the minimum salary for the position and of the length-of-service bonus for night work, right to work half-time for six months while breastfeeding, supplement to the maternal care allowance offered by the public social security system, use of the AEBU day-care center and preschool, and low-interest loans.

In this negotiating framework, bank wages outstripped the average private wage at an ever faster rate, especially since the end of the decade (Figure 4.8). This performance has not been improved upon in any other industry. In 1988, monthly compensation in banking was the highest in the private sector (16 percent higher than the second highest-paying sector), and at present this sector has further increased its lead.

One of the AEBU's main objectives has been job security, which eventually evolved into permanent tenure. Tenure appears as an outstanding achievement of that organization, a success not duplicated by other unions despite many efforts in that direction. In that sector, therefore, employers regard dismissal as impossible. In the past, a reduction in staff in one institution would lead to the reassignment of employees in the rest of the system. Until 1982, the public banking system played a valuable role by absorbing workers who lost their jobs whenever a private bank went out of business. However, as the relocated employees retained their salaries—higher than those in the public banks—distortions arose in the pay structure, affecting the AEBU's internal cohesion. The downsizing that came

---

[11] The agreement provides for 85 percent of the minimum wage agreed for the private banking system. However, since one twelfth of vacation pay is added to this wage (only in the private sector), the practical result is 100 percent parity.

Figure 4.8. Uruguay: Real Wages of Bank Employees Compared with Average Private Sector Wages, 1985-92
(Index 1984=100)

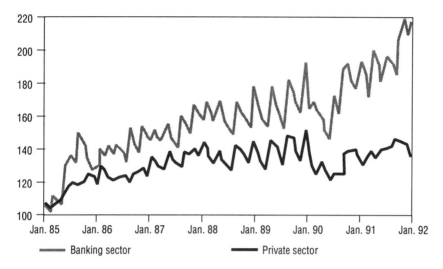

Banking sector   Private sector

Source: Wage Survey and National Institute of Statistics.

with the financial crisis of the early eighties and the technological restructuring of the last few years could not be dealt with by the same method as in the past. From the mid-eighties on, the emphasis on trimming the public sector and improving its efficiency made it even more difficult to relocate personnel in the public banks, and in 1990 a freeze on new public sector hiring finally made it impossible.

Against this background, the downsizing of the private banks, which was proceeding at a fairly brisk pace, could not be carried out by firing and then relocating workers. The solution was left to the banks themselves, which offered incentives for early retirement under schemes they devised without the AEBU's participation. The evidence nevertheless suggests that the existence of a powerful union, which had traditionally fought to protect jobs, ensured the sector's willingness to pay a very high monetary cost to avert a conflict. The amount offered under the incentives consisted of a fixed sum and additional emoluments, with different offers for different classes of employees in the same bank: distinctions might be made, for instance, between those eligible for retirement and those not, and between various grades and salary levels. On average, the amounts offered were similar from one institution to the next. The profiles of the employees who took advantage of the incentives varied widely, with no one age group, sex or grade predominating. Finally, considering that the general law provides for severance pay amounting to up to six months' compensation, it is obvious that what the banks offered easily surpassed that limit. A comparison of the real cost incurred in the departure of 240 workers in 1986 with what would have been paid under the law to a worker earning a management-level salary and with substantial time in service to his/her credit shows that the cost was almost seven times higher.

In summary, banking stands out as a sector which, with strong and effective employee and employer unions, has maintained and even increased its positive wage differentials by negotiating additional benefits, even in the public banking system. Furthermore, when restructuring affected employment, the threat of a showdown with the union was sufficient reason to offer the redundant workers retirement incentives that represented a significantly higher amount than that provided for by law.

Conclusions and Policy Recommendations

This chapter has examined the dynamics of the Uruguayan labor market in the period 1975-92 and the institutional issues affecting it. The labor market appears relatively flexible at the macroeconomic level, though with some difficulties in adjusting at the microeconomic level. From the institutional point of view the legal framework does not appear as a barrier. Hiring procedures, severance pay, and unemployment insurance do not play a central role in the dynamics of employment and unemployment. Nor would changes in supply explain the unemployment trend of the last several years. Collective bargaining and the unions, on the other hand, have introduced rigidities since their reemergence in 1985. The minimum compensation levels provided for in collective agreements, the meticulously defined work rules laid down by the Wage Councils, and the high severance pay required in strongly unionized sectors constitute institutional hurdles to adjustment. The public sector presents a situation quite different from that of private business: hiring is subject to several layers of approval, while the principle of permanent tenure makes firing practically impossible. Finally, labor costs, which are currently at their highest historical levels, may be contributing to a diminished use of the labor factor. The following policy recommendations are framed in the context of these considerations.

- *Eliminate legal rigidities with respect to work schedules.* The legal framework in general and legal and administrative practices appear relatively flexible where formalities about hiring and types of contract are concerned. Mechanisms for dismissal in the private sector do not require prior notice or compliance with rigid rules as to cause, and their costs are comparatively low. The jurisprudence has developed the concept of abusive dismissal, which applies to exceptional situations and entails significantly higher severance pay. In current judicial practice this concept is applied under exceptional circumstances. However, legal rigidities remain as regards work schedules, a fact that complicates the development of more flexible forms of work (flexible schedules, etc.) when the result of an activity is difficult to specify contractually. These rigidities grew markedly worse in the recent period.

• *Encourage collective bargaining at the company level in order to include specifics.* The practices of the industrial relations system impose rigidities through collective agreements, both because of certain elaborate rules that do not allow adoption of new technologies and because of the minimum wage levels provided. This situation is aggravated where agreements cover a broad range of firms and subsectors that are affected differently by external shocks because of the different degrees to which they are integrated into the global marketplace. Recent experience following the state's withdrawal from collective bargaining and changes in market conditions for certain firms indicates that this type of negotiation at the company level is taking place more often.

• *Develop a regulatory framework to resolve the legal uncertainty to which the practical operation of collective bargaining gives rise.* The econometric results obtained indicate unequivocally that union activity impacts wage levels and employment. Collective agreements are the institutional mechanism through which that impact is channeled. Paradoxically, this is the least regulated and least legally circumscribed area. The transaction costs associated with this legal uncertainty are increasing as the macroeconomic context changes. In this sense, a regulatory framework would have to be set up that (1) recognizes the normative effect of the collective agreement; (2) establishes the obligation to negotiate, under certain conditions; (3) resolves the lack of provisions ensuring the parties' right to information and their juridical legitimation; and (4) supplies mechanisms to review collective agreements. Given the recent changes in union structure—dwindling membership and decentralized bargaining—the prospects for achieving a consensus with regard to such a regulatory framework have improved.

• *In the short term, use selective incentive mechanisms to restructure the public sector.* In spite of permanent tenure, thanks to the sector's wage policy the recent incentive schemes have proved relatively effective in encouraging retirement, at a cost no higher than that in highly unionized sectors, though with some deterioration of human capital. Continuing this approach requires a design that does not disadvantage professionals with specific human capital. To this end it would be well to reduce wage compression, even though this may be difficult to accomplish because of union resistance.

- *In the long run, deemphasize the principle of permanent tenure and limit its application in the public sector.* Deemphasizing the principle of permanent tenure would improve the sector's ability to adjust. Once ways are found to deal with the practical difficulties of carrying out this directive, which requires constitutional changes, permanent tenure should be applied to more limited areas of an employee's career, without jeopardizing the safeguards offered by the principles, as exemplified in other comparable cases of public service.

- *Explore possibilities of redesigning unemployment insurance as an institution.* Unemployment insurance, which exists only for the private sector, has drastically reduced its benefits in the recent period, and it has lowered its caps by tying them to the minimum wage. It covers no more than 20 percent of the actual unemployed, and 60 percent of the beneficiaries are furloughed workers. It thus serves to subsidize certain businesses, with the manufacturing sector receiving the greatest net transfer. There appear to be no institutional reasons for this, although the question needs more detailed analysis. While that is pursued, an appropriate institutional design should seek to induce the sectors that make the most use of the insurance to contribute accordingly.

- *Reform the social security system so as to permit lower contribution rates.* In addition to the previously mentioned effects on labor demand, higher costs and contribution rates encourage underdeclaration of social security, since all the benefits are capped and both employer and employee therefore have an incentive to make no further contributions once those caps are reached. Since the caps are pegged to the minimum wage, their steep drop in real terms has aggravated the problem. In addition, the high tax encourages approaches other than hiring permanent workers. This situation is obvious in the case of professionals, for the value-added tax to which they are subject does not cost the firm anything. That can only point to the desirability of reducing the tax and other charges in conjunction with a reform of social security. Such a reform should probably aim at dovetailing social security with the retirement system and at promoting competition among health care providers, in order to cut costs. However, detailed discussion of this reform goes beyond the scope of this work and should be part of the public debate that has been taking place in Uruguay since 1989.

Bibliography

Abraham, K.G., and S.N. Houseman. 1988. Employment and Hours Adjustment: A US/German Comparison. University of Maryland. Mimeo.

Alfie, I. 1994. El Seguro de Desempleo. Centro de Estudios de la Realidad Económica y Social. Montevideo.

Allen, S. 1991. *Changes in the Cyclical Sensitivity of Wages in the United States, 1891-1987.* Working Paper No. 3854. National Bureau of Economic Research.

Allen, S., and G. Labadie. 1995. Labor Market Flexibility and Economic Performance in Uruguay and Chile. Advance report for Centro de Estudios de la Realidad Económica y Social and the Tinker Foundation, Montevideo. Unpublished.

_____. 1993. Labor Market Flexibility in Uruguay and Chile. Advance report for the Centro de Estudios de la Realidad Económica y Social and the Tinker Foundation, Montevideo.

Ameglio, E.J. 1994. Normativa laboral y formas de contratación in el Uruguay. Report for the Project of the Red de Centros de Investigación Aplicada: Reformas del mercado laboral ante la liberalización de la economía: el caso de Uruguay. Grupo de Estudios en Economía, Organización y Políticas Sociales. Montevideo. Mimeo.

_____. 1993. La indemnización por despido: su incidencia in la caracterización del mercado de trabajo uruguayo. *Revista de derecho laboral* (No. 17). Montevideo.

Ameglio, E., and A. Francés. 1994. Normativa laboral. Report for the Project of the Red de Centros de Investigación Aplicada: Reformas del mercado laboral ante la liberalización de la economía: el caso de Uruguay. Grupo de Estudios en Economía, Organización y Políticas Sociales, Montevideo. Mimeo.

Barbagelata, H.H. 1978. El despido abusivo y la reciente jurisprudencia. *Revista de derecho laboral* (No. 108).

Blanchard, O., and L. Summers. 1986. Hysteresis and the European Unemployment Problem. In *National Bureau of Economic Research. Macroeconomics Annual 1986,* ed. S. Fischer. Cambridge, Mass.: The MIT Press.

Bucheli, M. 1994. Los trabajadores del sector público. Report for the Project of the Red de Centros de Investigación Aplicada: Reformas del mercado laboral ante la liberalización de la economía: el caso de Uruguay. Grupo de Estudios en Economía, Organización y Políticas Sociales, Montevideo. Mimeo.

_____. 1992. Diferencias sectoriales de salarios in el Uruguay. *Suma* (No.7). Centro de Investigaciones Económicas, Montevideo.

Bucheli, M., A. Cassoni, R. Diez de Medina, and M. Rossi. 1993. *Los recursos humanos in el proceso de ajuste: el caso uruguayo.* Working Paper No. 2/ 93. Department of Economics, Faculty of Social Sciences of the University of the Republic, Montevideo.

Bucheli, M., and D. Dominioni. 1994. El sector bancario: un mercado de trabajo altamente sindicalizado. Report for the Project of the Red de Centros de Investigación Aplicada: Reformas del mercado laboral ante la liberalización de la economía: el caso de Uruguay. Grupo de Estudios en Economía, Organización y Políticas Sociales, Montevideo. Mimeo.

Cassoni, A. 1993. Employment Adjustment Process: 1975-1991. Report for the project on Labor Market Flexibility and Economic Performance in Uruguay and Chile. Centro de Estudios de la Realidad Económica y Social-Tinker Foundation, Montevideo.

_____. 1993. Wage Adjustment Process: 1968-1991. Report for the Project on Labor Market Flexibility and Economic Performance in Uruguay and Chile. Centro de Estudios de la Realidad Económica y Social-Tinker Foundation, Montevideo.

Centro de Estudios de la Realidad Económica y Social (CERES). 1995. El seguro de desempleo. Montevideo.

_____. 1990a. Algunos problemas de la administración pública: el envejecimiento de los funcionarios. *Informe y Propuestas* (No. 3, July). Montevideo.

_____. 1990b. *Reforma de la administración pública: posibles efectos del proyecto de ley de servicios personales.* Legislative Analysis No. 4. Montevideo.

Coe, D.T. 1985. Nominal Wages, the NAIRU and Wage Flexibility. *Economic Studies* (No. 5). OECD.

Dertouzos, J.N., and L.A. Karoly. 1990. Labor Market Responses to Employer Liability. Rand Corporation.

Ermida, O. 1984. El concepto de despido abusivo. *Revista de derecho laboral* (No. 135).

Forteza, A. 1991. *Contratos salariales e inflación, 1990.* Working Document No. 14/91. Department of Economics, Faculty of Social Sciences of the University of the Republic, Montevideo.

Frenkel, R., and M. Damill. 1988. *Concertación y política de ingresos in Uruguay, 1985-1988.* Working Paper No. 13. Centro de Estudios del Estado y Sociedad, Buenos Aires.

Greene, W.H. 1990. *Econometric Analysis.* New York: Macmillan Publishing Co.

Hamermesh, D.S. 1993. *Labor Demand.* New Jersey: Princeton University Press.

_____. 1990. *Aggregate Employment Dynamics and Lumpy Adjustment Costs.* Working Document No. 3229. National Bureau of Economic Research.

_____. 1990. *A General Mode of Dynamic Labor Demand.* Working Document No. 3356. National Bureau of Economic Research.

Heckman, J. 1979. Sample Selection Bias as a Specification Error. *Econometrica* (No. 47).

Holzer, H.J., and E.B. Montgomery. 1990. *Asymmetries and Rigidities in Wage Adjustment by Firms.* Working Document No. 3274. National Bureau of Economic Research.

Klau, F., and A. Mittelstädt. 1986. Labour Market Flexibility. *Economic Studies* (No. 6).

Layard, R., S. Nickell, and R. Jackman. 1991. *Unemployment. Macroeconomic Performance and the Labour Market.* New York: Oxford University Press.

Macadar, L. 1988. Protección, ventajas comparadas y eficiencia industrial. *Suma* (No. 3). Centro de Investigaciones Económicas, Montevideo.

Mangarelli, C. 1992. *Despido abusivo e incumplimiento contractual: criterios para la estimación del daño.* Montevideo: Faiza Editor.

Mangarelli, C., and J. Rosenbaum. 1988. El despido abusivo en el derecho uruguayo. *Revista de derecho laboral* (No. 151).

Pérez del Castillo, S. 1992. *Manual práctico de normas laborales.* Seventh edition. Fundación de Cultura Universitaria. Montevideo.

Rama, M. 1993. Institucionalidad laboral y crecimiento económico en Uruguay. Academia Nacional de Economía, Montevideo.

_____. 1992. Trade Unions and Protectionism. Research report. Centro de Investigaciones Económicas, Montevideo.

_____. 1988. ¿Qué es el pleno empleo? Una cuantificación de la desocupación voluntaria, de desequilibrio y de segmentación. *Suma* (No. 4).

_____. The Labor Market and Trade Reform in Manufacturing. In *Essays on the Effects of Protectionism on a Small Country: The Case of Uruguay,* eds. M. Connolly and J. de Melo. World Bank. Forthcoming.

Trylesinski, F. 1991. Los diferenciales salariales entre empleados públicos y privados: el caso uruguayo. Presented at the Sixth Annual Workshops on the Economy of the Central Bank of Uruguay, Montevideo. Mimeo.

Appendix Table 4.A.1. Uruguay: Estimation of the Impact of Union Activity on Private Wages

Equation 1
Dependent variable is LVW 1975-92

Variable	Coefficient	Standard error	Statistic T	Sigma of 2-queues
C	0.2452454	0.1002494	2.4463513	0.0308
D85	0.0887254	0.0284605	3.1174952	0.0089
U	-1.7864587	0.5590658	-3.1954353	0.0077
LINF	0.6649903	0.1115128	5.9633562	0.0001
LINF(-1)	0.2739453	0.1184527	2.3126983	0.0393
LWR(-1)	-0.4645663	0.1112351	-4.1764363	0.0013

R-square	0.948159	Average of the dependent variable 0.489245
R-adjusted square	0.926558	Standard deviation of the dependent variable 0.166844
Standard regression error	0.045215	Sum of the residual squares 0.024533
Logarithm of verisimilitude	33.84212	Statistic T 43.89498
Durbin-Watson statistic	2.642355	Prob(statistic F) 0.000000
Serial correlation LM Test: 1 lags		Statistic F 1.81000 Prob. 0.2056

LVWM: rate of change of the nominal wage of the manufacturing sector (in logs); C: constant; D85: binary equal to 1 of 1985 to 1992, 0 in the rest; U: unemployment rate; LINF: inflation rate (in logs); LWMR: real wage (in logs); (-1): lagging variable i periods.

Equation 2
Dependent variable is LVM 1975-92

Variable	Coefficient	Standard error	Statistic T	Sigma of 2-queues
C	0.2455504	0.1069095	2.2968051	0.0404
U	-1.9502993	0.6141446	-3.1756352	0.0080
UD	0.7958872	0.2873216	2.7700224	0.0170
LINF	0.6778145	0.1167695	5.8047239	0.0001
LINF(-1)	0.2788540	0.1248206	2.2340381	0.0453
LWR(-1)	-0.3965407	0.1233077	-3.2158636	0.0074

R-square	0.942768	Average of the dependent variable 0.489245
R-adjusted square	0.918921	Standard deviation of the dependent variable 0.166844
Standard regression error	0.047508	Sum of the residual squares 0.027084
Logarithm of verisimilitude	32.95176	Statistic F 39.53432
Durbin-Watson statistic	2.667006	Prob (statistic F) 0.000000
Serial correlation LM Test: 1 lags		Statistic F 2.10623 Prob. 0.1746

LVW: Rate of change of the nominal wage of the manufacturing sector (in logs); C: constant; D85: binary equal to 1 of 1985 to 1992, 0 in the rest; U: unemployment rate; LINF: inflation rate (in logs); LWR: real wage (in logs); (-1): lagging variable i periods.

Appendix Table 4.A.2. Uruguay: Estimation of Union Activity on Manufacturing Wages

Equation 1
Dependent variable is LVW 1975-92

Variable	Coefficient	Standard error	Statistic F	Sigma de 2-colas
C	0.2197331	0.1250997	1.7564638	0.1068
D85	0.0734390	0.0398355	1.8435565	0.0923
U	-1.7224648	0.6924798	-2.4873863	0.0302
LINF	0.8064921	0.6924798	5.5363680	0.0002
LINF(-1)	0.2757605	0.1456717	1.8251062	0.0952
LWR(-1)	-0.5004978	0.1353895	-3.6967261	0.0035

R-square	0.482925
R-adjusted square	0.181971
Standard regression error	0.033989
Logarithm of verisimilitude	32.09291
Durbin-Watson statistic	0.000003
Serial correlation LM Test: 1 lags	0.3475

Average of the dependent variable
Standard deviation of the dependent variable
Sum of the residual squares
Statistic F
Prob (statistic F)
Statistic F 1.81000 Prob.

LVWM: Rate of change of the nominal wage of the manufacturing sector (in logs); C: constant; UD: binary equal to U of 1985 to 1992, 0 in the rest; U: unemployment rate; LINF: inflation rate (in logs); LWR: real wage (in logs); (-1): lagging variable i periods.

Equation 2
Dependent variable is LVM 1975-92

Variable	Coefficient	Standard error	T-statistic	Sigma de 2-colas
C	0.2148302	0.1283871	1.6733001	0.1224
U	-1.8478111	0.7332034	-2.5201890	0.0285
UD	0.6641302	0.3979618	1.6688292	0.1233
LINF	0.8242128	0.1466735	5.6193720	0.0002
LINF(-1)	0.2708386	0.1573913	1.7207975	0.1133
LWR(-1)	-0.4402558	0.1536657	-2.8650232	0.0154

R-square	0.932991	Average of dependent variable	0.482925
R-adjusted square	0.902532	Standard deviation of the dependent variable	0.181971
Standard regression error	0.056811	Sum of the residual squares	0.035502
Logarithm of verisimilitude	28.33467	Statistic F	30.63126
Durbin-Watson statistic	2.438390	Prob (statistic F)	0.000004
Serial correlation LM Test: 1 lags		Statistic F 2,10623 Prob.	

LVWM: Rate of change of the nominal wage of the manufacturing sector (in logs); C: constant; UD: binary equal to U of 1985 to 1992, 0 in the rest; U: unemployment rate; LINF: inflation rate (in logs); LWR: real wage (in logs); (-1): lagging variable i periods.

Appendix Table 4.A.3. Uruguay: Estimation of the Impact of Union Activity on Manufacturing Wages (panel estimation)

Dependent variable is LVRH 1982.1-1991.4
Number of observations: 280

Variable	Coefficient	Standard error	Statistic F	Sigma of 2-queues
U	-0.9562967	0.2035828	-4.6973346	0.0000
LINF	0.7471313	0.0774369	9.6482589	0.0000
LINF(-1)	0.2416564	0.0663168	3.6439693	0.0003
LINF(-4)	0.2111687	0.0528317	3.9970041	0.0001
LRHR(-1)	-0.2622038	0.0280340	-9.3530554	0.0000
OBRP	-0.2574079	0.1322719	-2.0216530	0.0442
CE	29.277788	4.4456841	6.5856654	0.0000
VTASL	-0.0421726	0.0649997	-0.6488128	0.5170
GS	0.1062276	0.0136939	7.7572913	0.0000
I31	-96.305575	14.635601	-6.5802269	0.0000
I32	-53.356482	8.1153144	-6.5747893	0.0000
I34	-27.698878	4.2153740	-6.5709183	0.0000
I35	-55.454341	8.4321578	-6.5765303	0.0000
I36	-26.467924	4.0154157	-6.5915775	0.0000
I37	-9.5102626	1.4469583	-6.5725894	0.0000
I38	-20.925155	3.1792218	-6.5818481	0.0000
T1	0.0432670	0.0052062	8.3106589	0.0000
T4	0.0602819	0.0052594	11.461774	0.0000

R-square	0.748506	Average of the dependent variable	0.147957
R-adjusted square	0.732188	Standard deviation of the dependent variable	0.063823
Standard regression error	0.033029	Sum of the residual squares	0.285815
Logarithm of verisimilitude	566.9052	Statistic F	45.86905
Durbin-Watson statistic	1.238192	Prob (statistic F)	0.000000

LVRH: Exchange rate of the nominal wage per regular hour worked per worker of the manufacturing sector (in logs); LINF: inflation rate (in logs); LRHR: compensation per real regular hour (in logs); (-i): lagging variable i periods; OBRP: unskilled laborers as a percentage of all workers; CE: capital intensiveness measured by the consumption of electric power, in kilowatts; VTASL: membership as a percentage of all workers; 131 to 138: manufacturing industries (131: foodstuffs; 132: textiles; 134: paper and printing; 135: chemicals; 136: nonmetallic ores; 137: base metals; 138: machinery and equipment); T1, T4: quarters 1 and 4.

Appendix Table 4.A.4. Uruguay: Estimation of the Impact of Union Activity on Private Employment

Dependent variable is VLE 1976-91 Variable	Coefficient	Standard error	Statistic F	Sigma of 2-queues
C	9.9887127	1.8208859	5.4856335	0.0003
D85	0.1180974	0.0210478	5.6109256	0.0002
LQ(-1)	0.3691085	0.1256335	2.9379791	0.0148
VLQ	0.3972907	0.0854500	4.6993955	0.0009
LE(-1)	-1.0536086	0.2290486	-4.5999339	0.0010
DVLQ85	-0.3162121	0.1896154	-1.6676496	0.1263

R-square	0.866034	Average of the dependent variable	0.014825
R-adjusted square	0.799050	Standard deviation of the dependent variable	0.031878
Standard regression error	0.014290	Sum of the residual squares	0.002042
Logarithm of verisimilitude	49.02817	Statistic F	12.92912
Durbin-Watson statistic	2.257148	Prob (statistic F)	0.000424

VLE: Exchange rate of the level of employment, total private sector; C: constant; D85: equal binary variable to 1 from 1985, 0 in another case; LQ: GDP (in logs); VLQ: exchange rate of the GDP (in logs); DVLQ85: D85 by VLQ; (-i): lagging variable i periods.

Appendix Table 4.A.5. Uruguay: Estimation of the Impact of Union Activity on Manufacturing Employment

Dependent variable is VLE 1976-91

Variable	Coefficient	Standard error	Statistic F	Sigma of 2-queues
D85	0.3602795	0.1399893	2.5736211	0.0128
LTEND85	-0.0969986	0.0361166	-2.6857115	0.0095
LTCRUA	0.0192767	0.0082228	2.3564601	0.0220
LQM(-4)	0.0649667	0.0163628	3.9703850	0.0002
LQM	0.2336254	0.0554962	4.2097586	0.0001
LQM(-4)	-0.1202145	0.0405771	-2.9626176	0.0045
VLQM(-1)	-0.0933098	0.0370474	-2.5186575	0.0147
LEM(-1)	1.1419679	0.1162366	9.8245098	0.0000
LEM(-2)	-0.2624532	0.1232935	-2.1286863	0.0378

R-square	0.971212	Average of dependent variable	4.724395
R-adjusted square	0.967025	Standard deviation of the dependent variable	0.101243
Standard regression error	0.018385	Sum of the residual squares	0.018590
Logarithm of verisimilitude	169.7959	Statistic F	231.9387
Durbin-Watson statistic	1.901440	Prob (statistic F)	0.000000

LEM: Employment level, manufacturing sector; D85: equal binary variable to 1 from 1985, 0 in another case; LTEND85: logarithmic trend since 1985, 0 in another case; LTCRUA: Uruguay-Argentina relative exchange rate (in logs); LXQM: proportion of exports in the GDP, manufacturing sector; LQM: manufacturing GDP (in logs); (-i): lagging variables i periods.

Appendix Table 4.A.6. Uruguay: Estimation of the Impact of Union Activity on Manufacturing Employment
(Panel estimation)

Dependent variable is LEM 1982.1-1991.4
Number of observations: 288

Variable	Coefficient	Standard error	Statistic F	Sigma of 2-queues
C	0.8259059	0.1961760	4.2100244	0.0000
I31	0.1220661	0.0129559	9.4216879	0.0000
I32	0.1498920	0.0191470	7.8284708	0.0000
I34	0.1403868	0.0218717	6.4185469	0.0000
I35	0.2711410	0.0270316	10.030508	0.0000
I36	0.0510458	0.0148008	3.4488613	0.0007
I37	-0.1225337	0.0127562	-9.6058176	0.0000
I38	-0.0311492	0.0118786	-2.6222838	0.0092
GS	0.0424254	0.0171356	2.4758619	0.0139
OBRP	0.3914983	0.1757167	2.2280092	0.0267
LQM	0.4047007	0.0254002	15.932954	0.0000
VLQM	-0.2144344	0.0277714	-7.7142078	0.0000
VLQM(-1)	-0.1046401	0.0251167	-4.1661467	0.0000
LEM(-4)	0.3428239	0.0333026	10.294206	0.0000
TEND	-0.0040824	0.0003853	-10.594973	0.0000

R-square	0.925772	Average of the dependent variable	0.592114
R-adjusted square	0.921965	Standard deviation of the dependent variable	0.170514
Standard regression error	0.047633	Sum of the residual squares	0.619398
Logarithm of verisimilitude	475.7891	Statistic F	243.2026
Durbin-Watson statistic	1.459167	Prob (statistic F)	0.000000

LEM: Employment level, manufacturing sector (in logs); C: constant; I31 to I38: manufacturing industries (I31: foodstuffs; I32: textiles; I34: paper and printing; I35: chemicals; I36: nonmetallic ores; I37: base metals; I38: machinery and equipment); GS: unionization (members as percentage of all workers); OBRP: unskilled laborers as a percentage of all workers; LQM: manufacturing GDP (in logs); VLQM: exchange rate of manufacturing GDP (in logs); TEND: linear trend; (-i): lagging variable i periods.

CHAPTER FIVE

VENEZUELA

Samuel Freije Rodríguez
Keila Betancourt
Gustavo Márquez

The Venezuelan economy is highly dependent on its oil industry. During the 1980s, exports of petroleum products accounted for more than 85 percent of total exports. Meanwhile, tax monies collected from the oil industry accounted for more than 60 percent of the central government's ordinary revenues. Obviously, this excessive reliance of tax revenue and business activity on a product subject to abrupt price fluctuations makes the country very susceptible to macroeconomic instability.

Recognition of the undesirability of that dependence, together with the huge inflow of resources produced by the oil boom of 1973, prompted the Venezuelan state to expand public investment in industry in order to diversify the economy. The characteristics of the investment programs (large-scale projects, many of them in basic industries), combined with the downward rigidity of budgeted public outlays, led to external borrowing in order to continue the expansion even in the years when oil revenues stabilized or declined.

The public sector's expansion of its endeavors as producer (while neglecting social services and infrastructure) and its inability to balance its finances resulted in shrinking private investment from 1979 on and increasing capital flight from year to year. In 1982 the international debt crisis reduced the availability of external credit to cover the deficits, so that in February 1983 the rapid loss of reserves compelled the government to suspend the exchange stability and free convertibility that the country had enjoyed for more than 20 years.

In 1983 a "differential exchange regime" was established, consisting of a system of currency quotas at different exchange rates. The economic program also included controls on prices and interest rates as well as public spending cuts. The program was successful as a stabilization plan, and by 1985 the fiscal and trade deficits of 1982 gave way to substantial surpluses. The stabilization program achieved its objectives through broad controls and recession. Real GDP fell at an average annual rate of 2.2 percent, the number of unemployed doubled, and inflation stabilized at around 11 percent.

In 1986 and 1987 an initial agreement was reached on restructuring the external debt, and the government decided to use the reserves accumulated in the first three years of adjustment to revive the economy through expanded public spending. However, oil prices fell and the restructuring accord did not produce major access to new credits; fiscal and trade imbalances consequently reappeared as the price of the revival. Real GDP grew at an annual rate of 5.4 percent from 1986 to 1988 and unemployment decreased, but inflation heated up to 30 percent per year (across-the-board price controls notwithstanding). Meanwhile, the accumulated current account deficit surpassed $9 billion and the fiscal deficit exceeded 7 percent of GDP.

In 1989 the macroeconomic situation was critical, and the new government decided to adopt a stabilization and structural adjustment plan with the institutional and financial support of the International Monetary Fund (IMF) and the World Bank. It was clear that the nation's economy was constrained by a multitude of controls and institutional rigidities and that these had precluded structural changes which would have brought more stable trade and fiscal balances. The choice was made to unify the exchange rate, let the bolivar float (which led to a nominal devaluation of more than 100 percent), free prices and interest rates, and introduce trade and tax reforms.

With respect to the external sector, all quantitative restrictions on trade were lifted, the average tariff was lowered and simplified, foreign investment rules were liberalized, and the external debt was refinanced under the Brady Plan. As regards the public sector, the prices of services and inputs produced were raised, a privatization program was launched, and a tax reform proposal was presented to Congress.

The year 1989 saw a marked contraction of GDP (down 7.9 percent). Annual inflation exceeded 80 percent, and unemployment grew by more than 40 percent. But the fiscal and trade imbalances disappeared. In 1990 the economy began to grow again, thanks to a new expansion of oil revenues as a result of the Gulf War, new investment in the oil industry, and a new macroeconomic environment more favorable to entrepreneurial initiative.

The economic growth experienced in 1990 and 1991 and the political opposition to the public sector reforms prevented full implementation of the tax reform and the privatization program in those years. In 1992 political instability paralyzed the reform program, with the result that the fiscal deficit reappeared in 1993. As political uncertainty continued in 1993, a new slide in oil prices greeted the transition government, which attempted unsuccessfully to introduce some fiscal measures (such as a value-added tax) in the midst of a highly rancorous electoral contest. The year 1993 ended with a 1 percent drop in GDP, inflation outpacing the previous three years at 42 percent, and the reemergence of deficits

Figure 5.1. Venezuela: Unemployment, Real Wages and Economic Growth, 1980-92

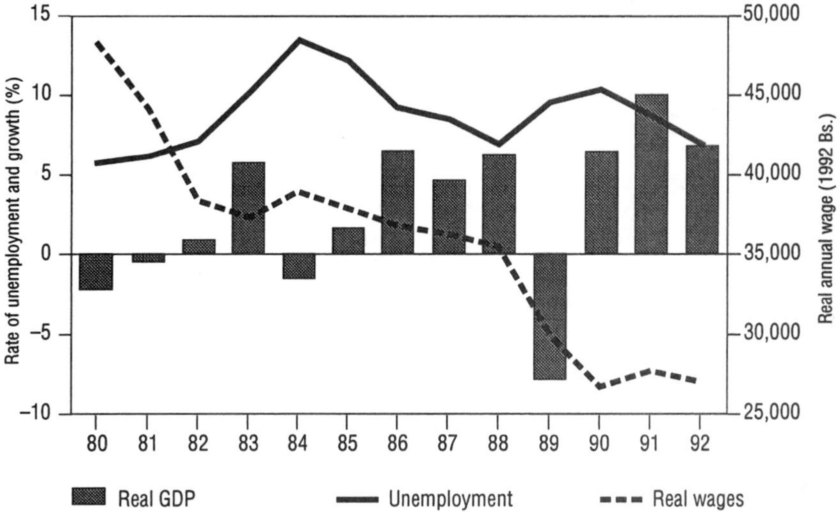

Sources: BCV (1993); Antiveros (1992); OCEI (1980-92b); Márquez, et al. (1993).

in the fiscal account (3.6 percent of GDP) and the current account ($1.8 billion) (Table 5.1).

Against this macroeconomic backdrop, the behavior of the labor market can be divided into two periods. The first, from 1980 to 1985, was marked by economic stagnation with low inflation and growing unemployment. The second, 1986-92, brought economic growth with high inflation and decreasing unemployment, except in 1989 when the adjustment measures were adopted. The increase in unemployment, particularly when economic adjustment programs were introduced (1983-84 and 1989-90), would seem to indicate downward rigidity in real wages (Figure 5.1).

The traditional argument is that if real wages fall enough, the lower labor costs will make it possible to maintain production without any need to reduce employment. Therefore, unemployment should reflect the fact that real wages have not been reduced. However, real wages diminished persistently, falling 25 percent from 1984 to 1992.

The simultaneous existence of unemployment and declining real wages is due to various mechanisms for adjustment among the different segments that make up the labor market. Three occupational segments can be distinguished: formal, divided into public and private, and informal. The public sector accounts for 20 percent of total employment and encompasses government workers and

Table 5.1. Venezuela: Basic Macroeconomic Results, 1980-92
(Percentages)

Year	Real GDP	Open unemployment	Consumer inflation	Public deficit[1]	Current account deficit[2]
1980	-2.0	5.7	21.4	0.0	4.7
1981	-0.3	6.1	16.2	-1.4	4.0
1982	0.7	7.1	9.6	-4.3	-4.2
1983	-5.6	10.2	6.2	-1.5	4.4
1984	-1.4	13.4	12.3	3.3	4.7
1985	1.4	12.1	11.4	5.3	3.3
1986	6.3	9.3	11.5	-2.0	-2.2
1987	4.5	8.5	28.2	-5.5	-1.4
1988	6.2	6.9	29.5	-7.3	-5.8
1989	-7.8	9.6	84.3	-1.2	2.5
1990	6.5	10.4	40.8	0.7	8.3
1991	9.7	8.7	34.2	-5.8	1.7
1992	6.8	7.1	31.4	-3.6	-3.4

Sources: IMF (1992); BCV (1993); Antiveros (1992).
[1] As a percentage of GDP (state enterprises excluded).
[2] In billions of U.S. dollars.

workers in public enterprises. The private formal sector accounts for around 40 percent of all employment and includes workers of businesses with more than five employees and self-employed, university-trained professionals. The informal sector absorbs the remaining 40 percent of those employed, including workers in microenterprises (with fewer than five employees) and all self-employed nonprofessionals (domestic servants, taxi drivers, plumbers, etc.).

The formal public and private sectors are subject to labor law and collective bargaining with the unions. The informal sector, by contrast, is characterized by its lack of labor organization and receives less attention from the law. As a result, the informal sector is more flexible in wage-related matters than the other sectors. In addition, the informal sector has no entry requirements: anyone can go to work for himself or in a microenterprise in the service sector without having accumulated much in the way of material or human capital. Employment in the formal sector, by contrast, requires that the worker undergo a selection process to verify the possession of human capital (appropriate training relevant in the sector) or, in the worst case, personal contacts with employers in the public or private formal sector. It is also easier to leave the informal sector: all one needs is to find a better-paying job in the formal sector. But in the latter, the severance pay that must be provided when the labor contract is terminated is burdensome, so reduction of formal employment has a cost. In some cases regulations even

Table 5.2. Venezuela: Employment and Wage Fluctuations, 1980-92

	Average	Typical deviation	Fluctuation rate (%)
Total			
Employment[1]	5,643.3	764.5	13.5
Real wages[2]	35,661.4	6,257.6	17.5
Public sector			
Employment	1,126.8	93.7	8.3
Real wages	40,408.2	6,982.8	17.3
Formal private sector			
Employment	2,213.0	403.6	18.2
Real wages	39,580.0	6,268.6	15.8
Informal sector			
Employment	2,303.5	319.8	13.9
Real wages	29,414.1	6,567.7	22.3

Source: OCEI (1980-92b).
[1] Thousands of persons employed.
[2] Monthly wages in 1992 Bolivars.

transitorily prohibit the termination of formal employment (permanent tenure).

These features are reflected in Table 5.2, which shows that employment in the public and the informal sectors fluctuates less than in the formal sector. At the same time, fluctuations in average real wages are less pronounced in the informal than in the formal sector. In other words, the informal sector is adjusted by prices, avoiding abrupt drops in employment, while the formal private sector allows wide swings in employment in order to avert such swings in real wages. The greater stability in employment shown by the public sector is due to the legal conditions governing hiring in that sector.

The coexistence of adjustment and unemployment in the formal private sector and of adjustment and real wage reduction in the informal sector causes rising unemployment to coincide with falling real wages. In periods of stagnation the informal sector increases its share of total employment. It then serves as a cyclical shock-absorber in the labor market, as many people who lose their jobs in the formal sector or cannot find work there in a recession take jobs in the informal sector rather than remain unemployed (Figure 5.2). The only ones who remain unemployed are those who can afford the opportunity cost of being unemployed, especially those who have high expectations that they will find a job in the formal sector. Concurrently, the growth of informal employment drives down informal wages because of the increased competition which that creates in the sector. This causes real wages in the informal sector to decline relative to the formal sector (which has remained stable), and this, in conjunction with the expansion of informal employment, drives down total average wages.

Figure 5.2. Venezuela: Economic Growth and the Informal Sector, 1980-92
(Percentages)

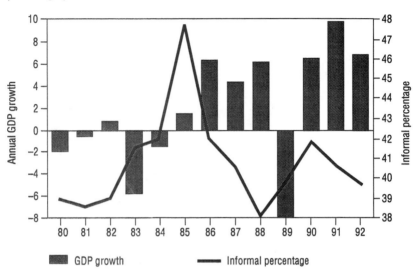

Sources: Antiveros (1992); BCV (1993); OCEI (1980-92b).

The foregoing would explain the decline in real wages accompanying the rise in unemployment in the period 1980-86. But why did real wages continue to fall from 1987 to 1992? The answer is because the nominal wage increases in the formal sector resulting from collective hiring or governmental decree did not offset the period's rising inflation. Thus, although informal employment and the wage differential between formal and informal jobs shrank, real wages in the formal sector fell and the total average wage fell with them (Figure 5.3). This was due to several factors, two of which stand out: the reluctance of the government installed in 1989 to decree general salary and wage increases, and the custom of letting collective bargaining culminate in three-year contracts, which makes it difficult to foresee the nominal wage increases needed to preserve real wages.

All the foregoing data indicate that the Venezuelan labor market is efficient at least in the sense that it is not characterized by inflexible wages that make it impossible to adjust the market without creating unemployment. Perhaps wages did not fall as much or as fast as necessary to eliminate any rise in unemployment, but ultimately they declined in order that unemployment should also diminish. Still, it must be asked to what extent this "flexibility" helped the 1983 and 1989 adjustment programs. In this sense, the recovery of fiscal and external balance requires a flexibility that would permit a reallocation of resources from the nontradable goods sector to the tradable goods sector, and from the public to the private sector.

Figure 5.3. Venezuela: Economic Growth and Income Spread, 1980-92
(Percentages)

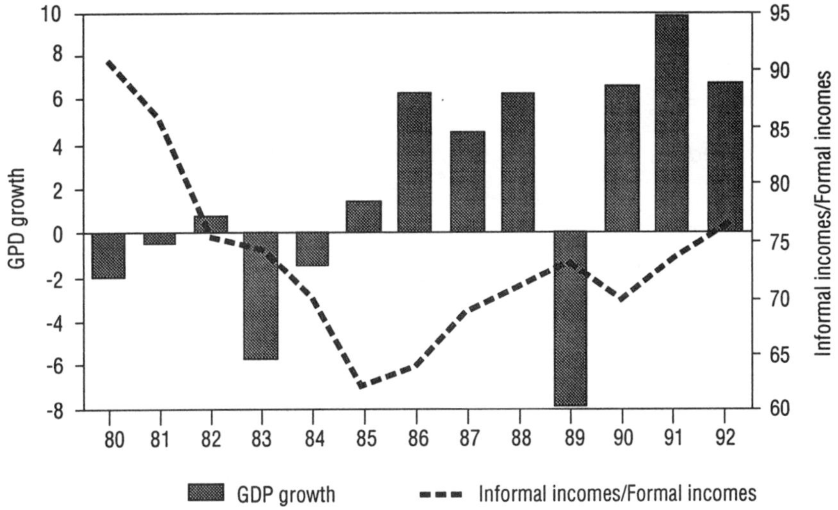

Sources: Antiveros (1992); BCV (1993); OCEI (1980-92b); Márquez, *et al.* (1993).

During the period 1980-92, the breakdown of employment by branches of economic activity shows that substantial changes in resource allocation did actually take place (Table 5.3). First, the data show a drop in agricultural employment and a corresponding rise in employment in financial services and trade. This entails a reallocation of resources from the tradable goods sector to the nontradable goods sector— the opposite of the desired outcome for our purposes. Second, the participation of the public sector has declined slowly but steadily, from a high of 22 percent in 1983 to a low of 18 percent in 1992.

A more detailed reading of the breakdown of employment further discloses a change in the proportion of informal workers in each sector. In the tradable goods sectors, formal employment has increased because of the declining number of informal workers in agriculture (displaced by the liberalization of trade, which has brought more agricultural imports), which has offset the rising number of informal workers in manufacturing. Nevertheless, informal employment has increased in nontradable goods sectors because of the increase of this type of occupation in areas with more employment opportunities, such as trade and financial services.

The Venezuelan labor market is clearly incapable of creating many jobs in the tradable goods sector and the modern private sector. Of all jobs created from 1980 to 1992, only 47 percent were in the formal private sector and 20 percent in

Table 5.3. Venezuela: Employment: Breakdown by Sector, 1980, 1985 and 1992
(Percentages)

Sectors	1980	1985	1992
Agriculture	14.8	16.3	10.9
Informal sector	68.0	70.3	59.8
Mining	1.5	1.3	1.1
Informal sector	5.0	3.6	2.8
Manufacturing	16.0	15.3	16.2
Informal sector	20.0	34.9	23.8
TOTAL TRADABLES	32.2	32.9	28.2
Informal sector	41.3	51.2	37.0
Electricity	1.2	1.2	0.9
Informal sector	2.1	3.5	0.9
Construction	9.1	7.0	8.8
Informal sector	31.9	56.2	41.5
Trade	19.0	19.8	21.9
Informal sector	54.3	66.6	60.5
Transport	7.1	6.6	6.2
Informal sector	48.9	59.2	58.7
Finance	4.4	5.2	6.0
Informal sector	13.3	31.2	22.9
Services	27.0	27.3	28.0
Informal sector	30.6	30.3	54.8
TOTAL NONTRADABLES	67.8	67.1	71.8
Informal sector	37.7	46.2	41.0

Source: OCEI (1980-92b).

the tradable goods sector. These results cast doubt on the "flexibility" of the labor market when it comes to reallocating work among sectors. This phenomenon has two explanations.

First, the difficulty in increasing employment in the tradable goods sector may be due to the insufficiency of the adjustment. In other words, the relative price changes arising from the devaluations of the bolivar begun in 1983 have not triggered a reallocation of factors toward the production of tradable goods. In this sense the labor market would be reacting appropriately to the revaluation of the bolivar beginning in 1989 with reduced employment in the tradable goods sector. Figure 5.4 shows that the rise or fall of employment in the tradable and nontradable goods sector reflects the devaluation or revaluation in real terms of the bolivar throughout the period 1980-1992.

Second, the difficulty of creating jobs in the formal private sector stems from the institutional features that define it. In effect, the formal private sector is subject to the labor laws and is therefore vulnerable to pressure from the govern-

Figure 5.4. Venezuela: Employment in the Tradable Goods Sector and the Real Exchange Rate, 1980-92
(As a percentage of total employment)

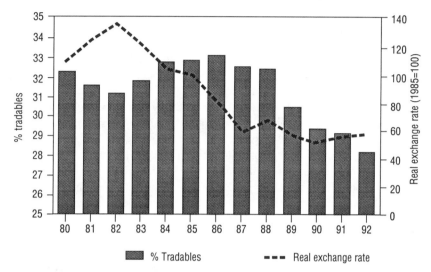

Source: IMF (1993); OCEI (1980-92b).

ment and the unions with respect to setting wages and providing employment.

The foregoing means that the formal private sector has to be very careful in hiring new workers. The formal sector requires workers with the training and experience that will add to the sector's accumulated capital. They must therefore be sufficiently productive to enable the firm to meet the standards established by labor laws with regard to compensation and job security. Labor rules thus affect the ability to generate formal employment. Our study focuses on this aspect of the problem, and in the second section we shall explore in greater depth the effects of the regulations on employment and labor costs.

It can also be argued that the segmentation of the labor market makes it more difficult for new workers to enter the formal sector, which rations jobs in order to protect the wages of those employed in it.

The topic of segmentation is controversial and difficult to contrast empirically. For segmentation to exist, the compensation of two workers with similar characteristics must be different owing to their working in different "segments." It must further be shown that barriers of some sort impede the workers' ability to move from one segment to the other.

Estimations by Márquez, *et al.* (1993) show appreciable differences in the performance of the human capital of the segments that make up the labor market.

Their findings show that education and gender are the most important variables determining a worker's placement in the formal or informal sector, and that some form of self-selection exists among workers. People with higher levels of education tend to find jobs in the formal sector, in which training is better rewarded. Women with little training tend to be employed in the informal sector. If they do succeed in finding work in the formal sector, it tends to be in the public sector. This pattern suggests that the labor market allocates workers efficiently with the aim of maximizing the complementarity between capital and work. The formal private sector, better endowed with physical capital resources, absorbs the most qualified workers. The public sector, preponderantly geared to services and providing the most effective regulations to protect female workers, absorbs a higher proportion of women.

The second aspect of segmentation, the existence of barriers to the mobility of workers between sectors, could not be verified empirically for lack of data. Usage and custom in the labor market do seem to entail some hindrances to mobility between sectors, due mainly to recruitment and selection practices. People who have been employed in the informal or public sectors for a long time do not seem to be easily accepted into the formal private sector.

For the moment we can conclude that "the differences between equilibrium wages and returns on education in each segment indicate that productivity is lower in the informal sector and, therefore, the expansion of the informal sector tends to lower the average productivity of the economy" (Márquez, *et al.* 1993). We do not know whether differences in productivity are aggravated by barriers to mobility, but we can be sure that they reflect a certain difference in the productive characteristics of each sector. Therefore, the elimination of barriers or the reallocation of resources from the informal sector would increase the productivity of the entire economy and help it to overcome its macroeconomic imbalances.

Labor Regulations

In this section we shall evaluate two aspects of Venezuelan labor law. We will start by analyzing the consequences that hiring and firing conditions have for labor costs by examining types of contract, wages and benefits. We will then go on to study the regulations concerning collective disputes and the impact of those regulations on the country's labor relations.

Hiring and Firing

Types of Labor Contracts

Venezuelan law broadly defines labor relations to cover the rights and obligations deriving from the legal ties between employer and employee. These arise from any service personally rendered against compensation, regardless of whether the work originates in a contract or other explicit agreement.

The *Ley Orgánica del Trabajo* (LOT, Organic Law on Labor) provides for three types of contracts: indefinite term, fixed term, and specified work. The last two can be converted into indefinite term contracts: a fixed contract when it has been renewed twice, and a specified work contract when a new contract is signed the month following completion of the former.

Five types of work schedules are provided for, but the most important one involves regular daytime work for eight hours a day, up to a maximum of 44 hours a week. In addition to regular working hours, provision is also made for overtime work hours as permitted by the *Inspectoría de Trabajo* (Office of the Labor Inspector). In this case the number of hours worked per day may not exceed 10, and no more than 10 hours overtime may be worked per week, or 100 per year. Overtime work must be paid at a rate 50 percent higher than regular wages. However, this does not apply to public employees, who are governed by the *Ley de Carrera Administrativa* (LCA, Law on Administrative Careers).

The question is whether these regulations have generated more secure jobs or less use of overtime. Unfortunately we lack precise figures on overtime and job security. However, we can gain some insight into the matter by looking at the number of hours worked per week, as reported by workers in the household survey (Table 5.4). According to this source, the proportion of persons working more than 45 hours a week has gradually declined in recent years.

Throughout the period, the areas showing the most persons working more than 45 hours a day are trade in the case of women, and agriculture, trade and transport in the case of men. These data must however be treated with caution, for a long work day does not necessarily mean that the worker is actually receiving overtime pay.

Minimum Wage

Even though wages can be set under the Law on Labor ever since its original version of 1936, the government has only sporadically made use of this power. Since 1985, accelerating inflation has made such intervention more frequent. In many cases a new minimum wage was accompanied by general salary and wage increases, and other compensation in the form of vouchers. In 1991 the government stopped using these mechanisms and since then has limited itself to setting the minimum wage. The most recent minimum wage was set in May 1994: 5,000 bolivars a month for rural workers and 12,500 for urban workers.

The minimum wage data show that it has lost real value, in bolivars and in dollars, as inflation and devaluation have eroded its purchasing power. Table 5.5 indicates that since 1985 the changes in the minimum wage have not succeeded in maintaining its real value at around Bs.10,000 and $90 a month.

Table 5.4. Venezuela: Workers Working More than 45 Hours per Week, 1982, 1987 and 1992
(Percentages)

Year	Private sector employees		Public sector employees	
	Women	Men	Women	Men
1992	22.6	31.4	12.1	24.8
1987	21.3	37.9	6.7	24.4
1982	35.1	43.2	17.4	31.4

Source: OCEI (1980-92b).

The impact of the minimum wage on the efficiency of the labor market depends on the distance separating the minimum wage from market equilibrium. Theoretically, a minimum wage over the market equilibrium will lead to increased unemployment, since it will leave workers prepared to work for a lower wage jobless. In Venezuela, although average wages declared by workers are above the nominal minimum wage, the percentage of workers with incomes near the minimum wage is not negligible (approximately 30 percent of private sector wage-earners in 1992). Fixing a minimum wage can therefore have some effect on the labor market's efficiency by displacing workers with less experience and training (especially first-time job seekers). An indication of this phenomenon is that during the past decade the unemployment rate among young workers aged 15 to 24 years was at least twice the unemployment rate of those over 24. Likewise, the highest unemployment rates are those for workers with primary education (unskilled laborers).

Payroll Taxes, Wage Vouchers and Nonwage Benefits

Venezuelan labor law establishes several levies on wages designed to finance social and labor protection systems. The following payroll taxes are currently on the books:

- Mandatory social security: in existence since 1946, it consists of contributions to finance cash benefits for disability or partial disability, old age, survivors, and weddings (partial regime), as well as health insurance for workers and their families (general regime), all paid for by the *Instituto Venezolano de Seguridad Social* (IVSS, Venezuelan Social Security Institute).
- Involuntary unemployment insurance: in existence since 1989, it consists of contributions to fund severance pay.
- Housing policy law: in existence since 1990, its contributions accrue in a fund placed in financial institutions devoted to the financing of construc-

Table 5.5. Venezuela: Current Minimum Wage, Real and in Dollars, 1980-92
(In bolivares and U.S. dollars)

Year	Urban minimum wage	Real minimum wage[1]	Wage in US$[2]
1980	900	12,857.1	209.3
1981	900	11,111.1	209.3
1982	900	10,112.4	209.3
1983	900	9,473.7	82.8
1984	900	8,490.6	67.9
1985	1,500	12,711.9	108.8
1986	2,010	15,227.3	90.3
1987	2,010	11,893.5	71.2
1988	2,610	11,972.5	76.7
1989	4,000	9,925.6	101.9
1990	4,000	7,054.7	85.1
1991	6,000	7,884.4	105.3
1992	9,000	9,000.0	132.4

Source: Data originally calculated for this study.
[1] At 1992 prices.
[2] At the free exchange rate.

tion (mortgage banks and savings and loan institutions) with the object of financing homes purchased by contributing workers.

- *Instituto Nacional de Cooperación Educativa* (INCE, National Educational Cooperation Institute): created in 1959 as an autonomous agency under the Ministry of Labor, it provides training and staff development services for the workers of contributing firms.

The contributions by employer and employee, as well as the contribution limits, are shown in Table 5.6. Two considerations about payroll taxes are important in this respect. First, these taxes are paid partly by the worker and partly by the employer. However, the tax burden depends on the elasticity of the labor supply and demand for different groups of workers, regardless of the proportion specified by law. Second, the caps on contributions make these taxes extremely regressive.

Many of these services are perceived by the public as poor in quality and inefficient. As a result many of them are used only by the less well-off workers, while the rest, individually or through collective bargaining, secure private services in these areas.

Three other benefits are paid to workers in addition to those covered by payroll taxes: leave, profit-sharing and transport. The first comprises two parts: one in kind, the other in cash. Payment in kind consists of 15 days' paid vacation

Table 5.6. Venezuela: Payroll Taxes
(Percentages)

	Maximum charge	Employee contribution	Employer contribution	Total
Mandatory social security	Five times the minimum wage	4	Between 11 and 13 (depending on job-related hazards)	15 to 17
Involuntary unemployment insurance	Five times the minimum wage	0.5	1.7	2.2
Law on housing policy	15 times the minimum wage	1	2	3
INCE	Businesses with more than five workers	0.5 of the profit sharing bonus	2 of payroll	

Source: Prepared by the authors.

from the first year of work. The number of days off increases with time in service: one day per year, up to 15 days. Payment in cash consists of seven days' pay plus one additional day per year, up to 21 days. The profit-sharing bonus consists of the worker's share of 15 percent of the firm's liquid profits. The bonus may not be lower than 15 days' or higher than four months' wages (if the business's capital is less than a million bolivars or if it has fewer than 50 employees, the upper limit is reduced to two months). Finally, the transport allowance (Decree 2052, February 21, 1992) consists of Bs. 900 per month for workers earning up to Bs. 9,800 a month and Bs. 500 a month for workers earning Bs. 9,800 to Bs. 15,000 a month.

Other available nonwage benefits are based on firm size, such as day-care centers, cafeterias, study grants, basic schools, transport, residential facilities, and health centers.[1]

---

[1] See LOT, Arts. 108, 224, 241, 242, 243, 245 and 391. Administrative career employees are entitled to receive housing credits from INAVI, bail money, retirement pensions, and training, under Articles 27, 22 and 47-49 of the LCA.

Termination Costs: Prior Notice, Seniority and Double Pay

There are four ways in which a labor contract can be terminated, with differing implications for severance pay: voluntary resignation, resignation for cause, dismissal for cause, and dismissal without cause.

In the case of voluntary resignation, the worker decides of his own accord to resign for personal or work-related reasons. In the case of dismissal for cause, the worker is dismissed for reasons that constitute just cause in terms of conduct or irresponsibility in the performance of his duties. In the case of involuntary resignation the worker decides to resign because of an objectionable action by the employer with regard to the worker's person or work situation, such as reduction in pay, transfer to a lower position, or assignment of work differing from or incompatible with the worker's abilities. Such cases are deemed to constitute "indirect dismissal" and entail the same severance rights as dismissal without cause. Dismissal without cause was defined in the law by exclusion, i.e., termination of the work relationship on the employer's initiative on arbitrary grounds. Just cause for dismissal does not include difficulties encountered by the firm in connection with a downturn in business activity or technological change.

On the other hand, workers are afforded very specific protections against dismissal, transfer, or a worsening of working conditions; these make dismissal impossible under such circumstances as maternity and union privilege.[2] In the former case, a female worker who is pregnant or adopts an infant three years old or younger enjoys tenure during pregnancy and for up to one year following the birth of the child. Union privilege protects workers representing their union as well as those engaged in collective action in defense of their interests.

The National Public Administration (APN) provides only two ways of terminating the work relationship: resignation for cause and removal from office. Severance pay is calculated in the same manner in either case: under the time-in-service provision the worker receives 15 days' wages per year or a fraction of at least eight months, and up to 15 days wages more, depending on time in service, as unemployment assistance. In the APN, resignation for cause has a different meaning because it arises out of a mutual accord between the parties for established causes: desire of the worker, reduction in force, disability, or retirement. Removal from office is the equivalent of dismissal for cause in the LOT. The problem presented by these causes is the tedious and complex administrative procedure required for proof, so that in practice it is found preferable to retain the employee or transfer him or her to another office rather than go through the time and trouble of completing the procedures.

---

[2] Although the LCA does not provide specifically for tenure in such cases, beyond paid leave, it guarantees career civil servants job protection.

While there is no permanent tenure, termination of the labor contract in Venezuela incurs two main costs: prior notice and seniority. Prior notice entails notifying the worker in advance that the contract is to be terminated. It is required only in cases of dismissal without cause or voluntary dismissal, and it varies according to seniority. If prior notice is omitted, the firm must pay the worker an amount in cash equal to the wages of the corresponding period.

Seniority is of greater importance, both in terms of the amount involved and the controversy it has generated.[3] This right is vested in every worker with more than three months of service, and it consists of 10 days' wages if time in service does not exceed six months, or one month's wages for each year of service or a fraction larger than six months. The amount of the social benefits is deposited in an account in the worker's name, either in the firm's accounting office or in an external trust, and accrues interest at a rate determined by the Central Bank of Venezuela.

Seniority-based benefits are paid out only at the time the work relationship is terminated. Advances on it may be granted at the worker's request for the purchase of a home or to pay educational expenses for the worker or the worker's children. These advances, however, do not alter the firm's labor liability, which is calculated only upon completion of the work relationship and from which any advances made are discounted.

It is also important to note that the wages on which calculation of the social benefits is based are "the compensation to which the worker is entitled by virtue of his/her service and include both what is specified by unit of time, by unit of work, or by piece and any commissions, bonuses, gratuities, profit sharing, supplementary wages, and leave allowance, as well as legal or conventional supplements for holidays, overtime, or night work, subsistence allowance if applicable, and any other remuneration or emolument received by the worker for the work performed" (*Ley Orgánica del Trabajo* [LOT], Art. 133). With this provision the law complicates any form of payment that might diminish or evade the generation of seniority-based benefits.

This wage benefit has a substantial impact on the total labor cost and has given rise to a significant difference, in level as well as behavior, between wages and total labor cost. To simplify the analysis, let us ignore other wage and nonwage benefits for the moment and evaluate the total labor cost as the sum of the year's wages and the accrued time-in-service benefits for that year plus the annual interest on the accrued benefits. The total labor cost can be defined by means of the following equation:

---

[3] The term "social benefits" is widely used in the debate on this topic. However, these benefits include not only the time-in-service benefit but also prior notice and leave. For the sake of clarity, therefore, the reference here will be to the time-in-service benefit rather than to "social benefits" in general.

$$CL_t = S_t + VPS_t + CFPS_t$$

where CL_t is the labor cost in the period t, S_t is the annual wage in the period t, VPS_t is the variation in the accrued time-in-service benefit for the period t, and $CFPS_t$ is the financial cost of the accrued benefits. Adding the three components and then the various algebraic transformations and deflating (see Appendix), we see that the real total labor cost is equal to:

$$CLTR = S_1 (1 + s)^{A-1} \{ 1 + \frac{1/12[1=A(p + s + ps) + (A-1)(r-i)]}{(1 + p + s + ps)} \}$$

where the annual inflation rate (p) and real wage increase rate (s) are constant; A represents the worker's years of service in the firm; S_1 is the annual wage at the start of the work relationship, and r,i correspond to the interest rates paid to the workers and obtained by the firm, respectively, through the labor liability accumulated in the preceding year.

In the first place, this formulation shows us that the total labor cost depends on different variables, the inflation of which is beyond the control of the contracting parties, the worker, and the firm. In the second place, the labor costs are a growing function of the worker's time in service, which allows us to infer a very important consequence of this wage benefit: the longer the worker serves with the firm, the greater the difference between what he earns for his work (total labor cost) and what he regularly collects.

A result of this phenomenon is not only that Venezuelan law compels the creation of a deferred wage benefit, but that the benefit as a share of the worker's total income grows with his seniority. It seems difficult to justify a benefit that absorbs, under law, a growing part of the worker's total income, as it may not coincide with the preferred timing of the workers or the firm.

The foregoing assertions are moreover verified by the workers' widespread practice of applying for advances on their benefits. These advances are taken out for many different reasons (often other than those strictly defined by the law), but confirm that the workers' preferred timing does not coincide with the schedule laid down by the law.

Another important point to note is the growth of total labor costs throughout the labor contract. The percentage increase of the real total labor cost is defined as

$$\%CLTR_t = (CLTR_t / CLTR_{t-1}) - 1$$

Following a series of algebraic transformations (see Appendix), it can be demonstrated that for the real labor cost to grow more rapidly than real wages, it suffices for

$$p > [(i-r) - s] / (1+s)$$

Assuming, for simplicity's sake, that the interest rates are equal, the foregoing inequality implies that, given a rate of increase of the real wage equal to zero, any inflation over zero percent will lead to growing real labor costs. In other words, the total labor cost will grow even if the real wages do not grow. It may be inferred that cases could be conceived in which the real wage diminishes even as the real total labor cost grows.

These characteristics of the behavior of wages and labor cost under the system of seniority-based benefits have important consequences for the labor market. In the first place, workers and employers are led to have different views of the same problem. It can happen that the increase (decrease) in wages as perceived by the worker will be smaller (larger) than the increase (decrease) of the real labor cost as perceived by the employer. Obviously, these different perspectives greatly complicate the wage negotiation process. Furthermore, the mechanism for calculating seniority-based benefits has the effect of making real wages much less flexible. This explains employers' reluctance to raise wages significantly, since each wage increase has disproportionate effects on real labor costs: it makes labor costs rise with inflation and seniority.

The law contains elements that seem to intuit the expansive effect of the calculation of seniority-based benefits, as they impose some limits on it. The executive branch can order wage increases in excess of 30 percent not to be considered, in whole or in part, in calculating the benefits.[4] The employers and the unions can also decide, in collective bargaining, that the excess over 20 percent of a wage increase may not be considered in the worker's social benefits. However, these provisions have not been made use of to date.

All the foregoing applies to voluntary resignation and dismissal for cause, but in cases of dismissal without cause or involuntary resignation the cost of terminating the labor contract is known as "double payment." That is to say that in these two cases severance pay consists of 200 percent of the social benefits for seniority and prior notice. If we interpret dismissal without cause as a random event (whose determinants we shall examine further on), labor costs can also be defined as a random variable whose expected value is

$$E [CLT_t] = S_1 + \pi (2PS_t - PS_{t-1}) + (1- \pi) (PS_t - PS_{t-1})$$

where π represents the probability of dismissal without cause. In fact, the greater the probability of dismissal without cause, the greater the expected value of labor

---

[4]As this study was being published, the national government announced an increase in the minimum wage that limited to 30 percent its effect on the accumulation of benefits.

costs. Two sets of factors, economic and legal, may be seen as influencing that probability.

First, economic conditions: recessions or greater foreign competition lower demand by business for labor and therefore increase the need to dismiss workers. Since these economic causes for dismissal are not deemed to be just cause, rising economic instability increases the expected labor cost. By the same token, the Law on Labor specifies that any change in "the existing working conditions" (Art. 103, paragraph 1-1) must be considered an "indirect dismissal," which has the same prerogatives as dismissal without cause. This may require that technological improvements which bring changes in working conditions be considered as giving rise to indirect dismissal.

Formally, the effect of an increase in the probability of dismissal for economic cause is expressed as follows:

$$\frac{\partial [E(CLT_t)]}{\partial \pi} = A/12S_t > 0$$

The foregoing indicates that the greater the worker's seniority, the greater the increase in expected labor costs as a result of the increased probability of dismissal without cause. Therefore, technological changes or an increase in uncertainty and economic risk significantly affect the firms that offer their workers the most job security. Since such firms tend to be the ones that invest the most in staff training, we can infer that the mechanism also affects the incentives to such investment. Theoretically, investment in specific training requires that the present value of the difference between labor cost and its marginal productivity should equal the cost of the training offered. The smaller that difference as a consequence of the increase in the expected labor cost, the less will be invested in training.

In the second place, the characteristics of the law with respect to dismissals and the decisions of labor tribunals in this area can affect the probability of dismissal. Firms must report each dismissal, for or without cause, to the *Tribunal de Estabilidad Laboral* (Labor Security Tribunal), under whose jurisdiction they fall. Following a series of waiting periods and procedures, the court determines whether the dismissal is without cause. However, the process generates a system of incentives to unequal litigation between the parties inasmuch as, for workers earning less than three times the minimum wage or workers who have requested associated judges, the costs of legal counsel are assumed by the Ministry of Labor, even if the workers incur no risks in filing a complaint for dismissal without cause. This gives the worker an incentive to file, which means that the probability π will be high.

This mechanism leaves many firms preferring to pay double severance at the time of dismissal, thus saving themselves legal costs and wages while the case is in process. Ultimately, some observers feel that the mechanism creates incentives to low performance on the workers' part, who can thus seek to induce dismissal with "double pay."

Summary of Hiring and Firing Costs

All of the foregoing information enables us to develop an estimation of labor cost per worker. To that end we apply to the basic wage all payroll taxes and wage and nonwage benefits entailed in hiring the worker and keeping him employed. We assume two workers, both with three years of seniority and earning the minimum wage, one in the public sector and the other in the private sector. Table 5.7 brings out the central points of our analysis throughout the section: less labor cost of the public employee under the Law on Administrative Careers; a small rate of additional cost for female workers; disposable income constituting a low percentage of the worker's total income (76.3 percent for the private sector worker); and accumulated costs for benefits growing with seniority.

Collective Conflicts

Existing Regulations

Public sector workers and public officials enjoy the rights to bargain and engage in collective disputes, contest management measures affecting working conditions, seek redress for noncompliance with collective agreements, petition for a collective agreement, or act in solidarity with another strike.

The law provides for an initial bargaining stage before the conflict is initiated. The purpose of that stage is to seek conciliation based on the previous procedures or with the intervention of the labor inspector participating in the conciliation, without restricting the union's freedom to file a grievance.[5] The demands are collective conflicts when the union, representing the majority of the workers, files the grievance with the Office of the Inspector.

The inspector presents the complaint to the employer and requires that the latter and the union appoint two representatives (plus an alternate for each delegation) to set up the *Junta de Conciliaciones* (Conciliation Board). The inspector presides over the board and has the right to intervene in its deliberations.

---

[5] The employer may file a conciliatory statement based on the firm's economic circumstances, requesting changes in working conditions. This is what is known as *paro patronal* (employer's inability to provide work). The conciliation proceeding may not exceed 15 business days, and if an agreement is reached the changed conditions cannot outlast the period needed to terminate the collective contract, while the workers are protected by tenure.

Table 5.7. Venezuela: Structure of Labor Costs
(Percentage of annual compensation)

	Private employee	Public employee
Basic wage	100.00	100.00
Profit sharing	16.67	12.50
Leave allowance	2.50	0.83
Wage for benefits	119.17	113.33
Transport allowance	10.00	10.00
Day-care centers[1]	16.20	16.20
(Minus) employee's contributions:		
Mandatory social security	4.77	2.27
Involuntary unemployment insurance	0.60	0.57
Law on Housing Policy	1.19	1.13
INCE	0.08	
Worker's disposal income	138.73	135.56
Employer's contributions:		
Mandatory social security	14.30	4.53
Involuntary unemployment insurance	2.03	1.93
Law on Housing Policy	2.38	2.38
INCE	2.38	
Benefits based on seniority[2]	9.93	4.72
Total labor cost	176.39	152.98
Payments in kind (days off):		
Vacation	4.72	4.72
Pre- and postnatal leave[3]	0.80	1.46
Final total labor cost	181.91	159.16

Source: Prepared by the authors.
[1] Equivalent to the maximum amount of compensation (i.e., 38 percent of the minimum wage), multiplied by the probability that a worker will have a child less than six years old in 1992 (the under-six population divided by the economically active population).
[2] This calculation is the minimum cap, since, as explained in the preceding paragraph, the cost for seniority benefits depends on inflation, the increase in the minimum wage, and seniority. Let us assume for simplicity's sake that both inflation and the real wage increase equal zero.
[3] Equivalent to total leave (18 weeks, which represent 34.6 percent of the annual cost), because of the probability of female employment in each sector for 1992 (26.7 percent for employees in the formal private sector and 48.9 percent for public sector employees), and because of the fertility rate weighted by the age distribution of women employed in 1992 (8.61 percent).

In conjunction with those procedures, the workers may exercise their right to call a strike, defined as a collective work stoppage, once 120 consecutive hours have passed following the filing of the complaint with the Office of the Inspector. The workers are protected by tenure as of that moment. Although the period occupied by the strike counts in computing seniority, the work relationship is suspended during the conflict and consequently the employer is not obligated to pay compensation, while the workers are not obligated to perform services. The workers may indeed not stay in the workplace unless they are performing health services or services connected with the upkeep and maintenance of equipment.

The life of the Conciliation Board depends on whether unanimous agreements are reached or conciliation is found to be impossible, so that the strike can be indefinite. The board's recommendations can take the form of specific settlement terms or suggest arbitration. If the latter is not agreed upon, the board's president must propose it, and the acceptance of the proposal entails the creation of the *Junta de Arbitraje* (Arbitration Board) in the office of the labor inspector,[6] which has the same investigative powers as a regular court. Questions are decided by majority vote, or otherwise the president's vote prevails.

A particular case arises from conflicts arising in public services, as the executive branch may suspend strikes that might endanger the lives and security of the public, and submit the matter to binding arbitration.

Contradictions and Gaps in the Regulations

The regulations governing collective conflicts are very complex and not altogether clear. In this connection the ILO (1992) has pointed out two problems: the diversity of standards and peaceful settlement bodies, and the excessively prominent role of the inspectors.

The first problem can be illustrated by the fact that in major conflicts such as, for example, the cases in 1993 involving VIASA, PDVSA, and the Ministry of Education, it was the minister or the vice minister who directly intervened as mediator in the Conciliation Board. In other cases the Office of Labor, the National Office of the Inspector, the Office of Policy Coordination and Legal Services, and other departments of the Ministry of Labor were brought into the proceedings without clear mandates, causing overlap in the board's efforts.

Agency officials can also intervene in conflicts between and within unions brought before the labor courts. Similarly, disputes over the interpretation of clauses in collective contracts can be handled by the tribunals through declaratory action but also in the ministry's legal services office. This shows how many agencies can get involved without proper coordination, with consequent confusion between administrative measures and judicial decisions.

---

6 With one member chosen by the employer from a short list presented by the union, another by the union, and the third by both (president). If no agreement is reached on the short list, the inspector may take a "summary" decision and make the appointment. The arbitrators may not be individuals directly related to the parties in the conflict, nor may they be connected by bonds of kinship in the fourth degree of consanguinity or the second degree of affinity.

The decision-making functions assumed by the Ministry of Labor in settling disputes, which should properly be left to judicial authorities, have indeed been found to be in conflict with the principle of the separation of the three powers of the state (ILO, 1992).

In addition to these problems, analysis of the implications of the regulations raises questions concerning their consistency in the light of certain contradictions and gaps. We shall examine the most important ones.

The main source of confusion lies in the combination of bargaining, collective conflicts, and the collective agreement under a single system. The logical structure presents difficulties in interpretation. In fact, the collective agreement is approached after the bargaining and the collective conflicts, and since it is also subject to disputes, it also calls for settlement measures. The sequence would seem to indicate that the strike is a mechanism following conciliation and arbitration; but the time limit for launching the strike is 120 hours, so that it can be called almost immediately after the formal conciliation has begun.

The marked preference for union action has eliminated the possibility that unorganized groups of workers might bargain, handle conflicts, and conclude collective agreements. Nor can workers at small businesses exercise these rights, as they necessarily entail union intervention, but forming a union in turn requires a minimum of 20 workers.

As the ILO (1992) points out, no distinction is made between bargaining (as a process voluntarily engaged in by the social partners) and the conflict itself as a subsequent step in the intervention of a third party. This is because, despite the importance of the initial collective bargaining prior to the conflict, in most cases intervention by the Office of the Inspector occurs once it has been declared.

Furthermore, the short time available for finalizing agreements before the strike encourages their indiscriminate use. In practice the conflict and the strike are declared without the employer having refused to negotiate. Nor is there any limit on the duration or on the actions that the workers can carry out.

Arbitration appears to get short shrift in the proceedings, and this is reflected in the few cases that normally occur, unless they have been mandatory. Nor do the regulations clarify what ought to be submitted for arbitration; generally they decide on issues that have not been brought to conciliation, and the arbitrators tend to split the difference when considering the parties' proposals.[7]

The gaps and contradictions in the collective rights of the public sector workers begin with the failure to define the employees on whom those rights are conferred. Apparently they apply to those who hold "career positions," which implies that not only the national civil service but also provincial, municipal and local public employees are included.

---

[7] Interview with Dr. Juan Carlos Larrañaga.

The problem is how to pinpoint "public agencies" in general. It must be asked if this means that the workers of public agencies with special regulations and excluded from the administrative career laws, regulations, and directives (such as faculty members of the national universities) also enjoy these rights under the LOT.

One of the substantive problems in regard to bargaining and strikes for public employees is the incompatibility of these rights with the powers of the unions. The latter are regulated by administrative standards with innocuous functions such as the protection of rights established in the LCA. By contrast, making use of the collective rights conferred by the LOT entails union intervention as well as surpassing the established benefits. This shows that there are discrepancies between the standards applied in different jurisdictions.

The confusion is greater in areas subject to collective bargaining. Everything pertaining to income, promotion, transfer, furlough, separation, compensation, job security and jurisdiction as set forth in the LOT must be governed by the LCA. In this sense it has been felt that their regulation through collective contracts "is simply unconstitutional" (Caballero, 1991), since what ultimately counts is what the law specifies. Apparently a large number of collective contracts are unconstitutional because one of the most frequent clauses has to with compensation. Nevertheless, some sectors long prominent in union activities, which have succeeded in establishing parallel labor regulations such as education and health, legally escape this restriction. The pertinent question is whether other issues drive public employees to initiate the lengthy and tedious collective bargaining process in which so many government agencies make their weight felt.

Interpretations and opinions diverge widely on the subject of gaps in the treatment of strikes in public agencies. It is not known when collective rights can be deemed "compatible with the type of services" performed by the workers. "Public services" are not defined, and it is not spelled out which ones are "subject to this law," or what types of injury are "irremediable to the public or to institutions" (LOT, Art. 496). It may be assumed that the public would name health and some urban services such as water supply, but it is not known whether it would include education, communications, etc., and it is more difficult to speculate as to what the term "institutions" refers.

There are also unanswered questions in the area of processing. The LOT prescribes that when a conflict is declared in some public service or agency, the inspector must inform the Office of the Attorney General of the Republic "for the appropriate purposes" (Art. 474). It is not clear what purposes and procedures are referred to, for apart from this law there is only a partial regulation specifying the steps to be taken in the negotiation of collective contracts covering public employees. But, as we have seen, a conflict can also arise for other, different reasons, and not every bargaining procedure necessarily implies a conflict.

The participation of the Attorney General's office as mediator and representative of the nation also makes it more difficult to ensure the neutrality of the third party intervening in the conflict. This tends to engender intransigence on the part of the union.

Another problem is the failure to define the parameters by which to measure a strike's scope, seriousness and length. This has created uncertainty as to when and under what circumstances the executive branch can order strikers back to work and call for binding arbitration.

These difficulties are compounded by the nonenforcement of disciplinary measures aimed at illegal strikes. No references exist regarding penalties applied to illegal strikers (five to 20 days of police detention, LOT Art. 640). The penalties established by the Penal Code (Art. 209) for public employees in improper strikes (fine and suspension from their jobs for up to two years) are not enforceable either.[8]

Even in legal strikes, the forfeiting of wages is not complied with. This creates an incentive for the indiscriminate use of strikes, for in the final analysis the costs are borne, on the one hand, by the state through the administrative expenditures of the Ministry of Labor and other agencies concerned and, on the other, by businesses, which in addition to having to halt production, pay back wages and contribute so-called "union expenses" to workers' organizations.[9]

Quantification of Strikes

During the democratic period (1959-92) only 175 legal strikes were recorded as against 2,655 illegal ones, with an average of 131 grievances filed annually. According to the ILO (1992), these figures show a low degree of labor unrest in comparison with other Latin American countries.

In historical terms, conflicts are tied more to political than to economic factors (Figure 5.5). During the first 10 years of the democratic regime (1958-68) the *pacto de punto fijo* (fixed-point pact) ensured a period of labor peace. That alliance between the state and the various economic and social sectors that had taken part in the overthrow of the dictatorship of 1958 was intended to perpetuate democracy. It promoted development designed to achieve industrialization through import substitution, modernization, and economic and social diversification.

The unions became an appendage of the political parties, especially AD, and their leaderships were increasingly co-opted by the pact, so that the labor movement lost much of its contentiousness.

---

[8] References exist regarding isolated cases of dismissal or harassment of union activists after a conflict.

[9] A report that union expenses are apparently used for the personal benefit of union officers (interview with the attorney Francisco Iturraspe) could not be corroborated.

Figure 5.5. History of Collective Conflicts in Venezuela, 1959-92

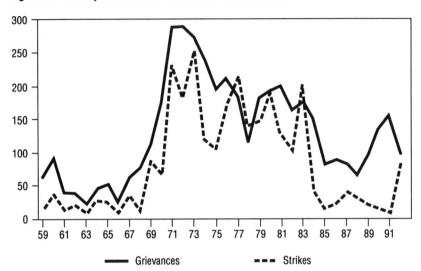

Source: Ministry of Labor (1958-92).

Surprisingly, the number of grievances began to increase in 1969. In that year the AD was voted out of office after governing the country for two presidential terms, and Rafael Caldera, founder of the Social Democratic Party COPEI, became the new president. Caldera reestablished control over the labor movement, replacing the union militants who had founded the MEP party in 1967. Labor resisted the new government, calling strikes in several sectors of the country. CODESA, the workers' confederation created by COPEI, split in 1971 with the creation of the CGT. This weakened union support for the governing party. Given those circumstances, it is no accident that the years from 1969 to 1973 saw the largest number of grievances and strikes in the history of the country.

With the election of Carlos Andrés Pérez, AD's dominant role in the labor movement was reinforced, despite the fact that the party's Labor Office leaned more toward a faction that supported former president Rómulo Betancourt. It should be noted that in the first Pérez administration (1974-78) the state expanded its role as producer and the oil and iron industries were nationalized in conjunction with the effort to maintain political unity, which was cracking.

Some analysts have attributed this fact to the internal contradictions of that government's socioeconomic development model, which was causing splits among the sectors that had backed the "tacit pact." The government was promising economic and social democracy with measures like a minimum daily wage equivalent to $3.60, a full employment policy, and price controls on basic necessities, to name a few. But at the same time it was devising economic restructuring plans to develop the third phase of the import-substitution industrialization process, with the state as producer (Sontag, 1984).

During this period, some workers' movements not tied to the CTV sprang up, as the latter was showing signs of weakness in the correlation of forces that had been dominant since 1958. The labor situation continued along the same path during the presidency of Herrera Campins (1979-83), despite the aggressive attitude of the unions toward a government in which the AD was not the ruling party. In the midst of that strife, COPEI and AD came to an understanding over control of the CTV, which then attained complete dominance (Larrañaga, 1993).

Collective conflicts abated considerably during the administration of Jaime Lusinchi (1984-88), in spite of the recession. The reasons were basically the entire support of AD's *Oficina Sindical* (Union Office) as soon as Lusinchi announced his candidacy, and his relative success with the social pact (Ellner, 1990). That party's practically absolute control of the executive committee of the CTV in 1985 was what ensured labor peace.

The situation varied substantially during the second presidency of Carlos Andrés Pérez (1988-93). Labor leaders did not figure prominently in his nomination, as they had in the case of other AD candidates (Ellner, 1990). This became a factor in the increase in grievances and, surprisingly, legal strikes numbered 55 in 1992, after never having gone over seven in the two preceding decades. It should be noted that two attempted military coups took place in the country that year, accompanied by intense protest actions and popular demonstrations.

Agency Interventions in Labor Relations

Decision-making in labor matters is in the hands of the executive branch. The Ministry of Labor handles administrative affairs and the Central Personnel Office (OCP) supervises the LCA. Areas subject to dispute, except for conciliation, arbitration and issues assigned to the labor inspection offices, are under the jurisdiction of the labor and job security tribunals, while the administrative career tribunal and the judicial bodies handling administrative disputes have jurisdiction over the APN.

Ministry of Labor

The administration of labor is excessively centralized. The Ministry of Labor acts as go-between in complaint proceedings and conflicts. It supervises, monitors and sanctions, and at the same time must take part in designing employment and wage plans and introducing bills in that regard. Its institutional capacity is questioned, as it experiences difficulties in applying controls and asserting leadership in mediating labor relations.

Figure 5.6. Venezuela: Budget of the Ministry of Labor, 1980-92
(Millions of 1992 bolivares)

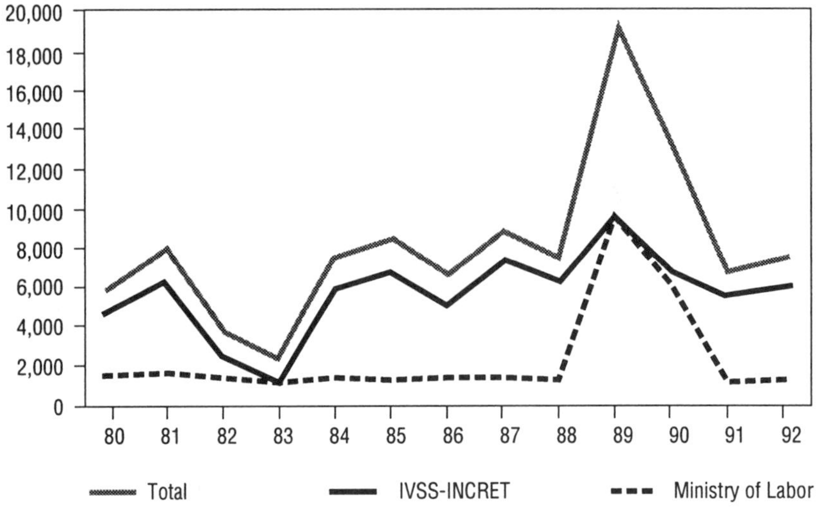

Source: OCEPRE (1980-93).

Budgetary Resources

One of the problems of labor administration in several countries is scarcity of resources (Sheehan, 1992). Such is the case in Venezuela. From 1980 to 1992 the ministry's total revenues amounted to only 0.16 percent, because of the strong absorption by part of the social security program (Figure 5.6).

Human Resources

Administrative personnel predominates: there are three for every professional. The majority have a low educational background (up to 11 years of school) and earn low pay. Some have positions involved with important programs, such as the commissioners of the inspection offices and the industrial safety inspectors (Figure 5.7).

The technical staff consists mainly of lawyers. Their pay is low (Bs. 17,520 and Bs. 30,599) (Table 5.8) in comparison with the national average in the private sector (Bs. 26,487) and self-employed professionals (Bs. 52,568) (OCEI, 1980-92b).

High- and mid-level supervisory staff also includes professionals. They are freely appointed and removed based on political considerations or the decisions of their superiors. This, added to the high turnover among senior staff, does not ensure operational continuity.

Figure 5.7. Venezuela: Employees of the Ministry of Labor, 1993

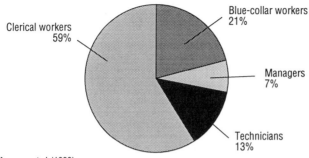

Source: Marquez, *et al.* (1993).

Despite the low pay and staff qualifications, there are no incentives or training programs. In 1992, no more than 2.4 percent of staff were promoted (Ministry of Labor, 1993a), and from 1990 to 1992 the already tiny number taking courses decreased by 50 percent (Table 5.9).

Labor Inspection Offices

These are part of the *Dirección General Sectorial del Trabajo* (Sectoral General Directorate of Labor), which receives a sizable budget allocation (21.8 percent in 1992) to run the largest but not necessarily the most effective program. Beyond formalities, the labor inspector acts as conciliator, administrative judge, union registrar, mediator, inspection chief,[10] and administrator of personnel (ILO, 1992).

Over-emphasis on mediation of labor-management relations, as reflected in the inefficient system for the collection of fines,[11] has weakened labor inspection, with the result that inspection does not constitute an effective means of protection (Figure 5.8).

The installed capacity is inadequate. Until 1992 only 42 labor inspection offices were in place in all of Venezuela to cover at least 2,751,800 modern private sector workers. With the highest percentage of nonprofessional employees—82 percent (Ministry of Labor, 1993b)—the program is also short of qualified staff, and the chief inspector as well as the operative division coordinators hold posts under party and union control.[12]

---

[10] The social security and involuntary unemployment insurance programs are inspected by IVSS, and a general directorate of the ministry oversees industrial safety.

[11] Some studies have revealed possible corruption during inspections (ILO, 1992; Pérez, 1985b).

[12] The divisions include Inquiries and Claims, Women and Minors, Union Privilege, Collective Contract, Union, Sanctions, and Conciliation.

Table 5.8. Venezuela: Wages in the Ministry of Labor, 1993

Staff categories	Salary range
Managers and supervisors	7,488 - 99,800
Technicians (mid-level and university graduates)	17,520 - 30,599
Clerical and support personnel	9,000 - 17,384
Blue-collar workers	11,340 - 18,660

Source: Márquez, *et al.* (1993).

Table 5.9. Venezuela: Staff Training, Ministry of Labor, 1990-92

	1990	1991	1992
Participating departments	7	13	16
Attending employees	250	159	125
Courses	14	33	32
Hours of instruction	2,911	1,411	1,544
Most frequent course (% of trainees)			
Spelling	62.8		
Secretarial improvement		35.2	
Information technology			52.8
Total cost (thousands of Bs)	121.9	395.4	782.8
Percentage of budget[1]	0.005	0.04	0.06

Source: Márquez, *et al.* (1993).
[1]Ministry of Labor without IVSS and INCRET.

Labor Attorneys

Free legal aid to workers is a service offered by the ministry under the Organic Law on Labor Tribunals and Procedures. Prior to LOT, the ministry intervened weakly to defend workers with individual claims after the labor relation was completed.[13] When the tripartite commissions[14] were eliminated, their personnel joined the attorneys' offices. Hence the latter were elevated from a marginal slot in the Sectoral General Directorate of Labor to a category of similar rank. They started with 62 attorneys' offices, but by late 1992 there were 111.

---

[13] The APN is not served by the attorneys.

[14] These came into being with the Law Against Dismissals Without Cause (1975) and consisted of a workers' representative, an employers' representative, and a chair appointed by the ministry.

Figure 5.8. Venezuela: Fines Assessed by the Labor Inspection Offices, 1980-92

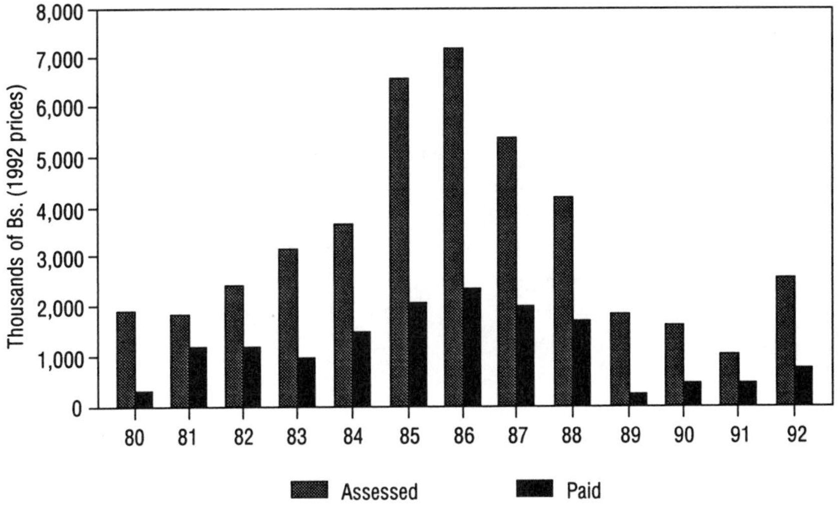

Source: Ministry of Labor, 1958-92.

Lawyers in the attorneys' offices are not required to have experience in litigation and some are recent law school graduates, so a first-rate defense is not guaranteed. Defendants, by contrast, hire private, specialized counsel. The performance by the attorneys' office lawyers in the courtroom has not greatly impressed the labor and union attorneys.[15] The attorneys' increasing participation in these proceedings is due more to changes in the treatment of job security, hence their activity expanded by 86 percent from 1989 to 1992. But for the latter year 49 percent of the accumulated claims were in process (Ministry of Labor, 1958-92).

The attorneys often perform the task of furnishing legal opinions. It should be noted that there is also an inquiries and claims division in the inspection offices, but communication between the two entities is rather poor. In a further overlap, the ministry's office of legal services also answers inquiries from the unions or other officials of the agency.

---

[15] Pérez (1985b) and the interviews with the lawyers Alejandro di Silvestro and Francisco Iturraspe coincide in these assessments.

Unemployment Insurance

Shortcomings in implementation are a continuing concern. Coverage is very low, and expenditure in relation to GDP is tiny (Table 5.10). The very role of unemployment insurance is being questioned: beneficiaries are not receiving payments cn time, public employment agencies are doing little to help or find new work for the unemployed, and training plans are nonexistent.

The problems stem from imprecise definitions of insurance and institutional limitations. With respect to the former, insurance has been viewed more as a palliative to ease the plight of the unemployed than as a coherent means of fighting unemployment. Its proper operation cannot be ensured if the agencies charged with managing and administering it (Ministry of Labor and IVSS) are not appropriately structured for those purposes.

The institutional limitations are of two types: administrative and coordination-related. IVSS's administrative problems have affected the financial situation of the involuntary unemployment insurance program because of the absence of an internal control system, shortcomings in billing and collection, transfer of funds for medical assistance, and weaknesses in the reporting system.

Four problems exist from the standpoint of institutional coordination: (i) management, monitoring and control have been overlooked; (ii) working guidelines have not been clearly laid down; (iii) authorities within the responsible agencies have not provided interagency coordination; and (iv) no training of beneficiaries of unemployment insurance has been initiated despite the existence of an agreement between the ministry and INCE.

Labor and Job Protection Tribunals

Superior and first instance labor tribunals and the job security tribunals are under the authority of the *Consejo de la Judicatura* (Judicature Council). The former date from the Law on Labor of 1936 and the latter arose from LOT, but both are currently merged and have jurisdiction in matters of job security.

Handling job security through administrative channels did not prove efficient. The process was exceedingly slow in the tripartite commissions; by 1990 more than half the cases filed since 1976 had not been settled and only 19 percent had been formally decided (Ministry of Labor, 1993a).[16]

Currently the procedure begins with the employer notifying the tribunal, within five business days, of the cause for the dismissal. In that same period the worker may file a grievance alleging that the dismissal was without just cause, but only if he/she did not receive double severance pay.

---

[16] The 158,081 cases pending in 1990 were referred to the inspection offices Their present status is unknown.

Table 5.10. Venezuela: Involuntary Unemployment Insurance, 1990-92

	1990	1991	1992
Coverage			
Contributors	2,431,694	2,524,443	2,448,289
Unemployed	655,097	626,134	481,717
Coverage (%)	26.9	24.8	20.0
Beneficiaries	463,394	364,510	309,294
Severance payments (millions of Bs.)			1,902
Paid	3,182	1,895	4,371
Pending		1,929	
Unemployment insurance/ OIB expenditure (%)	—	0.0	0.0

Sources: Comisión de Reestructuración del IVSS (1993); BCV (1993); IVSS (1991-92); OCEI (1980-92a, 1980-92b).

When the grievance has been filed, the judge cites the employer to reply within five business days. If conciliation is unsuccessful, the case is opened to evidence, or the judge may rule that the decision will be rendered without taking evidence. In the former case there will be three business days to introduce evidence. The parties may also request, within a time limit of five business days following the evidentiary period, that a panel of judges be seated.[17] A decision in favor of the worker entitles him to reinstatement and back pay,[18] but if the employer insists on dismissing him, he has to pay double severance pay and give prior notice.

Job security proceedings would appear to be short. However, they last no less than two years in first instance.[19] Others of a different sort, such as those requiring a calculation of benefits, last three years and six months on average.[20] Other studies also indicate that a labor proceeding generally lasts between two and four years (Pérez, 1985b). No reliable data exist on their actual duration or on the types of final decision. The only information available shows that not all cases filed with the tribunals are resolved in that same year (Table 5.11), but there are even fewer "resolutions" because lapsed (not pursued by the parties), adjudicated, and discontinued cases, as well as cases settled by compromise, are included.

---

[17] If the employer requested the panel or his arguments fail, he must pay the panel's fees, but if the worker requested the panel or his allegations are rejected, the ministry pays the costs should the court rule against reinstatement.

[18] Reinstatement does not apply for businesses with fewer than 10 workers.

[19] Interview with Leida Cerezo, Coordinator of Labor Attorneys of the Federal District, and attorney Alejandro de Silvestro.

[20] Of 80 cases in process assigned to a private consultant, all have been ongoing for more than three years since the grievance was filed (interview with attorney Alejandro di Silvestro).

Table 5.11. Venezuela: Labor Tribunals, 1984-92

	1984	1985	1986	1987	1988	1989	1990	1991	1992
First instance									
Filed	4,836	4,677	4,889	4,404	4,815	5,160	5,768	20,398	35,302
Settled	3,579	3,662	4,234	4,726	4,628	4,388	5,593	8,012	16,561
Superior									
Filed	873	930	1,078	1,201	1,236	1,349	1,472	2,394	2,652
Settled	879	807	1,016	1,227	1,137	1,160	1,339	1,874	2,553
Intervention Attorneys' Offices (%)	2.4	1.9	2.7	3.0	3.3	9.7	—	—	—

Source: OCEI (1980-92a).

Venezuela has 31 superior labor and job protection tribunals and 68 tribunals of first instance (Consejo de la Judicatura, 1993), so that each may potentially be required to cover at least 27,618 private sector employees and workers. The needs are much greater than the means available to meet them.

Administrative Career Tribunal[21]

The Administrative Career Tribunal dates from 1970. It is part of the administrative disputes settlement system and it is governed by the Organic Law of the Supreme Court of Justice and the Code of Civil Procedure.

There is only one Administrative Career Tribunal, located in Caracas, and in 1991, for example, it was faced with a potential nationwide demand of 221,070 public employees (OCP, 1992b). [22] It has three judges who are members of the bar, and the basic average salary of the staff in 1993 was Bs. 21,563, or less than the average income of the public sector (Bs. 29,674).

Trials in the Administrative Career Tribunal last no less than one year and have been known to last 10 years, with the average at approximately four years. Among the factors explaining the length of these proceedings are the small num-

---

[21] Interviews with Dr. Jorge Dugarte, Presiding Judge of the Administrative Career Tribunal, and attorney Belkis Briceño.

[22] Workers can file their grievances with the civil courts and then go on to the court with jurisdiction over their case. But usually they go to Caracas personally, which again reflects the excessive centralization and concentration of the judicial system.

ber of judges in relation to the caseload, the low qualifications of the attorneys assisting the workers,[23] and the scarcity of equipment.

Filings doubled in the period from 1990 to 1992. Grievances pour in relentlessly and the judges, unable to dispose of their caseloads in one year, have increased from three to four the number of cases in process for each judgment handed down (Tribunal de Carrera Administrativa, 1990-92). At present the situation is even more serious: according to the presiding judge, in May 1993 there were about 3,000 cases outstanding.

The slow pace of the process has prompted complainants to give up on their cases, and the number of cases halted between 1990 and 1992 climbed by 32.5 percent. Execution of judgments is not immediate either. Only 302 were executed in 1992, out of 618 handed down, in addition to those that had not been enforced in previous years (Tribunal de Carrera Administrativa, 1990-92). This costs the nation money, for if reinstatement is decreed, which is the usual outcome, the state has to give the employee severance pay for the entire period of litigation until the execution of the judgment.

Union Organizations

Union freedom is guaranteed in the National Constitution (Arts. 91 and 92) in the form of a set of rights, guarantees and powers. One of the more important rights is free association in union organizations (LOT, Art. 400).

Mechanisms for control by the state exist in spite of union freedom. Unions must be legalized by the Office of the Labor Inspector (LOT, Arts. 425 and 426) or, in the case of public employee unions, by the Ministry of Labor (Arts. 6 and 13).[24] They are required to disclose changes in their bylaws, submit an annual administrative report and a complete membership list, and provide information on their legal obligations (LOT, Art. 403).

Financing comes from four sources. The first two are dues by members and the solidarity contributions or collective bargaining fees charged to nonmembers who benefit from the collective contract. The latter source is not available to public employee unions, but their regulations include the acquisition of property for any purpose. The other two sources are not legal: employers' contributions to pay for collective bargaining costs incurred by unions,[25] and the state subsidy.

---

[23] Of 1,000 attorneys who generally defend public employees before this tribunal, only 10 percent are considered of "good quality" (interview with Presiding Judge Jorge Dugarte).

[24] In matters of unionization, public employees are governed by the regulations concerning public employee unions (1971).

[25] These funds usually cover personal benefits for union officers (interview with attorney Francisco Iturraspe).

At present the size of unions in Venezuela is not known. The only available statistics come from the ministry's legalization records, and the exact level of union membership is therefore impossible to state. Some have estimated it at 20 to 30 percent of the labor force, but more conservative estimates, such as that of Rafael Alfonzo Guzmán, put it at 10.73 percent for 1986. The greatest union strength is apparently found in the public enterprises, in some sectors of the civil service, and in professional associations (ILO, 1992).

Two features are particularly important in union organization in Venezuela: the marked pluralism and the close and dependent connection with political parties and the state. Pluralism is reflected in the existence of four federations, each with a different ideology.[26]

The various groups are supported and strongly dominated by a political party. The most visible point of contact between the largest confederation (CTV) and party activity consists of 10 AD leaders with seats on the 17-member executive committee. The relationship is a reciprocal one, with the *Oficina Sindical* (Union Office) also playing a leading role in the internal affairs of AD since 1958.[27] This is not a new development, however, for the development of the union movement is directly related to the history of the political parties (Larrañaga, 1993).

The unions are tied not only to the parties but also to the state. State subsidies are based on the specific considerations of importance and parliamentary representation, and many union officers are members of parliament (22 regular deputies and 28 substitutes between 1984 and 1989). It is not a coincidence that the regional officers of the Ministry of Labor are nominated by the party's union office, and even the minister needs the support of the CTV and the union office (Ellner, 1990).

This high degree of politicization has given rise to a number of problems mentioned by Larrañaga (1993). Some of these are elections of the third and fourth grade with little rank-and-file participation; dual political discourse with incoherent public action; leadership, representation and credibility problems; educationally and technically ill-prepared leaders; lack of consultation in decision-making; and a lifestyle among the top leadership inconsistent with their mission and social role. All this has tended to weaken the capacity to mobilize members and advance their interests, and it has concurrently encouraged bureaucracy and undermined the unions' credibility.

---

[26] The social democratic CTV, the Christian democratic CGTV, the humanist and independent CODESA, and the socialist and communist CUTV. There is also a Coordinating Committee of Independent Union Organizations or *Coordinadora de Organizaciones Sindicales Independientes* as well as some groups called New Unionism or *Nuevo Sindicalismo*, under the banner of the *Causa Radical* party.

[27] AD's union office has supported the candidates who were subsequently selected by the party for four of the six presidential elections (until 1988), and it has also had a hand in the appointment of labor leaders to the party's general secretariat (Ellner, 1990).

Policy Recommendations

Raising the productivity of workers is imperative if the Venezuelan economic crisis is to be resolved. This can be changed in two ways: first, by reallocating jobs from less productive to more productive sectors (from nontradable to tradable goods, from the public to the private sector, and from the informal to the formal sector); and, second, by increasing investment in worker education and training. However, as we explained in the first section, reforms adopted up to now have not enabled the labor market to achieve those objectives. That has been due both to inadequate macroeconomic adjustment and to the nature of existing labor law.

An extensive debate on how to bring about adequate macroeconomic adjustment is in progress. However, the assessment made in the second and third sections of labor law and the institutions that play a part in the labor market point to a field of action different from that of macroeconomic policy. The existence of a body of rules that makes it difficult to raise productivity signals a need for change. By the same token, changing the rules is not enough if the institutions applying and supervising them are not changed as well.

Our analysis demonstrates that the regulatory and institutional framework of the labor market needs reform in three general areas:

- The conditions governing hiring and firing must be reformed so as not to put obstacles in the way of formal employment, investment in training, and cooperation between the social partners.
- The rules governing collective conflicts must be reformed to make them more specific and avert arbitrary decisions or disparate interpretations of the process, and also to provide incentives not to resort to strikes.
- The agencies supervising and enforcing labor law must be reformed so that they will permit the creation of a safety net for workers as an efficient replacement for current protection mechanisms.

With respect to the conditions governing hiring and firing, a first recommendation is that the seniority-based benefits system be modified. These benefits, originally designed as an unemployment insurance and retirement compensation system, do not fully meet either of those purposes. On the contrary, they only reduce workers' take-home pay and raise labor costs in ways neither the employee nor the employer can control. Furthermore, the "double payment" of benefits greatly raises the propensity of both sides to dissolve the labor contract while lowering their propensity to work in concert and to invest in training.

Elimination of seniority-based benefits, the inclusion of economic and technological grounds as just cause for dismissal, and changes in the conditions governing job security proceedings will lead to more disposable income for workers, facilitate labor negotiations (by simplifying the way both sides view labor costs and encouraging them to work in concert), and spur invest-ment in training.

Obviously, this course may lessen job security by making workers more vulnerable to fluctuations in business activity, but it will reduce insecurity due to incentives created by regulations. It is therefore necessary to create institutions capable of doing effectively what the current system is not: providing unemploy-ment insurance, retirement and health insurance, and incentives and facilities for investment in training and staff development.

To that end, payroll taxes must be revised to correct the regressive nature of the present system as well as strengthen the finances of the entire security sys-tem. Whether through private unemployment, retirement and health insurance, or through mixed public and private systems, the current payroll taxes should be replaced by a set of contributions chosen by the worker and representing true value for the services mentioned.

A special feature of that network of social services is an unemployment insurance system combining severance pay, training, and a return to work. As we explained in the third section, the basic objective is to raise the technical potential of human capital, reshape it in accordance with the needs of the mar-ket, and reduce the period of unemployment as much as economic circum-stances will permit. Unlike the penalties for dismissal, this would make the firm's labor costs independent of unfavorable changes in demand through a charge on the value of the payroll. The following institutional changes are needed (Márquez, *et al.*, 1993):

- Separate the involuntary unemployment insurance program administra-tively into an agency with legal personality and its own infrastructure. It ought to have an adequate internal control system and streamlined ad-ministrative procedures for handling the financial resources produced by employee and employer contributions.
- The *Servicio Nacional de Empleo* (National Employment Agency) must become a competitive and decentralized body, linked to its regional and local counterparts, in which the unemployed or anyone seeking a job can choose the best offer. The job-seeker will be required to pay the agency a minimal charge once it has found him or her a job, the amount of the charge varying with the type of employment, and this revenue will pay part of the costs of upgrading service, staff and infrastructure.
- The National Employment Agency will channel the training of the unem-ployed through INCE, especially to users with low skills or expertise that does not match the requirements of productive restructuring. This entails reviewing INCE's institutional capacity and training plans as well as forg-ing ties with this institute's decentralized civil associations, NGOs en-gaged in educational programs, and businesses.

Rather than draw up new regulations concerning the collective conflicts discussed in the third section, an effort should be made to ease existing regulations and to reduce as much as possible the red tape that inhibits labor-management negotiations. The reforms will be aimed primarily at redirecting the scarce resources of labor agencies toward inspection, legal assistance, and programs to support job placement, and secondarily at facilitating collective bargaining by reducing the state's role in the settlement of labor disputes.

The Ministry of Labor should be decentralized in order to give local bodies a greater voice in labor affairs. As the central organ in labor administration, the ministry ought to develop policies in the following areas:

- Overall monitoring and supervision in industrial safety, labor relations, and social matters, leaving the labor inspection offices free to focus on inspection as such. The technical criteria and mechanisms for imposing sanctions in this connection must be clearly laid out.
- Counseling and legal assistance for low-paid workers.
- Job placement support, with a view to strengthening employment agencies and coordination mechanisms with training schemes.

From a labor-management point of view, the reforms should stress collective bargaining without intervention by third parties, with the state serving as an external facilitator. This would strengthen the workers' negotiating capacity without making them dependent on a "protector state" or on a union with close party ties to the government in power. Formal conciliation, in the quasijudicial sense established by LOT in arbitration, should be used only in "extreme" situations.

In order to ensure the transparency of the state's participation in the process of resolving collective conflicts once the bipartite collective bargaining process has been exhausted, clear and expeditious procedures must be established with respect to:

- State authorities that take part in formal conciliation based on the scope of the conflict or the type of workers involved. In the public sector, the mediator should be an external agent who can ensure an impartial proceeding.
- Issues to be negotiated in regard to administrative career employees.
- A limit on how long an issue can remain under consideration by the Conciliation Board as a preliminary procedure which, once completed, must lead automatically to arbitration.
- Issues requiring arbitration and cases subject to binding arbitration, which should be limited to extreme situations in public agencies.
- Precise definition of "essential services."

The low rate of unionization and manifest lack of protection in small businesses make it imperative to facilitate access to collective rights in that sector. As regards union freedom, LCA regulations must be made compatible with those of the LOT, in order to give this sector's unions adequate and appropriate power to exercise their collective rights. Finally, the legalization of unions requires more expeditious procedures that leave less decision-making power in the hands of inspectors.

Bibliography

Antiveros, I. 1992. *Series estadísticas de Venezuela en los últimos 50 años.* Caracas: Central Bank of Venezuela.

Banco Central de Venezuela (BCV). 1993. Year-end statement by the President of the Central Bank of Venezuela. Caracas. Mimeo.

Betancourt, K., and Y. D'Elia. 1993. *Menores trabajadores en las calles (estudio en el area metropolitana de Caracas).* Serie Cuadernos de Investigación 7. Fundación Escuela de Gerencia Social, Ministry of the Family, Caracas.

Bronstein, A. 1990. La protección contra el despido injustificado en América Latina. *Revista internacional del trabajo* 109 (2).

Bruzual, G. 1992. *Derecho laboral. Estudio sistemático de la ley orgánica del trabajo en Venezuela.* La Guaira, Venezuela: Colección IUTIRLA.

Bulatao, R., R. Bos, P. Stephenes, et al. 1991. *Latin America and the Caribbean (LAC Region Population Projections).* World Bank Working Papers, WPS 329, Washington, D.C.

Caballero, O. J. 1991. *Incidencias del artículo 8 de la ley orgánica del trabajo en el régimen jurídico del funcionario público.* Caracas: Editorial Jurídica Venezolana.

Consejo de la Judicatura. 1993. Listado de tribunales en Venezuela. Mimeo.

Comisión de Reestructuración del IVSS. 1993. Informe financiero del 01-04-92 al 31-12-92. Caracas. Mimeo.

Ehremberg, R., and R. Smith. 1991. *Modern Labor Economics.* New York: Harper Collins Publishers.

Ellner, S. 1990. La influencia política y los lazos partidistas del sindicalismo venezolano. In Las *relaciones de trabajo en los noventa (Desafíos y propuestas),* eds. H. Lucena and F. Calero. Valencia, Venezuela: Instituto Latinoamericano de Investigaciones Sociales (ILDIS), Asociación de Relaciones de Trabajo, and the Universidad de Carabobo - Nueva Sociedad.

Ermida, O. 1993. La intervención estatal en las relaciones colectivas de trabajo latinoamericanas. *Nueva Sociedad* 128. Caracas.

Fields, G., and G. Jakubson. 1991. Labor Market Policies and Functioning in Venezuela. Cornell University, Ithaca, New York. Mimeo.

Godio, J. 1986. *50 años de la C.T.V. (1936-1986)*. Caracas: Instituto Latinoamericano de Investigaciones Sociales (ILDIS).

——————. 1980. *El movimiento obrero venezolano*. Vols. I, II, III. Caracas: Editorial Ateneo de Caracas - Instituto Latinoamericano de Investigaciones Sociales (ILDIS).

Hernández, O. (ed). 1992. Comments on the Organic Law on Labor. *Legislación Laboral Venezolana* 1. Caracas.

Hernández, O., and H. Lucena. 1985. Condicionantes políticos y económicos de la negociación colectiva en Venezuela. *Revista internacional del trabajo*. 104 (2).

Instituto Latinoamericano de Investigaciones Sociales (ILDIS). 1990. El movimiento sindical venezolano y el reajuste estructural de la economía: retos y desafíos. Caracas. Mimeo.

Instituto Venezolano de los Seguros Sociales (IVSS). 1991-92a. Estadísticas del seguro de paro forzoso. Caracas. Mimeo.

——————. 1992b. *Memoria y cuenta*. Caracas: IVSS.

International Labor Organization (ILO). 1992. Las relaciones laborales en Venezuela. Caracas. Mimeo.

International Monetary Fund. 1993. *International Financial Statistics*. Washington, D.C.

Iturraspe, F. 1992. Conflictos colectivos, reglamentación legal y realidad social. *Revista fundación de la procuraduría general de la república* 6. Caracas.

Larrañaga, J. 1993. Legislación, sindicatos y relaciones laborales. Proyecto Venezuela Competitiva-IESA. Caracas. Mimeo.

Liemt, G. 1993. La mundialización de la economía: posibilidades al alcance de los trabajadores y estrategias de empresas en los países de costos laborales altos. *Revista internacional del trabajo* 112 (1).

Márquez, G. 1993. Legislación laboral y mercado de trabajo en Venezuela. In *Reglamentación del mercado de trabajo en América latina*, ed. G. Márquez. Caracas. Unpublished.

_____. 1989. El impacto del proyecto de Ley orgánica del trabajo sobre la competitividad de la economía venezolana. Caracas. Mimeo.

Márquez, G. (ed.), K. Betancourt, and S. Freije. 1993. Cui Bono?: Regulation and Outcomes in the Labor Market. World Bank, Washington, D.C. Mimeo.

Ministry of Labor. 1993a. Relación de funcionarios que asistieron a los cursos de adiestramiento (1990-92). Caracas. Mimeo.

_____. 1993b. Nómina del personal (al 15/05/93). Caracas. Mimeo.

_____. 1991. *Anuario estadístico*. Caracas.

_____. 1958-92. *Memoria y cuenta*. Caracas.

Oficina Central de Personal (OCP). 1993. *Compilación legal para el área de recursos humanos* (leyes, reglamentos, decretos y procedimientos en la administración pública). Caracas.

_____. 1992a. *Informe estadístico*. (Distribución de cargos y costos de la administración pública nacional, período 1981-90). Caracas: Gráficas Chemar.

_____. 1992b. *Informe estadístico*. (Distribución de cargos y costos de la administración pública nacional, período 1991). Caracas: Gráficas Chemar.

Oficina Central de Estadística e Informática (OCEI). 1988-92. *Anuario estadístico*. Caracas.

_____. 1980-92a. *Encuesta de hogares por muestreo*. Caracas.

_____. 1980-92b. *Encuesta de hogares por muestreo*. Caracas.

Oficina Central de Presupuesto (OCEPRE). 1980-93. *Proyecto de ley para el ejercicio fiscal*. Caracas.

Pérez, R. 1985a. Asistencia jurídica y acceso a la justicia en Venezuela. In *Justicia y pobreza en Venezuela*, ed. R. Pérez. Caracas: Monte Avila Editores.

_____. 1985b. Los trabajadores de bajos ingresos y la justicia laboral. In *Justicia y pobreza en Venezuela,* ed. R. Pérez. Caracas: Monte Avila Editores.

Ramos, J. 1993. El problema del empleo: enfoques ortodoxos y estructurales. *Cuadernos de economía* 30 (90). Santiago.

Repúblic of Venezuela. 1993a. *Reglamento del seguro de paro forzoso.* Caracas.

_____. 1993b. *Ley del seguro social.* Caracas.

_____. 1991. *Ley orgánica del trabajo.* Caracas.

_____. 1975. *Ley contra despidos injustificado.* Caracas.

_____. 1961. *Constitución nacional.* Caracas.

_____. 1957. *Ley orgánica de tribunales y procedimientos del trabajo.* Caracas.

_____. 1936. *Ley del trabajo.* Caracas.

Sainz, C. 1990. *Comentarios al reglamento del seguro de paro forzoso.* Caracas: Editorial Lito Jet.

_____. 1989. *Los derechos y garantías de la próxima ley del trabajo.* Caracas: Editorial Lito Jet C.A.

Sheehan, G. 1992. Reorientación de la administración del trabajo a raíz de la crisis económica. *Revista internacional del trabajo* 111 (3).

Simmons, J. 1991. *La justicia laboral venezolana frente a la ley orgánica del trabajo: la estabilidad laboral.* Caracas: Instituto Latinoamericano de Investigaciones Sociales (ILDIS).

Sontag, H. 1984. Estado y desarrollo socio-político en Venezuela. *Cuadernos del CENDES* 4. Centros de Estudios del Desarrollo, Universidad Central de Venezuela, Caracas.

Storper, M., and A. Scott. 1990. La organización y los mercados locales del trabajo en la era de la producción flexible. *Revista internacional del trabajo* 109 (3).

Tribunal de Carrera Administrativa. 1990-92. Informe anual. Caracas. Mimeo.

Valecillos, H. 1993. *Estadísticas socio laborales de Venezuela. Series históricas 1936-90.* Caracas: Central Bank of Venezuela.

Villasmil, P. 1991. Precariedad, legislación y administración del trabajo. In *La flexibilización laboral en Venezuela (¿nuevo nombre o nueva realidad?),* P. Galin, *et al.* Caracas: Editorial Nueva Sociedad.

APPENDIX. MATHEMATICAL DERIVATION OF EQUATIONS FROM LABOR COSTS

Ignoring other wage and nonwage benefits, the total labor cost is the sum of the year's wages plus accrued seniority benefits for this year:

$$CL_t = S_t + VPS_t$$

where CL_t refers to the labor cost in the period t, S_t is the annual wage in the period t, and VPS_t is the variation in the accumulated seniority benefit for the period t. Assuming the rate of annual inflation (p) and real wage increase (S) to be constant, we can redefine the wage as follows:

$$S_t = S_1 (1 + p + S + pS)^{(A-1)}$$

where A represents the worker's years of service in the firm and S_1 the annual wage. Meanwhile, the cumulative balance of seniority benefits is

$$PS_t = AS_1 (1/12) (1 + p + s + ps)^{(A-1)}$$

The cost of accrued social benefits for the year t is the variation of the balance with respect to the previous year

$$\Delta PS_t = PS_t - PS_{t-1} =$$
$$S_1(1/12) A (1 + p + s + ps)^{A-1} - S_1(1/12) (A-1) (1+p+s+ps)^{A-2} =$$
$$S_1(1/12) (1 + p + s + ps)^{A-2} [1 + A (p + s + ps)]$$

In addition, the accrued benefits earns interest

$$CFN_t = S_t(1/12) (1 + p + S + pS)^{A-2} (A-1) (r-i)$$

where r,i represent the rates of interest paid to the workers and obtained by the firm, respectively, by the labor liability for the preceding year. Adding from the net financial cost (CFN_t) to the labor cost (CL_t), we obtain the total labor cost

$$CLT_t = S_1 (1 + p + s + ps)^{A-1} + S_t(1/12) (1 + p + s + ps)^{A-2} [1 + A(p + s + ps)] + ...$$
$$.... + [S_1(1/12) (1 + p + s + ps)^{A-2} (A-1) (=-i)]$$

Simplifying

$$CLT_t = S_1 (1 + p + s + ps)^{A-1} 1 + \frac{(1/12) [1 + A(p + s + ps) + (A-1) (r-1)]}{(1 + p + s + ps)}$$

In addition, the percentage increase of the real total labor cost is defined as

$$\%CLTR_t = (CLTR_t / CLTR_{t-1}) - 1$$

By substituting and simplifying, we will obtain

$$\%CLTR_t = S + (1+s) \; \frac{(1/12) \, [(p + s + ps) + (r - 1)]}{(1 + p + s + ps) + (1/12) \, [1 + (A-1) \, (p + s + ps) + A - 2) \, (r - 1)]}$$

or also,

$$\%CLTR_t = s + (1 + s) \, \alpha$$

For $\%CLTR_t > s$, it is necessary that $\alpha > 0$, and provided that $(r-i) < 1$, it suffices that

$$p > \frac{(i-r) - s}{(1 + s)}$$

Index